T0366015

Hearts for the Kingdom

Christ Revealed in the Hearts of His People

Cho Larson

WESTBOW
PRESS®
A DIVISION OF THOMAS NELSON
& ZONDERVAN

Contact: Cho Larson, cho@cholarson.com, or P.O. Box 1141, Cottonwood, AZ 86326

This book is a work of non-fiction. Unless otherwise noted, the author and the publisher make no explicit guarantees as to the accuracy of the information contained in this book and in some cases, names of people and places have been altered to protect their privacy.

All Scripture quotations contained herein are from New Revised Standard Version Bible NRSV® copyright ©1989 by the Division of Christian Education of the National Council of the Churches of Christ in the U.S.A., and are used by permission. All rights reserved. NRSV published by Oxford University Press, Inc., 200 Madison Ave., New York, New York 10016.™ All other Scripture quotations are as noted, from NIV, NLT, KJV and ESV and used within limits of specified and permissible use by publishers of each version.

♦ Cover image used by permission of Shutterstock.com

WestBow Press books may be ordered through booksellers or by contacting:

WestBow Press
A Division of Thomas Nelson & Zondervan
1663 Liberty Drive
Bloomington, IN 47403
www.westbowpress.com
1 (866) 928-1240

Because of the dynamic nature of the Internet, any web addresses or links contained in this book may have changed since publication and may no longer be valid. The views expressed in this work are solely those of the author and do not necessarily reflect the views of the publisher, and the publisher hereby disclaims any responsibility for them.

Any people depicted in stock imagery provided by Thinkstock are models, and such images are being used for illustrative purposes only.
Certain stock imagery © Thinkstock.

ISBN: 978-1-5127-1536-1 (sc)
ISBN: 978-1-5127-1538-5 (hc)
ISBN: 978-1-5127-1537-8 (e)

Library of Congress Control Number: 2015916736

Print information available on the last page.

WestBow Press rev. date: 10/14/2015

Contents

**Dedicated to my grandchildren
for the strengthening of their faith.**
Devon and Samuel.
Emma, Mia, Katherine, Diana.
Benjamin.
And all those yet to come.

Acknowledgments

My fellow writers, Christian friends, Bible study groups, family members and so many others have inspired me with words of encouragement. Many have prayed for me and helped me along the way. My editor helped me clarify what I was trying to say. Their support in this effort has been essential, or the book would never have come together as it has.

An overflow of strengthening, encouragement, instruction and inspiration from so many good people surrounded me to make this study book possible. Gratefulness overwhelms me when I think of how this book has come together. Like a conductor directing an orchestra playing a symphony, my Almighty Conductor has been instrumental in these words written here on these pages.

My precious wife Susie has encouraged me and prayed me through the process of study, research, writing, and rewriting. Her love, encouragement, and support have been a great help to me.

Your Mission Begins Here

Mission Impossible. That's what this study book is about. Not TV shows reruns, but the precious gift of a kingdom heart that is beyond our reach. This is impossible for one very simple reason: a kingdom heart is miraculous — a mystery too wonderful for human words to fully describe. It cannot be achieved in the strength we have, by our own effort, by our wits and willpower because it is a wondrous gift of saving faith that changes our hearts into Hearts for the Kingdom. It's as if the Bible says, "Don't try this at home." Attempt it by yourself and you'll fall on your face. Just as important, what you accomplish on your own will have no lasting worth. It will be of little eternal value in the Kingdom of Heaven.

The message of *Hearts for the Kingdom* is equally impossible to write. There are no "Ten Steps to a Kingdom Heart." You can't give assent to four spiritual laws to gain a Kingdom Heart. There is no methodical approach to achieve the objective. My task as teacher and writer is simply to be an instrument of the Holy Spirit to lead you to Christ who will give to you a new heart. And then, in your new heart, Christ is revealed.

As impossible as it is for you and for me, we have a very essential role in this kingdom heart process. It cannot be done without trusting the goodness of our Lord Jesus and jumping in with both feet. This requires a childlike faith, like a little girl who jumps into daddy's arms in the swimming pool, knowing beyond a doubt that he will catch her. We are powerless in this process, yet not without means to do our part. But the means are not our own. While a kingdom heart cannot be earned, effort is called for on our part. Jesus spoke of this when He said, "With man this is impossible, but with God all things are possible" (Matthew 19:26).

In his letter to the Corinthians, the Apostle Paul followed up his chapter on the gifts of the Spirit with the love chapter, directing our hearts to the kingdom of heaven in order to prevent the precious gifts of the Holy Spirit from being compromised with childish foolishness, human failings and selfish ambitions. Paul did not write a new set of laws or imperatives that Christians must follow. He was illuminating the words of Jesus: "Love one another. As I have loved you, so you must love one another" (John 3:35). Paul wrote his letters to the churches like he was peeling back an onion layer by layer to reveal the very nature of a kingdom heart. He showed us what it looks like at the very core of the heart. Paul was not saying, "you must" be productive he was tenderly saying, "you will" be like a well-watered tree naturally bearing fruit in season.[1]

Paul wrote the Corinthians love chapter in a way that may be compared to observing ants in depth. If you only pass by and give them a glance, you will see what is on the surface — busy bugs. You have to go deeper. When I was in junior high school, I made my own ant farm in a glass jar from mom's pantry and I was amazed at what these critters were doing underground. Their resourcefulness, organization and purposeful work surprised me. At that age I didn't know it was Biblical to consider the ways of ants and be wise (Proverbs 6:6).

Hearts for the Kingdom is an ant-farm-in-a-jar kind of observation, revealing the depths of your new heart. We must look deeper than the smiling faces people see at a glance. Join me in considering the changed heart, so we may be wise. "I will give you a new heart and put a new spirit in you; I will remove from you your heart of stone and give you a heart of flesh" (Ezekiel 36:26). A kingdom heart is indeed a circumcision of the heart. It is a baptism that penetrates to the depths of our hearts, making our hearts a new creation in Christ to the very core.[2]

Certainly, as we step into a priestly role among the priesthood of believers, it would be good to consider our ways so we don't become like an irritating "resounding gong" or "clanging cymbal." It's too easy to become like the two-year-old who gets toy drums for Christmas from grandma and grandpa who live too far away to hear them. He'll drive his parents to distraction with his drumming. He needs to grow

---

[1] We would be wrong to interpret this to mean that we should sit back in our deck chairs, sipping piña coladas and waiting for some fruit to pop out. We are called to action; we are compelled to stir up the precious gifts the Holy Spirit has given us and to do the work He has ordained for us to accomplish.

[2] Romans 2:28—29.

and mature so his drumming is a blessing to those around him and not an irritation.

Every time I read the Gospels, Jesus' message, work, and ministries overwhelm me with joy. Most often, people who saw Jesus do great and miraculous works immediately responded by giving glory to God (Matthew 9:8, 15:31).

When ministering using spiritual gifts, if you do so for your own glory, to be noticed, to be known as spiritual, or to be elevated in the ranks of the church, you will be just so much noise and quite irritating at that. You may at first be praised for being such a great instrument of the Holy Spirit. People will likely introduce you, presenting a long list of accolades for the great things you have done. You may well receive honorary plaques for the wall of your den; but these honorariums wear thin all too soon.

The greatest of all gifts from the Holy Spirit is love — the love of Christ flowing from hearts of the redeemed. The most treasured blessing from ministering in a spiritual gift comes from serving by means of the power of God's love through fruitful service that will blossom and flourish from the depths of a kingdom heart. This kind of serving is like a refreshing, clear mountain stream that naturally overflows from the Rock like a wellspring of life giving water.

You can't "make" it happen. It's not possible to train yourself to do it. Forget trying to force it. You can't visualize or speak it into being. Don't even think about attempting self-talk to get into it. This empowering work is the power of the Holy Spirit ministering through His servants. You and the Spirit of Jesus are brought together to minister to human needs around you. As you humble yourself you will be an all but invisible servant, for the glory and honor of the Name of our Lord and Savior, Jesus Christ.

Moses is one of the greatest examples of a man humbling himself before a Holy God and allowing God to work His mighty works through him. His model of humility is worth looking at to see that it was not natural to come to that point. It could be said that it took forty years alone in the desert with stinking herds of sheep to get him to that place of humility. But Moses style humility is not being a wilting flower, a doormat or having an "I'm good-for-nothing, I'm the dirt-on-the-floor" attitude. Humility knows its place before a Holy God and knows the might and power of God Almighty. Humility is stepping aside, putting your *self* away, and allowing God to work through you. Humility is God's power at work through you and under His authority. It is His power manifested in your weakness.

In Exodus chapter 13, God led the children of Israel into a trap near Pi Hahiroth, between Migdol and the sea. When the twelve tribes saw the clouds of dust from the Egyptian armies, they started shouting and crying out to Moses. "Weren't there enough graves in Egypt that you brought us to the desert to die?" Moses was between the proverbial rock and a hard place. The sea hemmed them in on one side and the angry tribes of Israel were facing him down while the armies of Pharaoh were descending upon them at full speed. Now we are ready to see one of the greatest acts of a man's humility in Scripture. In verse 16 God instructs Moses, "Lift up your staff, and stretch out your hand over the sea and divide it, that the people of Israel may go through the sea on dry ground."

Moses obeyed God, knowing that everything depended upon his Almighty God, and nothing depended upon Moses except to be God's instrument and stretch out the rod in his hand. Moses had to put aside his frustration with the people he was leading. He had to cast away fear as he looked in the angry faces of his people and then at the charging Egyptian armies. It was necessary for him to give it all up to Jehovah God and simply obey. I'm sure he raised his staff with a white knuckled grip and stretched it out over the water, steel faced with clenched teeth. In doing this, he put his fears and frustrations aside and simply obeyed.

This is the best part of the story. In verse 14, God reassures the people through Moses, "The Lord will fight for you; you need only to be still." And then in the very next verse God says, "Why are you crying out to me?" God issued the order: "Move on." My paraphrase, "Be still—stop your whining and move out." Mission impossible; yet totally possible as Moses put himself, his panicked feelings, and his fearful thoughts aside and was God's vessel to accomplish all the Lord proclaimed He would do.

We cannot go on without declaring the greatest act of humility of all time. "In the beginning was the Word, and the Word was with God, and the Word was God. He was with God in the beginning. Through him all things were made; without him nothing was made that has been made. In him was life, and that life was the light of all mankind" (John 1:1-4). Our Lord Jesus who was with God at the creation of all things, who is the Word, gave himself up to suffer at the hands of man to redeem man.

Begin your mission impossible and do what you never could before. Now, with a kingdom heart you will be prepared for a whole new life with a purpose. Your life and task are unique to you because God prepared these especially for you. Remember, trying to do this work on your own is impossible, yet it is totally possible in Christ who is strength in you. With each chapter that follows you will observe this kingdom heart layer by layer, and see the impossible mission you are called to become mission possible.

1

Redeemed by Grace

Considering first things first is vitally important. Nothing in *Hearts for the Kingdom* will make sense to you if you are not an adopted son or daughter of the Heavenly Father, who is Creator of all heaven and earth. He is the One who created you! The message here will be incomprehensible and doubly impossible unless you are totally in love with Jesus, the Bridegroom, Son of the Living God. There is no point to what is written here if you are uncomfortable in the presence of a Holy, Righteous, Awesome, Majestic God who dwells in light so blinding and bright that you cannot approach in your natural, mortal state. We cannot come close to a Holy God apart from being in Christ. Right now your Lord Jesus stands with open arms, calling to you.

This is my encouragement, if you have not received your new adopted name (Revelation 2:17), or if you're not completely sure of your eternal destination: Read through the following Scriptures, take them to heart and then consider the words. Read them again, out loud, skipping the comments after the verses. If you're then still not sure you "get it," have someone read the Bible verses to you. After truly hearing and coming to agreement with the truths of these Scriptures, this is a good time to pray to your Heavenly Father or find someone who will lead you in prayer. You will have Help from above right beside you as you do this. When you're ready, just start your prayer, "Heavenly Father..." The Spirit of God will help you pray.

Romans 10:17: "So faith comes from what is heard, and what is heard comes through the word of Christ." I encourage you to read and reread the Scriptures written here because it is by hearing them, not in a passive sense, but truly taking them in, examining them, testing them, meditating on them, praying over them, agreeing with them and knowing them, that you receive this gift of saving faith.

Romans 3:23: **"For there is no distinction, since all have sinned and fall short of the glory of God; they are now justified by his grace as a gift, through the redemption that is in Christ Jesus."** We are all guilty, we have all sinned, none of us measures up to who God is. We can't blame anyone else because we are personally guilty of sin. We have all lied, cheated, stolen what wasn't ours, yearned for what didn't belong to us, and we have spoken harmful words against our friends, family and neighbors. We haven't honored our parents as we ought, we have been unforgiving, we have not loved our neighbor, and we have been greedy. In dark moments, we've "murdered" people with our words, we're responsible for heated words spoken in anger, and the list goes on ad infinitum.

In our hopeless condition we find hope in Jesus Christ, for by His grace He justifies us freely and makes us right before a Holy God. By faith in Christ, we are redeemed, bought back from being bound up in sin, and then adopted as sons of our Heavenly Father.

Romans 5:12: **"Therefore, just as sin came into the world through one man, and death came through sin, and so death spread to all because all have sinned."** It's just not fair, you might think. How is it possible to be guilty of sin when it's all Adam's fault? It may help you to think of it in this way. When a person sells himself into slavery, every child born to him is naturally a slave. His offspring are conceived in bondage and are born into slavery. In Adam's original sin, he sold himself into slavery to sin and thereby sold all of his posterity into servitude as well. We all descend from Adam and therefore we are born into bondage to sin. The end result of our sin is death.

But we have the greatest of all hope, and that is Jesus Christ and His redemptive sacrifice on a cruel Roman cross on a hill called Golgotha. When you truly see your sinful state, you'll cringe at the thought of what you've done and grieve. Now turn to look upon the cross of Jesus Christ. Tell our Lord Jesus about your grief. What you're doing is called confession and repentance.

Romans 5:8: "But God proves his love for us in that while we still were sinners Christ died for us." The cross of Calvary, stained with blood and pierced with nails that were driven through Jesus' hands and feet, is proof positive that God loves you more than you can even imagine. Even while you were in the depths of your sin, Christ died to pay the penalty of your sin. His blood purchased you from your bondage. You may be thinking that you weren't even born when Christ died over two thousand years ago. But remember that the cross of Jesus is timeless, reaching back to the beginning of time and forward to the end of time. The saving work of the cross is not bound by the time and seasons of this world. The work of the cross is present today and ready to do a good work in you right now.

Romans 10:9-10: "...because if you confess with your lips that Jesus is Lord and believe in your heart that God raised him from the dead, you will be saved. For one believes with the heart and so is justified, and one confesses with the mouth and so is saved." Even before we believe, the Holy Spirit prepares our hearts to hear and receive His Word. It's like He is tilling the ground before He plants the seed. With the seed planted, the Holy Spirit helps us to understand and agree with the Word of God. When you truly hear, you come to believe that Jesus not only died, but rose again from the grave on the third day. Then, because of what is planted in your heart, the urge to talk about it bursts out of you like a spring of water; to tell people at every opportunity what God has done in you. The greatest declaration of this newfound faith that is planted in you is to obey Jesus command to be baptized in water.

Romans 10:13: "For, everyone who calls on the name of the Lord shall be saved." What do you do when you're caught in a tight spot or a life-threatening situation? You cry out, "Help! Help! Is anybody there?" Your life for all eternity is on the line. You are stumbling around in darkness and there is no light to show you the way out. Because of all the crazy stuff you've done, your life is a mess and there's no light at the end of the tunnel. You're isolated, alone and no one seems to care.

Be encouraged. There is a great hope that I hold out to you. Right here, in the mess you've made, call on the name of Jesus Christ. He will find you and lift you out. In fact, after you call on His name, you'll suddenly realize that all this time He has been calling out for you by name.

Will you answer?

John 3:16: "For God so loved the world that he gave his only Son, so that everyone who believes in him may not perish but may have eternal life." You see John 3:16 on placards at the stadium; it's on t-shirts and billboards. This incredibly familiar verse is often glossed over without taking a moment to see the depths of truth in it. Our Creator God loves all those whom He created in His image with a love that is beyond words. Can you imagine giving up your one and only son for some wretched souls who could care less about you? God sent His Son into a lost and dying world. His name is Jesus and He is called Immanuel, which means "God with us." Jesus taught the people, healed their sick, raised their loved ones from the dead, fed them with miracle food, and then was rejected, thrashed with whips, crowned with thorns, nailed on a Roman cross to die, and buried in a garden tomb.

But the story doesn't end there. In fact, it's a new beginning that changes everything, because after three days Jesus rose up from the dead. Even more than this, because He is the resurrected Christ, He is the first of many who will rise from the dead to have eternal life. Believe that His sacrifice paid the penalty for your sins and you will be saved from your lost, depraved condition. Believe that He rose from the dead, and you will not depart this life in a hopeless state, for now you hold the promise of eternal life with God.

Believe and receive.

Ephesians 2:8-10: "For by grace you have been saved through faith, and this is not your own doing; it is the gift of God — not the result of works, so that no one may boast. For we are what he has made us, created in Christ Jesus for good works, which God prepared beforehand to be our way of life." Try to imagine the wondrous truths of this Scripture. You have been given a gift by means of grace through faith in Jesus Christ our Lord and Savior. To be sure, you didn't do anything to deserve it; quite the opposite in fact. Some teach that salvation is conditioned on an obedient response. The truth is, salvation comes by faith alone, through Christ alone, by the cross alone; and obedience is no more than evidence that your salvation

4

is for real. God has adopted you into His family for a purpose, which results in "good works." You can be sure that God has a job waiting for you to accomplish in life.

Ephesians 1:7-8, "In him we have redemption through his blood, the forgiveness of our trespasses, according to the riches of his grace, which he lavished upon us." You may be a convicted felon, an embezzler, or a thief. Your record may be blemished by ruined relationships and divorce. You may have been fired from your job with good cause. The truth is, because of our sins, none of us, from felon to president to pastor, is redeemable on our own. We are totally dependent upon Christ Jesus and His gospel of grace. Grace proclaims that we are not stuck in our failures, weakness, and faults. Instead we are set free and given value in Christ, and His great love is held out to us without merit or condition. The word "lavished" says so much, because He gave His all for you and me. God showered us with the bountiful measures of His saving grace. And then your record is wiped clean, never to be remembered again.

Will you believe and receive His free gift?

Isaiah 52:7: "How beautiful upon the mountains are the feet of the messenger who announces peace, who brings good news, who announces salvation, who says to Zion, 'Your God reigns.'" Spread the news. Be God's messenger, tell someone of this marvelous, miraculous salvation. Indeed, saving a lost soul is the greatest of all miracles the Lord performs among His people. The Good Shepherd is prepared to bring you home in a great celebrative parade. The angels of heaven are prepared to sing your joyous song of deliverance. The Bridegroom will now prepare a place for you to dwell in His house for all eternity.

When you hear all these Scriptures so completely that these truths permeate the depths of your soul, a miracle happens. Because each one of us is uniquely and wonderfully made, we respond in a way that is delightfully special, according to the person God has made each of us to be. Our personal responses may be somewhat different, depending on our age, cultural roots, and personalities.

That said, let's look at what a typical response might be. When you truly hear God's Word, i.e. grasp hold of and receive the grace freely extended to you, first your heart will be torn with grief over your sinful condition, and you will see your need of Christ. When faith is sown like a seed in your heart of hearts by the hearing of the Word, by the grace of God and by the power of the Holy Spirit, you will burst at the seams, so to speak. You will feel like you can't wait to tell someone what has happened to you. And most certainly, you will desire to be joined together with Christ, obeying the Lord's command to all who come into saving faith to "believe and be baptized."

Many fabulous benefits are held out to you as you come into faith, and you'll snap them up like a hungry newborn baby.[3] A desire to hang out with your brothers and sisters in Christ will come over you. A hunger and thirst for God's Word, the Scriptures, will overwhelm you. You'll find yourself talking to God often, if not in every spare minute of the day. Your mouth will not shut when it comes to telling people the miracle God has done in you. Joy will wash over you like a flood.

You have been called out of a world of darkness into a kingdom of glorious light. You are cleansed to the depths of your soul and healed of the ruin of sin and degradation. You are washed in the blood of the Lamb of God and made spotlessly clean before God. You are received into Christ and the fellowship of His family, the church, by the waters of baptism. Jesus wraps His robe of righteousness around you. Now you may dwell in the very presence of your Heavenly Father. Your new name gives you a whole new family identity.

Do you truly believe in this great salvation, in agreement with the Scriptures you have read and heard? My encouragement to you is to believe it, receive it and now tell the world about your personal miracle of saving faith.

Rev. 2:17: "...and I will give a white stone, and on the white stone is written a new name that no one knows except the one who receives it." You are the only one who truly knows that the seed of saving faith in Jesus Christ is planted in you. No other person is able to discern it, except by the "fruit" of the seed planted in your garden.

The white stone imagery in this verse comes from an ancient Greek custom where the accused would come before the Judge to face

---

[3] Psalms 103 is the believer's benefit statement.

trial. If the accused was found to be guilty, he was given a black stone. If he was acquitted of the crime, he was given a white stone.

You have been found guilty of violating God's law, but in Christ, because He paid the penalty for your sin, because He paid the debt you owe, you are given a white stone with your new name engraved upon it. Hold out your hand to receive it. Treasure this white stone. Hold it in your hand to remind you of what has been done for you.

Romans 6:21-23: "So what advantage did you then get from the things of which you now are ashamed? The end of those things is death. But now that you have been freed from sin and enslaved to God, the advantage you get is sanctification. The end is eternal life. For the wages of sin is death, but the free gift of God is eternal life in Christ Jesus our Lord." Imagine being set free from being imprisoned in the dark and seeing the light for the first time in years — it would take a long time for your eyes to adjust to the light. This is how sanctification works. A beautiful picture is painted to describe this incredible, powerful word. Sanctification is relationship with our Lord Jesus Christ who gives us His Holy Spirit to "open [our] eyes, so that [we] may turn from darkness to light and from the power of Satan to God, that [we] may receive forgiveness of sins and a place among those who are sanctified by faith in [Him]" (Acts 26:18).

Sanctification is a process of restoring your soul, renewing your heart and coming to have a mind that thinks like our Lord Jesus. Sanctification is the means by which your heart becomes teachable and pliable. In the process of being sanctified, we come to know the mind of Christ and we learn to do what He is doing, say what He is saying and act as He would act if He were walking in our flip-flops. In sanctification you are blessed by God, separated for God's purpose, restored to fellowship with your Heavenly Father and with the community of your new brothers and sisters in Christ. Sanctification means that your purification has begun in earnest as our Lord Jesus Christ wraps His robe of righteousness around you. In sanctification your effort is important, and your cooperation is necessary. The writer of Hebrews says, "Work at living in peace with everyone, and work at living a holy life, for those who are not holy will not see the Lord"

(Hebrews 12:14 NLT). Paul agrees: "...work out your own salvation with fear and trembling" (Philippians 2:12).

Saving faith places you side by side with Jesus where He wraps His robe of righteousness around you. Now in Christ, you may come before a Holy God with great confidence. You are freed from darkness, your sin debts have all been paid, and you have been given a sure promise of eternal life with Him. This is a free gift, it didn't cost you anything; you didn't earn it. In sanctification you are coming into the fullness of Christ, which is made possible by faith. You are being called to work it out. You've been given a treasure of incredible value — be encouraged to treasure the generous wages you now receive in Christ.

Luke 14:28: "For which of you, desiring to build a tower, does not first sit down and count the cost, whether he has enough to complete it." Did you pick up on the key words in this verse? "Count the cost." Certainly, count the cost before you begin so that you may know whether or not you are willing to pay the price. Being a disciple of Jesus is going to cost you. Get your mental calculator turned on and add it all up. In total — it will cost you everything. It will cost you friends, it may cost your job, you could lose your present status in the community, your family may turn away from you, it may cost you lifetime habits you've enjoyed, it will cost you all of what you own, you will no longer be captain of your soul or master of your fate, it may mess up your weekends and it could cost you your very life. If you are not willing to pay the price in total, you should reconsider before you walk through the gate onto this narrow pathway. But count it all joy, for to walk in this way is to walk step in step with our Lord and Savior, Jesus Christ.

May I encourage you to count the cost, believe and receive — right now.

John 8:12: "Again Jesus spoke to them, saying, 'I am the light of the world. Whoever follows me will never walk in darkness but will have the light of life.'" Surrender[4] to God's call to follow in His footsteps. You may be strong willed. People may call you "bull

---

[4] This is a great mystery. We must surrender our hearts and our will to God who is calling us, yet even in surrendering to His grace this is not of ourselves but by the power and work of the Holy Spirit in our heart of hearts.

headed." That's your will at work in your life. Now is the time to surrender that will to Christ. Repent of your sins. Repent of your "I'll do it my way" kind of thinking and start doing it His way.

Now that you've received and believed this truth, tell somebody that Jesus is Lord of your life — that you're not the boss of your life anymore. Then be encouraged to continue, by faith, to walk in the Light. Jesus' final command to His followers was to "go therefore and make disciples..." (Matthew 27:19). Remember first things first. With the seed of faith now planted in you, you receive the indwelling Holy Spirit, who seals you, shielding you from God's just wrath. Now, wait for the promised empowering work of the Holy Spirit to be poured out upon you. Wait and receive. Pray with expectation. Pray with likeminded believers in Christ. Pray in agreement to receive all God has for you.

Before you can make disciples you must be a disciple. This means walking in the Light, being taught, enlightened, strengthened, nurtured, encouraged, admonished, and disciplined — this is being a disciple. But remember, in discipleship, there is a cost. Jesus spoke of this in Luke 14:25-36. In being a disciple of Christ there is a cross to bear; but indeed, His burden is light.

Now that you have been made a disciple of Jesus, I'll give you some disciple homework. Find your Bible or purchase a new one. My recommendation is the New Living Translation to start with.[5] Read the book of John first. Next, read and consider the books of Matthew, Mark, and Luke — read the words of Jesus as He taught the people. After these books, you're ready to branch out into the Psalms and Proverbs. For many years I began my morning studies by reading the chapter of Proverbs that corresponded with day of the month and I found great wisdom for my daily life. When you're ready for

---

[5] I'm not in favor of Bibles that have a lot of teaching footnotes because the reader often depends too much on the comments rather than asking for the Holy Spirit to teach them as they take time for quiet meditation in the scriptures. As you mature in your studies, an excellent study Bible is the NIV Thompson Chain Reference. This version will lead you in your study with helps that connect the whole of scripture together. Another excellent version for study is the ESV.

something to really chew on, work and study your way through the book of Romans.

My prayer: May your walk in the Lord be blessed, and your fellowship in Christ be sweet. Lord God, bring up your new children to be strong and mighty soldiers in the battle for the Kingdom of Light. Make them great witnesses of your power to save. I pray that their brothers and sisters in Christ will lift them up, strengthen them, and encourage them in the faith.

Q & A Chapter 1: Redeemed by Grace

1. How is the seed of Christian faith "planted" in you?

2. What must you do to be saved?

3. What is your new family name?

Your Mission Journal Notes:

2

Assurance of Salvation

Robin Willard stiffened. His heart pounded as he stood next to his dad, his mouth open and his blue eyes like saucers. Dad was holding out a set of keys, but Robin was so shocked he couldn't reach out to take them — but only for a moment.

"Happy birthday, son." Dad was all smiles.

"But, dad, this is your very own Mustang. I know how much it means to you."

"Yes, and you mean even more to me than this old car." Dad slapped Robin on the shoulder. "Let's take it for a spin."

The next day Robin got to drive his car to school. As he cruised along, the rules of the road flashed through his mind, the stuff he learned in Driver's Ed. Classes. This was the greatest day of his life and he didn't want to ruin it with a ticket or even worse, a fender bender. He parked the red Mustang, perfectly centered between the white lines, and then stood to admire his car until the class bell rang. Keys in his pocket and backpack slung over his shoulder, he ran to his first class. Before he sat down at his desk, he reached into his pocket to check for the keys. Yup, he really did have his own car.

After class, he checked for his keys again. "No doubt — my own car."

As he walked down the hallway, his best friend Thomas asked him, "Did I see you driving your dad's Mustang this morning?"

Robin reached into his pocket to be sure. "No way man. You saw me driving my own Stang this morning."

Thomas stopped in his tracks, grabbed Robin's arm and spun him around. "For real?"

Robin took the keys out of his pocket and held them up. "For real."

Throughout the rest of the day, Robin found himself reaching into his pocket to check his keys to be sure he really did have his own wheels now. In the hallway between classes and before and after every class. Even though he couldn't see his car in the parking spot, with the feel of the keys in his jeans pocket came waves of reminders that he really did have his own car, and a very cool one at that.

When you are gifted with saving faith in Jesus Christ, you get "keys" to offer assurance of your salvation. You are given proof that your salvation is for real — that you got the genuine article. You can't keep it in your pocket because it doesn't come in the form of a physical object. But in fact, there is all encompassing evidence that removes doubts and questions. Like the keys in Robin's pocket – the keys were not the car, but a reassuring evidence and a reminder that he had one.

What is rock solid proof of salvation? What evidence is there that yours is for real? Are adopted sons and daughters given indisputable witnesses who offer testimony of the gift of saving faith? Where do you find this assurance? "Those who believe in the Son of God have the testimony in their hearts" (1 John 5:10).

First we will look at what is not an assurance of salvation. Then there are three certainties we must consider: 1) You are given rock solid proof of your salvation. 2) You are given evidence of your salvation. 3) You are given a guarantee of your salvation. The proof is undeniable, the evidence comes as a result of true salvation, and the guarantee is unshakeable. All three are important and offer us God's blessed assurance.

Be aware that no other person can know and offer total assurance of your salvation. You are the only one who can truly know if God has written your name in the Book of Life.[6] If your claim to Christianity is based on a statement like: "I know I'm a Christian because I _____" (fill in the blank), you are on shaky ground. Nor can you say, "I know I'm a Christian because my parents _____" (fill in the blank). You cannot be assured of salvation by means of anything you have done or because of anything your parents did.

---

[6] Revelation 21:27

Salvation comes as a gift of grace, by faith alone and there is nothing anyone can do to earn it.

First you will find proof in His promise to give you a new name. That doesn't mean that you choose a new handle for people to call you, changing your name from Nancy to Hope. No! This is a family name. You are now called by the name of your new adopted family. Listen to this precious promise: "To everyone who conquers I will give some of the hidden manna, and I will give a white stone, and on the white stone is written a new name that no one knows except the one who receives it" (Revelation 2:17).[7]

Now that you are in Christ, His Holy Spirit protects you by putting His seal on your heart, soul and spirit. By sealing you, He becomes your shield, your fortress, and your life preserver from God's just wrath because of your past sins. Because you are sealed, shielded by Christ, you can stand tall, confident in the presence of a holy God.

Being sealed is not only an external thing. What happens inside you offers greater proof of your salvation. The following Scripture will open your eyes to this truth. The apostle Paul writes to the church, "Or do you not know that your body is a temple of the Holy Spirit within you, which you have from God, and that you are not your own?" (1 Corinthians 6:19). Why are you likened to a temple? Because God dwells in temples and He now has taken up residence in you and He makes His living, active presence known to you from within. Just as God reassured the people of Israel, He reassures you also. "...For the Lord your God goes with you; he will never leave you nor forsake you" (Deuteronomy 31:6). You are shielded, enveloped, and filled with the Spirit of Jesus, and in this you have great proof of your salvation.

When a baby is born, he's hungry. His hunger is an indication of a healthy, strong, thriving baby boy. In the realm of the kingdom of heaven, we are born spiritually hungry. Are you hungry for God's Word, for reading your Bible? This is evidence of your salvation.

An emotionally healthy child desires to be with those who love her. She coos when daddy is talking to her, she wants to be held close

---

[7] This doesn't mean no one knows your new name, it means that no person can know and offer you assurance of your new name or deny that you have the name. Only you can truly know.

to mommy, she laughs with delight when her silly brother talks to her. As the child grows, she desires play with her little friends. Now that you are a new creation in Christ, like this child, desiring to be with other followers of Jesus is evidence that you're alive in Him.

Now that Christ Jesus has changed your old heart to a kingdom heart, the things you want to do have changed. You're forgiven and cleansed and you will want to be with your new family.[8] Forgiveness of sins is like getting rid of that old baggage that dragged you down. Now you are lifted up, and the weight is gone because Jesus took the burden of your sins upon himself when He was nailed to a cruel Roman Cross. Now that you are in Christ, you are free of the weight of sin. This is further assurance of your salvation. It isn't a feeling, it's a reality, like the reassuring keys in Robin's pocket.

The apostle Paul wrote to the church in Rome, "But now that you have been set free from sin and have become slaves of God, the benefit you reap leads to holiness, and the result is eternal life" (Romans 6:22 NIV). Did you catch that incredible truth? The evidence you see is holiness. Think of holiness as a side effect of being set free from the clutches of sin.

There is another assurance — evidence of salvation that we may wish to avoid. But it is very important. Does God discipline you? "My child, do not regard lightly the discipline of the Lord, or lose heart when you are punished by him; for the Lord disciplines those whom he loves, and chastises every child whom he accepts" (Hebrews 12:5).[9] Are you an adopted child of the Heavenly Father? Sure evidence of His love and a solid confirmation that you are now called by His name is that God will discipline you, because He loves you, because you are family.

Isaiah offers us further evidence that God's righteousness is at work in us: "The effect of righteousness will be peace, and the result of righteousness, quietness and trust forever" (Isaiah 32:17). Is your heart at peace? Is there quietness in your soul? Has trust in Jesus become

---

[8] Please understand that my references to leaving baggage behind and turning to your *new* family does not in any way mean that you are to leave behind, ignore or push away the family you were given at birth. In fact, they may be the first ones to hear of your new faith in Jesus Christ.

[9] Also in Revelation 3:19.

part of who you are? Does your heart yearn to be hanging out with other Christians? Do you look forward to getting together with them to worship the God of your salvation? Are you totally hungry for God's Word? Do you want to talk to God in every moment possible? Does God tenderly discipline you and lovingly correct you? These things are typical of a new Christian and are indicative of a good, healthy and strong new life in Christ.

But you want more than proofs; you want undeniable guarantees of your salvation to drive out any shadow of doubt that tempts you. The evidence is strong, and the witnesses indisputable, but you want to be unshakably confident. God's Word fulfills that desire. "Faith is the confidence that what we hope for will actually happen; it gives us assurance about things we cannot see" (Hebrews 11:1 NLT). Confident hope that comes by means of faith in our Lord and Savior, Jesus Christ is undeniable. Indeed, Jesus Christ is the One who guarantees your salvation. "Truly he is my rock and my salvation; he is my fortress, I will not be shaken" (Psalms 62:6 NIV). In your heart of hearts, you find confident hope of your salvation even though your eyes do not yet see it. In this you know beyond doubt you have a risen, living Savior who is Guarantor of your salvation.[10] "We have this hope, a sure and steadfast anchor of the soul" (Hebrews 6:19). Hold onto this confidence and treasure this great hope.

Confidence in your salvation will increase as you hunger to join together with a gathering of your brothers and sisters in Christ around the communion table to partake together of the body and blood, the cup and the bread of the Lord's Supper. Your hunger is the result of the powerful, miraculous saving grace of our Lord Jesus Christ at work in you. Only those who are in Christ are beckoned to come join Him around the table. Do you hunger and thirst for the communion of the Lord's Table? Your assurance is strengthened in this blessed sacrament of the church.

It keeps getting better.

One of the most beautiful Scriptures is Psalms 103. In these inspired words you will see more blessings and benefits of salvation. Let me

---

[10] Hebrews 7:22.

encourage you to take a sheet of notepaper and list every blessing you see as you prayerfully read this Psalm. This is important because these blessings are yours — further evidence of your salvation.

> *"Bless the Lord, O my soul, and all that is within me, bless his holy name. Bless the Lord, O my soul, and do not forget all his benefits — who forgives all your iniquity, who heals all your diseases, who redeems your life from the pit, who crowns you with steadfast love and mercy, who satisfies you with good as long as you live so that your youth is renewed like the eagle's. The Lord works vindication and justice for all who are oppressed. He made known his ways to Moses, his acts to the people of Israel. The Lord is merciful and gracious, slow to anger and abounding in steadfast love. He will not always accuse, nor will he keep his anger forever. He does not deal with us according to our sins, nor repay us according to our iniquities. For as the heavens are high above the earth, so great is his steadfast love toward those who fear him."*
>
> *(Psalms 103:1—12)*

As if proof and evidence of your salvation isn't enough, God offers even more assurance. He gives you a written guarantee. It's written in the words of Scripture. This is better than the Good Housekeeping seal of approval. God's guarantee means more than a presidential seal or the president's signature, because it is a covenant sealed by His blood.

There are three that testify, guaranteeing your adoption as a son or daughter of the Living God. Your three witnesses are the Holy Spirit who indwells you, the waters of baptism that receive you into Christ and make you a new creation, and finally the cleansing work of our Savior, Messiah, who gave His blood to be shed to pay the penalty for your sins.[11] Further testimony is given of our salvation: "It was declared at first through the Lord, and it was attested to us by those who heard him, while God added his testimony by signs and wonders and various

---

[11] Paraphrased from 1 John 5:7-9.

miracles, and by gifts of the Holy Spirit, distributed according to his will" (Hebrews 2:3-4).

You can also take great comfort in the One who guarantees your salvation when His Holy Spirit imparts spiritual gifts, as you become a part of His church. Spiritual gifts are given for the effective functioning and ministries of the church and the manifestations of these gifts are assurance that the Good News of Jesus Christ has been truthfully proclaimed and truly received and believed. You can rest assured in your salvation as the Holy Spirit gives and empowers spiritual gifts in you.[12]

Consider also that you are given a guarantee beyond doubt when your heart compels you to obey His command to be baptized. In baptism, the power of God's Word is joined together with the waters of baptism and in this you are given an unquestionable guarantee of God's saving grace at work in you by faith in Jesus Christ. "But if anyone obeys his Word, love for God is truly made complete in them. This is how we know we are in him..." (1 John 2:5).

"In him you also, when you had heard the word of truth, the gospel of your salvation, and had believed in him, were marked with the seal of the promised Holy Spirit; this is the pledge of our inheritance toward redemption as God's own people, to the praise of his glory" (Ephesians 1:13-14). You have God's Word on it. When you heard the Gospel read, taught and preached and then given faith to believe it, you were marked and sealed by the Holy Spirit who Jesus promised to send to you. It's like an invisible mark, or seal, that only the light of Christ can reveal.

When the seed of faith is planted in your heart, the Holy Spirit seals your heart and marks you as His own until that great Day when He calls us to the wedding banquet as His bride. He guarantees it by His Word and seals you by His Holy Spirit for that coming day of His return.

---

[12] Be aware of a common error, mistaking what is common for what is holy. We must not confuse God-given natural gifts for true and real Holy Spirit-given and empowered spiritual gifts. Spiritual gifts are holy, while everyone born into this world is given natural gifts.

You can be sure of this great salvation. Welcome to the family of God.[13]

Q & A Chapter 2: Assurance of Salvation

1. What "keys" do you have to assure you of your salvation?

2. What are the three indisputable witnesses of the saving faith given to you?

3. What is baptism and why is it so important?

Your Mission Journal Notes:

---

[13] Anytime you're feeling the need for reassurance of your salvation, just turn to the book of 1st John. The apostle John's letter is full of assurances of your salvation.

3

Foundation of Repentance

Visiting home, where my roots were established, is always comforting to me. The sky drizzles, the land is wet, the air is misty and damp, the fields are green and the moss is thick on the north side of the trees. The Nooksack River Valley is where my ancestors settled and my parents grew up. I love visiting the valley even though it's a busy time, driving all around to see everybody. On one of those outings, traveling between the towns of Nooksack and Sumas, I always look for an old house in the middle of a pasture that's been abandoned for years. Apparently, it was built without a proper foundation; therefore, the south side of the house has sunk a couple of feet into the soggy ground, tilting the house rather dramatically.

Houses – anything we build – require a solid foundation. Especially in the work of the kingdom of heaven, a solid spiritual foundation is necessary. The church is established upon a foundation of the Apostles and Prophets.

> "So then you are no longer strangers and aliens, but you are citizens with the saints and also members of the household of God, built upon the foundation of the apostles and prophets, with Christ Jesus himself as the cornerstone. In him the whole structure is joined together and grows into a holy temple in the Lord; in whom you also are built together spiritually into a dwelling place for God." (Ephesians 2:19-22)

The church is built upon the solid Rock, Christ Jesus.

In the same way, to prepare a church to be restored and revived, a foundation must first be established. We see many precedents in Scripture of this foundation of repentance. In each example we find in the Bible, before the hand of God moves on behalf of His people, this foundation must be built.

Daniel got on his knees before God and repented of the sins of the nation of Israel as God prepared to bring them back to their promised land after seventy years of exile. When Nehemiah heard of the "great trouble and disgrace" of the people in Jerusalem, he sat down and wept; he mourned and fasted for days, confessing his sins and the sins of God's people. And again as the walls of Jerusalem and the temple were being rebuilt, upon hearing God's Word, the people humbled themselves and repented of their sins. The prophet Haggai called the people to repentance — the people repented, worshipped the Lord in earnest and completed the rebuilding of the temple. John the Baptist called the people to a baptism of repentance to make a way for the Messiah to come and minister among them. The apostle John writes the words of Christ Jesus in Revelation, calling the churches to repentance as the Bridegroom prepares His bride for His return.

This is an essential truth of orthodox Christian faith. The writer of Hebrews makes clear that repentance is both foundational and elementary: "Therefore let us move beyond the elementary teachings about Christ and be taken forward to maturity, not laying again the foundation of repentance" (Hebrews 6:1 NIV). But in this day and age we have neglected the most elementary basics of our faith.

The practice of repentance is too often forgotten among God's people. Throughout the history of the orthodox Christian faith there have been seasons of special repentance, even though it should also be a daily and weekly practice. The Jewish people have an appointed annual time for repentance on their Day of Atonement (Leviticus 23:27). Christians have a special season to remember the birth of the Christ child, his saving sacrifice and resurrection, and more frequent remembrances through the Holy Communion. We should also observe a season to center our attentions on the need for repentance. Historically this season for Christians is during Lent.

Will you stand with me in repentance? God has broken my heart with a call to repentance and a grieving over my sin and the sin of the church. I look to Daniel who did not repent saying "those sinners." He repented owning up to the sin that stained him as if he personally committed it. "We have sinned," he prayed. Likewise, the sins of the (universal) church stain us as if they were our very own.

Listen to Nehemiah's prayer: "I confess that we have sinned against you" (Nehemiah 1:4-7). We, too, are called to repent of sins even though we could rightfully say, "I didn't do that." We can't wash our hands of wrongdoing saying, "It was the church down the street." We can't point our fingers at the man sitting on the other side of the church saying, "He did it." No! We must own up to all sins of the church as our own. "We have sinned against You, God."

This is my prayer. Please join in agreement with me to fast, pray and repent for the sins of the church.

Oh Lord, great and awesome God, God of our salvation, forgive me, forgive us, your church, your people; for we have sinned against You, we have dishonored Your holy name, and we have brought shame upon your church.[14]

- We are selfish and ambitious; we cause quarrelling and backbiting (James 3:16).
- We rebel against discipline. We will not allow our pastors or elders or God's Word to discipline us. We don't allow anyone to hold us accountable (Proverbs 12:1, Jeremiah 17:31, I Tim 5:20, Titus 1:13, Galatians 6:1, Hebrews 12:9-10).
- We have itching ears. We only want to hear those things that are self-serving, uplifting and encouraging (2 Timothy 4:3, Micah 2:11).
- We are a people who refuse to be under authority (James 4:7, 2 Peter 2:10, I Peter 5:5, Jude 1:8).

---

[14] This is not a catalog of "must do" or "must not do." It is simply my personal list that I'm sharing with you. Sins of which I'm convicted and in need of repentance for the whole church, of which I am a part.

- We are self-indulgent. We want to have everything that the world has (I Peter 4:1-3, Ecclesiastes 6:7, Amos 6:4-5, Proverbs 23:17).
- We are not a people devoted to prayer. We do not live in a way that opens God's ears to our prayers (Psalms 34:15).
- We do not walk in the fear of the Lord (I Peter 1:17, 2 Corinthians 7:1).
- We presume upon the Lord's grace, mercy and patience toward us (Hebrews 10:29).
- We cover up our sins to create a righteous mask in our attempt to appear godly and pious (Proverbs 12:15, Proverbs 28:13).
- We do not know or seek to know what God requires of us (Jeremiah 8:7, Acts 17:30, Micah 6:8).
- The shepherds of the church do not strengthen the weak, heal the sick or bind up the wounds of the injured (Ezekiel 34:4, I Peter 5:1-4).
- We go our own way and ask God to bless us, fully expecting Him to do so (James 4:13).
- We are neither hot nor cold. We do not seek with all our hearts to know God (Revelations 3:15).
- We have dug our own wells, abandoning the Spring of Living Water (Jeremiah 2:13).
- We stifle the Holy Spirit (I Thessalonians 5:19-21).
- We have *more* faith in science than in the "Great Physician" (Exodus 15:26).
- We are building our lives, our nest eggs, our homes, our careers but not God's house (I Corinthians 3:9).
- We are chasing after things that lead us into sin (Ezekiel 14:3, I Corinthians 10:22).
- We attempt to use God's Word to enrich ourselves (Titus 1:11).
- We are conformed to this world (Romans 12:1-2).
- We have created a god that is all love, leaving out God's holy justice (Matthew 15:8-9).
- We do not know or accept the whole of salvation — body, soul and spirit (John 5:39-40, Psalms 27, Isaiah 12:2-3, Psalms 25:4-5).

- Christian dads do not stand up as the priests and spiritual leaders in their homes (Ephesians 6:4).
- Christian moms and dads do not fill the ever-important role of "evangelist" to their children (Isaiah 54:13, Joel 1:3).
- We hold onto our possessions too tightly — we don't see ourselves as only stewards of what belongs to God alone (I Peter 4:10, Luke 19:13, I Corinthians 4:2, I Corinthians 6:19-20).
- We allow things into our homes that don't belong there (Job 31:1).
- We use things that are attractive to the world in an attempt to draw people to Christ (John 12:32).
- We have no commitment when things get tough or when things go wrong (I Corinthians 13:7).
- We shun the disciplines of the historic orthodox Christian faith: fasting, meditation, secluding ourselves in times of prayer (1 Thessalonians 5:17, Psalms 104:34, Matthew 6:6).
- We do not see ourselves as a people set apart to the Lord (Isaiah 29:13, I Corinthians 6:19-20).
- We allow ourselves to be polluted by the world (James 1:27).
- We do not weep and sigh at the sins we see around us (Ezekiel 9:4, Lamentations 3:48, Proverbs 13:5, 2 Peter 2:7).
- We reinterpret the Scriptures, creating a theology that justifies our lifestyles (I John 1:6-7, I John 2:4).
- We have established churches by the volition of man and for self-serving purposes, rather than to worship, serve and honor God (Galatians 5:16).
- We have refused to enter into God's rest, and have caused God's day of rest[15] to become a distraction in our weekend (Ezekiel 20:12, 22:26, Hebrews 10:25, Hebrews 4:11).
- We do not distinguish between the holy and the common;[16] we teach that there is no difference between the unclean and clean (Ezekiel 22:26).

[15] God has given to us a weekly day of rest to remind us of His eternal rest that He has prepared for us from the creation of the world.
[16] This is most evident in spiritual gifts; when we teach there is no difference between God-given natural gifts and Holy Spirit-gifted and empowered spiritual gifts.

Our Prayer: Lord God, Maker of heaven and earth, break our hearts because of our sin. Give us hearts of repentance and make us servants worthy of Your glorious, almighty name. Father God, we ask You to renew us, restore us, rebuild your church, refresh us, and revive Your people. Hear our prayer, O Lord, and may we bring honor to Your name throughout all the earth. In Jesus name, Amen.

Q & A Chapter 3: Foundation of Repentance

1. What are the benefits of repentance?

2. Give examples of godly men who repented for the sins of God's people.

3. Why should we repent of something we didn't do?

Your Mission Journal Notes:

4

Overflowing with the Love of Christ

The fragrance of the cherry blossoms around the Eiffel Tower wafted through the morning breeze. Invisible waves carried the aromas to lovers who strolled the cobblestone pathways, hand in hand, arm in arm. Overwhelmed by the ambience of love, they often stopped, looked into each other's eyes and touched, cheek to cheek, lip to lip, and then walked on laughing and speaking love in whispers.

Beyond the fountains along the pathway, rustic wooden carts displayed flowers of every color. The little wagons overflowed with vibrant pink, yellow, red, orange, and purple blossoms of every variety and size. Another puff of cool air carried the perfume of cherry blossoms, blending it with the intoxicating scents of cut garden flowers. Lovers, holding each other close, were drawn to the vibrant floral displays, as if irresistibly, by heady aromas too rich to resist.

I watched as two young lovers strolled toward the flower carts, oblivious to all that was around them, yet pulled by the magnetic tug of fragrant bouquets on display. The gathering lovers, constantly moving about, began to drift toward one wooden wheeled flower cart in particular. I couldn't help but wonder about this and I moved along with those who were gathering there.

I stood with amazement, watching a girl beside her cart helping young men select flowers for their lovers. It was as if she became visible for just a moment and then invisible again, blending with the flowers. Her dress was adorned the same colors as the goods she was offering. With her bright red hair, her rosy cheeks and twinkling green eyes she appeared to be a flower among flowers. Then she opened her mouth and began to sing a sweet song. It was a song the flowers would sing, with words the blossoms would proclaim. The morning wisps of wind, warming in the sunlight, picked up the song with the springtime fragrances and carried them along to lovers along the way.

The scene was a beautiful delight, springtime for the eyes. The power of song and flowers, the fragrance of fresh garden bouquets, drew the crowds with an invisible power. The young girl was hidden among the beauty, blending in like a butterfly alighting upon colorful flower petals of a lily, opening to the light of day.

I walked on to gaze at the colorful flower carts at the edge of the square. There were but a few scarce couples gathered around them. The lady at the next cart I approached screeched in a loud, piercing voice, "Get your flowers. We got your fresh flowers. Best prices for flowers."

Her call disturbed the beautiful fragrance carried along in the air. Her iridescent pink apron was so bright my eyes could see little else. Her bleached blond hair was pinned up in voluminous curls on top her head. Her oversized chartreuse glasses made her blue eyes glare. She grabbed a bouquet of flowers in each hand and waved them about, desperately calling again and again as loud as she could, "Flowers. Get your fresh flowers. Discounts on fresh bouquets."

But the crowds gave her a wide berth. The grating sound of her voice drove them away. I watched as the sweet-smelling breeze and song of the flowers drew them back to the flower girl, cloaked with color among her aromatic displays of springtime radiance. Her every movement was like the dance of garden-fresh blossoms waving in the breeze as she offered her precious gifts to lovers who came her way.

The young girl illustrates the nature of ministering in our spiritual gifts through the power of the Holy Spirit, extending the hand of Jesus to those around us – to a lost and dying world. Like the lady in the bright pink apron, if our purpose is rooted in our own desire or if what we do is by the power of finite man, our gifts of servanthood come across as an irritating, clanging gong. Our service to our brothers and sisters will become little more than a grating noise.

For all of us who are called by Jesus' Name, it would be good to examine ourselves and check our motives. Are we doing what is right because of what we will gain from it? Do we serve God only because

He is of great benefit to us? Do we serve in our church and community because of the good will it creates for our business? The best way to do a self-check is to look at what is overflowing from our lives. The young maiden became almost invisible and sold flowers to serve young lovers in love. The bleached hair flower lady was there for a buck. She was there to sell all her flowers so she could get out of there.

But there is hope for those who desire to spill over with the love of Christ. And not just any hope, but an eternal hope. This expectation of hope is disguised in a mystery beyond human understanding. But that mystery has been fully revealed to us in Jesus Christ, the eternal Son of the Living God.

After Moses parted the Red Sea, the people of Israel lifted their voices in prophetic song before the Lord: "Then Moses and the Israelites sang this song to the Lord: 'I will sing to the Lord, for he has triumphed gloriously; horse and rider he has thrown into the sea. The Lord is my strength and my might, and he has become my salvation; this is my God, and I will praise him, my father's God, and I will exalt him'" (Exodus 15:1-2). The name of God's humble servant, Moses, wasn't even mentioned in the song and rightfully so. Even in his sister Miriam's spiritual song he's not mentioned, because the praise and glory were to God whose mighty hand accomplished great things for His people.

We are confronted with a great and glorious mystery. By the power of the Spirit this mysterious truth saturates every fiber of our being. Our Lord Jesus Christ is the very center of this mystery. The apostle Paul spoke of it, unfolding the secrets of this mystery:

> *"In former generations this mystery was not made known to humankind, as it has now been revealed to his holy apostles and prophets by the Spirit: that is, the Gentiles have become fellow heirs, members of the same body, and sharers in the promise in Christ Jesus through the gospel."*
> *(Ephesians 3:5-6)*
>
> *"I became its servant according to God's commission that was given to me for you, to make the word of God fully known, the mystery that has been hidden throughout the ages*

and generations but has now been revealed to his saints."
(Colossians 1:25-26)

The secret of the mystery of salvation have been opened to you; now walk in it by the power of the Spirit, overflowing with the love of Christ to those around you. Minister in the power of the Holy Spirit, by means of the gifting and empowering work of the Holy Spirit. In this you are allowing God to use you as His instrument to minister, in a sense, invisibly so that God may be glorified, receiving all the honor and glory. John the Baptist said it well: "He [Jesus] must become greater; I must become less" (John 3:30). You are simply a weak vessel God has chosen to use as His hand extended to manifest His living, active presence to all the people you rub elbows with every day. As you become more invisible, Jesus will overflow from your life even more than you can imagine.

Q & A Chapter 4: Overflowing with the Love of Christ

1. Describe the true heart of a servant.

2. What is the great mystery made known to us in Christ?

3. How is the love and power of Christ manifested in the world today?

Your Mission Journal Notes:

5

A Tsunami of God's Love

It's like body surfing on a tsunami wave. Like being swept along in an irresistible, powerful force, enveloped in the tide and carried along in the love of the One who made the wave. This love is a continuous, all-encompassing love that carries us day-by-day, hour-by-hour, and minute-by-minute as we walk, or should I say "surf," with our God in sweet, loving fellowship.

Not only is His loving sacrifice on a wooden cross, on a hill called Golgotha, a timeless and enduring sacrifice, it also reveals a love that covers all of His people through all of time. This includes every adopted child who becomes a part of His eternal kingdom.

God is present in the moment with you, desiring to hold you close to His heart. He desires sweet communion and fellowship with you because of His down-to-earth love for you. We don't have a Jesus who only loved us two thousand years ago. The same love that drove Him to die in our place and for our sins is alive and actively present today — and He wants you to be the recipient of His sacrificial love. In fact He wants you so full of His love that it overflows from you.

We do not serve a distant God who can only be reached if we pray long enough and get all of our friends praying with us until we rattle the god box in heaven. We serve a God who is as close to us as the air we breathe. Even closer. Our God pours out His heart of love, knowing our hearts may harden. We stand before a God who lovingly teaches us to walk, knowing we may walk away. He adopted into His family and given His family name, knowing that we may bring dishonor and shame to His name. When He loves us and receives us as His own. He gives up having total control of the outcome. He loves us completely, knowing His heart will be pierced as we despise Him:

> *"For it is impossible to restore again to repentance those who have once been enlightened, and have tasted the heavenly gift, and have shared in the Holy Spirit, and have tasted the goodness of the word of God and the powers of the age to come, and then have fallen away, since on their own they are crucifying again the Son of God and are holding him up to contempt." (Hebrews 6:4-6)*

This is vulnerable love. This is sacrificial love. This is like the love of the father who gave his wealth to a son who would distance himself and squander the gift in a full tilt, party hearty mode. This is the love of the father whose eldest son refused to welcome back his prodigal brother and join the party. This same God, Creator of heaven and earth, commissioned the people He created to fill and subdue the earth. God called them to fill the earth with righteousness and godly offspring, knowing they would reject Him and squander the gift. But it didn't take long for mankind to spoil the earth rather than subdue it. "Now the earth was corrupt in God's sight, and the earth was filled with violence. And God saw that the earth was corrupt; for all flesh had corrupted its ways upon the earth" (Genesis 6:11-12). This was not God's purpose and plan. It's certainly not the outcome He wanted. And yet, knowing full well the end result of it, God gave His created beings a job to do. In a sense, God set them on a pathway, a narrow and good pathway, giving them the capacity to walk upon it or to wander.[17] In giving His created beings the freedom to stay close or to drift away, God opened Himself to being pierced by those whom He loved. Now we see clearly that God has no desire for us to be like dogs on a chain

---

[17] What I'm presenting here is the opposite of Deistic beliefs. God did not set mankind on a path and then ascend into the heavens to await the outcome. God is actively present in His creation to walk with, to commune with, to strengthen, to encourage and to guide His people for the good of all mankind, for the good of His church and the Kingdom of Heaven.

or puppets on a string. His purpose also doesn't include leaving us to flounder on our own.

Today's churches have taught Christians to see God as omnipotent, omniscient and totally in control. This is completely true, but not the whole truth. If we stop at omnipotent, omniscient, and almighty we end up with a god who has a greater likeness to Greek gods. The Greeks portrayed their gods as mighty, awesome, and fearsome, but relationally distant, beyond time and out of touch with their subjects. What we've created in this day and age is God who has done great things in the past but is not actively present today. We have great Bible stories, but they aren't relevant in this day and age.

Please don't misunderstand me. Beyond any doubt, our Creator God *is* omnipotent, omniscient and sovereign. His hand is upon His creation and His Holy Spirit is at work in the world today to accomplish His purpose and plan among mankind. Yet God reveals the wondrous depth of His nature in overwhelming love for His created beings. God has placed before us choices — subdue or destroy, return His love or reject it. Scripture shows God in all His glory, enlightening us to His sovereign kingdom as a dominion that overflows with His love and compassion. Even so, apart from the fact that God first loved us, we cannot find in ourselves the capacity to love Him. In the overwhelming flow of His love and mercy, how is it that hearts are hardened in rebellion, finding the ability to reject His love?

Throughout all the history of mankind, God has come down to covenant with man, commissioning him to good works. The first people's disobedience in the Garden of Eden was a violation of God's covenant. The point is that God poured out His overwhelming love upon His creation, first to Adam and Eve, then to Abraham and Sarah, and then to the people of Israel. In our time, God pours out His love upon the church and through His people by initiating this loving bond of fellowship, in covenant with those He has chosen. He willingly becomes vulnerable, in a sense, setting Himself up to be rejected by the ones He has brought into loving fellowship with Himself.

What incredible love He has shown you. What will you do with this great love? What will you do with His covenant of love? Will you embrace the sweet, loving communion and fellowship God desires with you because of His down-to-earth love for you?

Be assured that when you determine to step into the fullness of God's love, His love will supernaturally overflow from you to all those your life touches. This is the New Covenant work He has given you to do. Will you do it?

Q & A Chapter 5: A Tsunami of God's Love

1. Describe your understanding of God's actively present love for you.

2. How would you depict God's vulnerable love?

3. What will you do with God's great love for you?

Your Mission Journal Notes:

6

Finding Treasure in the Rubble

In every book store with a Christian section there is a book on "Promises," and rightly so because the Bible is full of precious promises. And yet there are promises in the Bible that we'd rather forget. Like this one: "In this world you will have trouble. But take heart! I have overcome the world" (John 16:33 NIV). I have yet to find anyone from any persuasion who would not agree with the first part of this Scripture. The life we live on this planet is full of trouble. If you're fortunate enough to be without any troubles in your personal realm, just turn on the news and you'll find more than enough trouble in every corner of the world. Terrorism, disease, earthquakes, tsunamis, wars, refugees, famines and the list goes on. "Trouble, Bubble, Struggle, and that's today's news."

The greatest tragedies are those that greet us at our doorstep. How is it possible in times of great personal tragedy to find treasure? Is it just a matter of diverting our eyes? Is it only a matter of not focusing on the trouble? Putting it behind you? Do we ignore the elephant in the middle of the room? Do we just refuse to center our attentions on our circumstances and ourselves?

Not at all. We do well, as grief runs its course, to look to our Lord Jesus who has overcome the world and all its troubles. In Him, no matter the circumstances, we have great comfort, joy and peace. On your own it is impossible. Yet our Lord and Savior is more than able to bring you into victory in spite of any and all circumstances that force their way into your life.

The writer of Proverbs 30:8-9 understood the need to have just enough - not too much, not too little. He knew the importance of having just enough of a struggle, but not just lounging on easy street.

He wrote, "Keep falsehood and lies far from me; give me neither poverty nor riches, but give me only my daily bread. Otherwise, I may have too much and disown you and say, 'Who is the Lord?' Or I may become poor and steal, and so dishonor the name of my God."

God rescued Joseph from a dungeon prison, placing him in a position of authority so that he could rescue his family from a devastating famine. While oppressed as slaves in Egypt, Israel became a nation set apart to God. Through the trials of the desert, God led His people to the Promised Land. In spite of vicious opposition from Sanballat the Horonite and Tobiah the Ammonite, Nehemiah led the people to rebuild the city of Jerusalem and the temple. In a time of great persecution the foundations of the church were established.

Finding treasure in trouble may be like going fishing and reeling in a chunk of rusty metal instead of a sockeye salmon, only to find out you now own a valuable relic from an ancient sailing ship.

Or it may be like parents who have dreamt of a boy who will become a great basketball player. They shared a dream for their daughter to become a brilliant doctor. They planned for a child to follow in dad's footsteps as an engineer. But they have given birth to a child who has Down syndrome.

When they are given the news, a flood of sadness, anger and fear overwhelm them. They look for the cause, for someone or something to blame. They are angry with God. They are frightened of what lies ahead. They ask, "Are we being punished?" Their hearts overflow with love for their new baby and their hearts are heavy because they know this won't be easy. Their dreams are dashed and their lives forever changed.

The grief begins to change and fears subside when the baby is given a name. Grandpa stoops over the child as mom holds him in her arms. He whispers, "I would be so blessed if you would give him my name, Allan Sawyer."

Mom smiles and a tear streaks down her cheek. She looks at her husband and they agree. "Yes, he will be named Allan Sawyer McTaggart."

As the years pass by, the family finds a great treasure in raising a Down syndrome child. They look back on their initial reaction and feel foolish that they thought God was punishing them. In fact, their son has brought joy and happiness into their lives. He's a blessing that they wouldn't trade for anything. Mom often finds herself staring at her sleeping child and thanking God for the blessing. She's proud of her special child. She delights in his blue eyes and cherishes his cuddles. Dad dashes home right after work to enjoy his laughter and revel in his delightful and carefree approach to everything he touches.

I'm completely amazed as I watch the hand of God orchestrating my life and the lives of friends and family. All for good. Too often we see trouble in what has happened to us, when in fact, God is using it for good. In sorrow, the Lord gives gladness. When we are anxious, He gives us peace. When we are weary, He gives us strength. Yes, Jesus has overcome the world, and He lifts us up, blessing us, and He prepares us for a joyful eternity with Him. Our joy is complete because we have overcome, laying up treasures with Him for all eternity.

Q & A Chapter 6: Finding Treasure in the Rubble

1. What good does God accomplish in the troubles and trials we face?

2. How is it that troubles paved the way to great accomplishments for the heroes of our faith like Joseph and Nehemiah?

3. What good things does God accomplish when troubles come your way?

Your Mission Journal Notes:

7

Overflowing with Worship

Have you ever walked up to your car in the parking lot at the mall, balancing your shopping bags on both arms and fumbling to get your key fob and push the button? You do a double take when nothing happens. Then you realize that it isn't your car. It only looked like it. Same color, same model and year, but at second glance you see that your bumper stickers are missing.

As Christians, we are called to worship in a way that is spiritual and real, according to spirit and truth. Speaking to the wayward woman at the well, Jesus said, "God is spirit, and those who worship him must worship in spirit and truth" (John 4:14). What does it mean to worship in a way that is spiritual and real, to worship in spirit and in truth? Does this mean we must worship in a liturgical church? Are we supposed to clap with the music and lift up our hands as we sing? Are we truly worshipping when we are sitting cross-legged in the sand with a campfire lighting our faces, lifting our hands, eyes closed and swaying to the sounds of a guitar? Do we all have to speak in tongues and prophesy to make it real?

How often do Christians worship in a way that looks like the right thing, sounds real, feels true, but it's the "wrong car in the parking lot?" How do we know when our worship is in spirit and in truth? These are good questions for us to answer and in fact, when we see it, our lives will change — your key fob will unlock the door.

We worship and offer up our praises to God who is worthy of our praise and worship because of all He has done for us. Because of who He is, we are called to ascend before Him in worship. The Bible includes many examples of this call to ascend in worship and clear glimpses of true worship. The design of God's temple in Jerusalem is a model for the various forms of New Testament worship. The ascending temple courtyards depict common worship, i.e. natural forms of worship; then personal, worshipful prayer; then gatherings for worship; and then the highest worship we can offer: ministering to the body of Christ using our Spirit-empowered spiritual gifts. Finally, the Bible shows us how we can know if it's spiritual and real.

Numerous Psalms of ascent reveal to us that ascending to worship is a part of who we are as God's people. "I lift up my eyes to the hills—from where will my help come? My help comes from the Lord, who made heaven and earth" (Psalms 121:1). This is the Psalm Israelites would sing on their journey from Jericho in the valley to Jerusalem on the mountain of the Lord. Again in Psalms 122:3-4: "Jerusalem — built as a city that is bound firmly together. To it the tribes go up, the tribes of the Lord, as was decreed for Israel, to give thanks to the name of the Lord."

Again we read about worshipful ascent in Hebrews 12:22-24:

> "But you have come to Mount Zion and to the city of the living God, the heavenly Jerusalem, and to innumerable angels in festal gathering, and to the assembly of the firstborn who are enrolled in heaven, and to God the judge of all, and to the spirits of the righteous made perfect, and to Jesus, the mediator of a new covenant, and to the sprinkled blood that speaks a better word than the blood of Abel."

Upon arriving in Jerusalem, God's people became witnesses of this worshipful ascent in the very structure of the temple where God's people would first enter the temple courtyards and then ascend the steps of the temple to worship.

The Apostle Paul encourages us to ascend in worship with our minds and in spirit. "I will pray with my spirit, but I will pray with my mind also; I will sing praise with my spirit, but I will sing with my mind also" (1 Corinthians 14:15).

Christian worship is best defined as giving homage and reverence, living in awe, bending our knees, and honoring God in word and deed. Worship is acknowledging and glorifying God, His nature, His attributes, His marvelous ways, and His awesome acts on behalf of His people. Worship is serving God's people and His church. We worship as we return a portion of God's blessings, an offering to acknowledge God's bountiful provision. Worship is also walking as Jesus would walk if He were wearing your sneakers. Another dimension of worship is to be the person God has called you to be, what He has prepared you to be.

Our challenge is that the Bible does not provide a systematic theology or pattern for worship. It's likely that it isn't provided because we would then create a system of worship that would not be real. From a methodical doctrine, it is too easy to construct a box that worship must fit into. If we create a system or attempt to package worship, its purpose is lost. I'm in no way speaking against godly order in a church gathering, nor am I saying there is only one acceptable form of worship for the New Testament church.

We can further our understanding by observing those who came to worship Jesus. Imagine the spirit of worship in those who came to kiss Jesus' feet with a heart that was torn, grieving over their sin and coming before Him as Lord and Savior. Here is a beautiful picture of the true heart of worship in Luke 7:36-38:

> *"One of the Pharisees asked him to eat with him, and he went into the Pharisee's house and reclined at the table. And behold, a woman of the city, who was a sinner, when she learned that he was reclining at table in the Pharisee's house, brought an alabaster flask[18] of ointment, and standing behind him at his feet, weeping, she began to wet his feet with her tears and wiped them with the hair of her head and kissed his feet and anointed them with the ointment."*

---

[18] This alabaster flask was filled with ointment, a fragrant oil.

Matthew records an eyewitness account of another beautiful act of worship in Matthew 26:6-13:

> *"Now when Jesus was at Bethany in the house of Simon the leper, a woman came up to him with an alabaster flask of very expensive ointment, and she poured it on his head as he reclined at table. And when the disciples saw it, they were indignant, saying, "Why this waste? For this could have been sold for a large sum and given to the poor." But Jesus, aware of this, said to them, "Why do you trouble the woman? For she has done a beautiful thing to me. For you always have the poor with you, but you will not always have me. In pouring this ointment on my body, she has done it to prepare me for burial. Truly, I say to you, wherever this gospel is proclaimed in the whole world, what she has done will also be told in memory of her.*

There was a beautiful display of worship even in Bethlehem, Jesus' birthplace. The Magi came on a journey that required roughly thirty days on a camel to worship Jesus. They did not come empty handed. They offered gold as a symbol of Jesus divinity, frankincense as a symbol of holiness and righteousness, and myrrh as a symbol of bitterness, suffering and affliction. This act of worship was true and real (Matthew chapter 2).

With this clear definition of worship in mind, let's examine worship as a part of our everyday lives. Worshipping with our minds is completely possible for all those who are called by His Name. To worship in our spirit is not of ourselves because on our own it is, in fact, mission impossible.

We'll start with the most basic and common forms of worship that all of God's creation may take part in. The writer of Psalms 148 opens our eyes to this form of worship:

> *"Praise the Lord! Praise the Lord from the heavens; praise him in the heights! Praise him, all his angels; praise him, all his host! Praise him, sun and moon; praise him, all you shining*

stars! Praise him, you highest heavens, and you waters above the heavens! Let them praise the name of the Lord, for he commanded and they were created. He established them forever and ever; he fixed their bounds, which cannot be passed. Praise the Lord from the earth, you sea monsters and all deeps, fire and hail, snow and frost, stormy wind fulfilling his command! Mountains and all hills, fruit trees and all cedars! Wild animals and all cattle, creeping things and flying birds! Kings of the earth and all peoples, princes and all rulers of the earth! Young men and women alike, old and young together! Let them praise the name of the Lord, for his name alone is exalted; his glory is above earth and heaven. He has raised up a horn for his people, praise for all his faithful, for the people of Israel who are close to him. Praise the Lord."

In this beautiful Psalm, we are blessed to see how all of God's creation praises Him simply by doing what He created them to do. The stars shine forth, the moon glows in the night and the trees clap their hands as the wind stirs them up. This is the most basic and common form of worship. In this way, when we do our work as if we're working for the Lord, using our God given natural gifts, we do this as a form of worship. It is that simple and that beautiful.

We must not confuse this common means of worship with what is holy: our times of private prayer, praise and worship. This takes place in your closet, prayer room or wherever you can catch a moment to block out or get away from the chaos around you. In these quiet times, we offer up prayers of thanksgiving, lay our petitions before the Lord, intercede for our Christian leaders, plead for our brothers and sisters in the Lord, lift our hands to worship, and exalt the Lord in His majesty. We pray earnestly for those in need, and offer up our praise and worship to a holy God who is "God who Provides." This is one-on-one with God Almighty. This is Abba[19] time, talking

---

[19] Abba means, "Father." Jewish children may call their fathers "Abby" which means "daddy."

together, sharing your heart, and hearing the heart of God. During Abba times, Jacob wrestled with God, David played his harp and sang Psalms of praise before God, Elijah implored God on behalf of His people, Moses interceded before God for the tribes of Israel, and Jesus advocated for his own disciples on His knees before God in the quiet of the wilderness.

If a private form of worship is not a part of your life, today is a good time to begin. There is no need to become the greatest prayer warrior the world has ever known in your first week of making this spiritual discipline a part of your life. You don't need to be perfect in offering up praises before the Lord. Just come before Him with an honest, open heart in the best way you can. Don't make it too hard. Let it grow and flourish in a natural — supernatural - way.

This is Theresa's story of blessings in prayer and private worship. As Theresa[20] matured in her walk with the Lord, she began to sense a need for Abba time beyond little snippets of prayer in anxious moments and the formal prayers during Sunday morning church. She started by dedicating two or three minutes to prayer each morning before dashing out the door to join the daily grind. Over the next several months her prayer time naturally grew to ten or fifteen minutes. Then she started to set the alarm clock early to allow more prayer time. Her three minutes grew into a much longer time, because it was so sweet, beautiful and pleasant. It was like being led beside still waters, refreshment for the soul.

It wasn't long before Theresa began to want more prayer moments and she set aside a time before retiring for the night — just a few minutes at first. And then her prayer time went beyond praying through a list of prayer requests. During times of prayer, she began to lift up her hands to worship her God, her King, her Lord, Master and Friend. She was blessed with the gift of praying in the spirit and she matured in that gift as well.

Because she found these prayer moments with her Heavenly Father to be such an overwhelming blessing, she began to catch a few

---

[20] The name is changed and the story slightly altered so the real person in the story is not too recognizable.

moments in the middle of the day to stop what she was doing and come before the Throne of Grace to pray and worship. She still prayed while commuting to work and in those moments throughout the day when she felt anxious or in need of a protective hand. Her private Abba moments became like a root system growing deep into the Living Water to feed her relationship with her Heavenly Father.[21]

Indeed, just like Theresa, these private moments of prayer, thanksgiving, praise and worship that are just between you and Abba are some of the most precious moments of walking with the Lord. Your prayers, praise and worship are treasured as a sweet smelling fragrance to our Heavenly Father, for He stores the prayers of the saints as incense in golden bowls (Revelation 5:8). Truly, these private moments prepare you for gathering and worshipping together with your brothers and sisters in the Lord.

Another uncommon way to worship with our mind and our spirit is by singing hymns, songs and Psalms of worship and praise in a gathering of God's people. The congregation of God's people offers us a taste of heaven that is the beginning of the fulfillment of God's promise of gathering us from every tribe, nation, people and tongue to worship before His throne.

We find an awesome description of this gathering in this Scripture: "But you have come to Mount Zion and to the city of the living God, the heavenly Jerusalem" (Hebrews 12:22).

Rise up before God Almighty, Maker of all heaven and earth, to worship in spirit and in truth, worshipping God in all His fullness as He has revealed Himself to us in the words of Scripture. Join together with the congregation and give glory to our Awesome and Mighty God at His footstool. Hold nothing back from exalting Him in all that He has shown Himself to be to His people from the beginning to the end. This is true worship.

When we deny God's attributes, when we reject even a part of who He proclaims Himself to be, when we refuse His good gifts to His people, we begin the process of creating our own designer God

---

[21] Do not attempt to imitate Theresa or her style of private prayer and worship. God has made you to be unique and He will lead you in a way that works for you. Instead, imitate Christ.

made in our own likeness and according to our own likings, and we place ourselves in great peril, coming to a place where we are not worshipping God in truth. We will not be gathering according to truth, or in the fullness of His Holy Name.

The priestly courts show the highest manner of worship before a Holy God. Psalms 135:1-2 (NIV) introduces us to the nature of worshipful ministry: "Praise the name of the Lord; Praise him, you servants of the Lord, you who minister in the house of the Lord, in the courts of the house of our God." The Apostle Peter proclaims the priesthood of all believers: "...like living stones, let yourselves be built into a spiritual house, to be a holy priesthood, to offer spiritual sacrifices acceptable to God through Jesus Christ" (1 Peter 2:5-6).

This is the universal priesthood of the believer. We are each called to minister in the congregation according to the spiritual gifts the Spirit of Jesus has poured out into us for the good of the whole church, in your home church and throughout all the earth. The Holy Spirit will empower all His people to serve and minister in a holy gathering according to what He has given us to do.

As the apostle Paul encourages in Romans 12, if the Holy Spirit has gifted you to teach, instruct God's people with all your strength. If the Holy Spirit has gifted you with a ministry of helps, set up the chairs, make the coffee and serve the veggie trays and muffins with joy and gladness. If you are gifted in the spiritual gift of prophecy, minister God's active and living presence in the moment as He spontaneously speaks out to His people through you. If the Spirit of God has gifted you in discerning of spirits, keep your eyes clear and minister God's delightful jealous protection over His people. Should God gift you to be a doorman in the house of the Lord, greet the people at the door in the love of the Lord with a heart overflowing with His sacrificial love.

If we dismiss ministries by the gifts the Holy Spirit has distributed in the local church, we miss out on the fullness of worship. I encourage you to enter into ministries of spiritual gifts because these are the greatest and highest form of worship before our God and King. Indeed, ministries that are true and real take place when the Holy Spirit gifts and empowers a weak but willing vessel, who will be God's hand extended to reveal Jesus Christ to those in need of Christ. Humble yourself and be Jesus' hand in ministering to His church.

Now, how do we know if our worship is spiritual and real and according to spirit and truth? There is a sure way to know if our worship, in private, in a gathering of believers, or Christian service is proven to be real and true in our words, deeds and actions of our daily lives. We examine ourselves for no one else can do this for us. We must simply ask, "Is my faith proven to be true in all that I do and say? Is what I do at church, serving in my community, and the words I offer in worship consistent with my daily actions?"

We must consider Romans 12:1-2:

> *"I appeal to you therefore, brothers and sisters, by the mercies of God, to present your bodies as a living sacrifice, holy and acceptable to God, which is your spiritual worship. Do not be conformed to this world, but be transformed by the renewing of your minds, so that you may discern what is the will of God — what is good and acceptable and perfect."*

This Scripture is the only one that explicitly refers to what we ought to do as a spiritual act of worship, showing us how to truly live out your worship in everything you do. This is living a sacrificial lifestyle, committing our desires to Christ and serving others first and foremost. This is not setting up a new legalistic system for how to act. The Apostle Paul is saying, in essence, "This is the fruit that will sprout and grow and come to fruition on your branch that is grafted into the true vine." This is your spiritual act of worship.

You may be overcome with a sense of having failed miserably in this. You might feel like you're sitting in an ash heap, covered by soot with tears streaking down your face. I proclaim to you God's promise to give you splendor in place of ruins — even ruins you have created: "...[I will] bestow on them a crown of beauty instead of ashes, the oil of joy instead of mourning, and a garment of praise instead of a spirit of despair" (Isaiah 61:3 NIV).

At some point we all fail to live what we believe because we are fallible beings. My own sense of guilt in this drives me to Christ and in my failings I must stand with my Old Testament brother Job: "For I know that my Redeemer lives, and that at the last he will stand upon the earth" (Job 19:25). Repent of your sin, your failings, your weaknesses that drag you down, and then turn to your Living Redeemer to be forgiven and washed. Now get up and start fresh in the beauty of His holiness.

Be encouraged. You know what it is to ascend in worship before a Holy God. You worship God in common worship, doing what he has naturally gifted you to do and doing it as unto the Lord. Worship God in your prayer closet, in your Abba times, laying your petitions before Him, exalting and praising Him who is worthy of praise. Gather together with the congregation to worship in spirit and in truth, singing hymns, Psalms and spiritual songs. Offer up your body as a living sacrifice unto the Lord as a part of your worship. Above all, as God calls, gifts and empowers you, you may minister in the house of God, offering up the highest form of worship to God, of whom the angels of heaven sing out, ""Holy, holy, holy, the Lord God the Almighty, who was and is and is to come" (Revelation 4:8). And again, "You are worthy, our Lord and God, to receive glory and honor and power, for you created all things, and by your will they existed and were created" (Revelation 4:11).

Blessed be the Name of the Lord. May His Holy Name be glorified in all the earth.

Q & A Chapter 7: Overflowing with Worship

1. How does worship enter into the realm of being spiritual and real?

2. Can we worship in different ways and still worship in spirit and truth?

3. Describe worship in a gathering of believers.

Your Mission Journal Notes:

8

The Glory of Christ

A thunderous rush of rain water filled the forested gulley while a crack of lightening lit up the night sky. The crescendoing sounds, like crashing cymbals and rumbling drums, shook the third story balcony where I stood. From the depths of my being, a spontaneous shout rose – "Glory!" And my shout was a whimper, drowned in the roiling rumble within the low hanging mist.

The Lord God Almighty reveals Himself, showing His power and might throughout all the earth for the glory of His name. And what an awesome God we serve. I've often puzzled about why God, who is more than able to accomplish all that He wills — why does He need me? What is His reason for involving me when, in reality, He could do all that He wants to do without me? God revealed this desire to the first man and woman He created: "God blessed them, and God said to them, 'Be fruitful and multiply, and fill the earth and subdue it; and have dominion over the fish of the sea and over the birds of the air and over every living thing that moves upon the earth'" (Genesis 1:28).

Why does God include us in what He is doing? The answer began to come to me as I read John chapter 17, which is the prayer of our High Priest, Jesus. The words "glory" or "glorify" are used nine times in His prayer to the Father, and it is in His glory that we find the answer to this question. It's a beautiful succession of glory upon glory, and indeed, God includes us because we are His glory.

Before you continue here, read John chapter 17 in your Bible and specifically note verse 1: "Glorify your Son so that the Son may glorify you." Again in verse 4: "I glorified you on earth by finishing the work that you gave me to do. So now, Father, glorify me in your own presence with the glory that I had in your presence before the world existed."

God's glory is central to our faith and of great importance for the church. We read of God's glory in Exodus 24:17: "Now the appearance of the glory of the Lord was like a devouring fire on the top of the mountain in the sight of the people of Israel." We learn more of God's glory in this verse: "O Lord, our Sovereign, how majestic is your name in all the earth! You have set your glory above the heavens" (Psalms 8:1). The angels proclaimed God's glory as they announced the birth of the Christ child: "And suddenly there was with the angel a multitude of the heavenly host, praising God and saying, 'Glory to God in the highest heaven, and on earth peace among those whom he favors!'" (Luke 2:13).

What is this glory we are called to be a part of? How do we fit into bringing glory to God? Jesus prayed specifically for those given to Him as the sheep of His pasture: "All mine are yours, and yours are mine; and I have been glorified in them" (John 17:10). He gave up the glory that was His before the beginning of the world to come down here to walk among us (verse 5). He gave up His splendor and majesty and the grandeur of God's presence to come down to earth so that we too might glorify Him. Yes, the end result is that Jesus is now glorified in us. His Holy Name is glorified through those He has called. But how is He glorified in us?

Beyond a doubt, we glorify God as we worship Him. When we gather together as believers to proclaim Christ, to sing His praises, to lift up holy hands, to speak of His goodness, to speak words of faith in our creeds, to pray together, to read and declare the truths of the Holy Scriptures, and to preach the cross of Christ, we are (or ought to be) doing all this to the glory of God and His Holy Name.

But we must press on, for there is so much more our Lord Jesus has for us. Our first clue to these precious benefits is in Jesus' prayer: "I glorified you on earth by finishing the work that you gave me to do" (John 17:4). Jesus brought glory to the Father here on earth by finishing the work God gave Him to do. It's pure and simple. Jesus' work was completed and the disciples watched as the resurrected Christ Jesus ascended into heaven. Everything He did was to the glory of God and His work was complete. But how does that apply to us?

We are joined together with Christ in this powerful family of faith called the church. We glorify God when He is able to exhibit His divine attributes and perfections through us. When we speak what God is speaking. When we go where we see God going. When we extend our hand to do what He is doing, we do all this to the glory of God. God glorified His Son. The Son glorified the Father. And now when we complete the work God has ordained for us, glory comes to Jesus through those God gave to Him. This is the essence of the Great Commission, which is God's New Testament covenant with His people. God is glorified as we complete our part of His grand plan.

Again, the Father glorifies the Son, the Son glorifies the Father, and Jesus is my glory and the "lifter of my head,"[22] and therefore we glorify the Father and the Son. It's a wonderful, miraculous circle of fellowship.

Be encouraged. Humble yourself and step into this circle of fellowship and be blessed beyond all you can ask or imagine. "And all of us, with unveiled faces, seeing the glory of the Lord as though reflected in a mirror, are being transformed into the same image from one degree of glory to another; for this comes from the Lord, the Spirit" (2 Corinthians 3:18). I'm overwhelmed to think of how great is His glory, for indeed, before Christ returns for His bride, every tribe, nation, people and tongue will glorify His holy name.

Why does God use us when He could do all He desires without us? The Lord Almighty glorifies His name as He covenants with you and me to accomplish His plan in all the earth.

This is my desire: that with my last breath here on earth, I will join with the thunderous voices of a chorus of angels and shout, "Glory! For my work is completed, the work God has ordained for me to accomplish — and all to His glory. Amen!"

---

[22] Psalms 3:3

Q & A Chapter 8: The Glory of Christ

1. Why does God need me to accomplish His purpose and plan?

2. How is God glorified when we complete the work He has planned for us?

3. Describe the miraculous power of the circle of fellowship.

Your Mission Journal Notes:

9

Knowing God's Presence

Messages flash at every turn. "Walk. Don't Walk." Yellow — Caution. Red — Stop. Green — Go. Blinking lights assault our senses on every street. Neon signs shine, "OPEN." The marquee glares, "SALE! 50% DISCOUNTS! LAST DAY!" New spring fashions, artfully displayed and lighted are designed to pique our cravings. Background music in the store sets the mood to buy T-shirts, pants, hats - outfits of every kind, emblazoned with messages. Posters and billboards promise something better, making our old stuff seem so inadequate. We can't help but see the ads for the newest gadgets and the QR codes offering more information. Media, sounds, images, and messages of all kinds swarm our lives with an endless, overwhelming flood to overpower our senses. Everywhere placards declare, "Keep off the Grass," "Don't Feed the Bears," "Turn Right," "No U-Turn." My cell phone is ringing. My calendar beeps reminders of places I must be, appointments I have to keep. I'm late — step on the gas.

How do we know what is real and what is a sham? What is just a passing vapor and what is real enough to anchor me? How do we get clear of the fog? How do I get away from laser lights pulsing to music that makes my head throb? It's all so meaningless and the assault of noise leaves me feeling jittery and anxious.

In the noise of this world, in the glaring, flashing messages that inundate our lives, in overwhelming moments with emotions tugging at us, how is it even possible to know the presence of a Holy God? It's a matter of who you hang out with. The Bible calls this "dwelling in His presence." The Psalmist says, "He who dwells in the shelter of the Most High will abide in the shadow of the Almighty" (Psalms 91:1). He's way up there in heaven, right? He's so far away. Anyways God must agree with me. What I'm doing must be okay because I don't hear Him saying anything about it.

Knowing the presence of God in a crazy, busy world full of things tugging us in every direction is impossible, yet entirely possible. Once again, if we depend on our own means — impossible. When we call upon the Name of the Lord, totally possible. Not only is it possible, it is of critical importance to our walk in the Lord. Knowing His presence sets the stage for what is referred to as "the fear of the Lord," which is best understood as reverence, awe and delighted obedience. "I keep the Lord always before me; because he is at my right hand, I shall not be moved. Therefore my heart is glad, and my soul rejoices; my body also rests secure" (Psalms 16:8-9).

God doesn't do advertising campaigns – the voice of the Almighty resounds with the greatest thunder in all the earth. He doesn't write His name in neon lights to get our attention; the light of His omnipotent presence flashes from horizon to horizon. The Holy Spirit doesn't require modern merchandising methods to get our attention at every turn; He manifests Himself in flames of fire and rumbling thunder, shaking the very foundations of the earth. As awesome and fearsome as He is, God may come to us in a still, small voice, gently calling us to His side. He yearns to refresh us by still waters. He asks us to lie down and rest in cool, green pastures. He urges us to be quiet, to be still, and to listen to His sweet voice.

Prayerfully read and reread Psalms 119 and let it wash over you like a flood, as your eyes, ears and understanding are opened to great truths. Read it again and see that the whole chapter is, in essence, about the fear of the Lord. Read it again and hear words that proclaim the blessings of delighted obedience. Read it again and know the value of seeking God's living, active presence in every moment of every day.

David, as a boy, remembered God's presence as he marched out boldly and picked up five stones for his slingshot to confront Goliath, who towered over him.[23] As king, he forgot God's presence as he

---

[23] 1 Samuel chapter 17.

looked over his balcony at Bathsheba taking a bath.[24] With all of life's distractions, it is too easy to forget God's presence. We do well to stand with Joshua as he was given God's promise: "Be strong and courageous; do not be frightened or dismayed, for the Lord your God is with you wherever you go" (Joshua 1:9). In our vulnerable moments, it is too easy to forget and think, "God doesn't know. He doesn't see." But He has promised to be with you wherever you go.

Our human way of thinking is often like that of the beagle our kids grew up with. We never had trouble with her jumping up on the living room sofa, because she knew it was forbidden. But occasionally, when the weather was bad, we would let her stay in the house while we were gone. When we came home, she was right there to greet us with wagging tail. But she looked guilty. Sure enough, when I checked the couch it had a nice warm spot where she had been napping. God doesn't ever leave us. He is present with us in every moment, not to keep us off the couch, but to lovingly watch over us as a father watches over a much-loved child.

Take comfort because God knows the secrets of your heart. Rest assured – He watches over every step you take, day and night. Relax – your Creator God hears every word you speak. Chill – He knows what you seek, where you explore, the places you hang out, and what you search on your cell phone. Be at ease – He knows the desires that drive you. Remember, God is not hovering over you to condemn you, but to hold you in the hollow of His hands (Romans 8:1).

God is your loving, caring Shepherd, watching over you to protect you from the wiles of the enemy and the deception of this world, to keep you from being tempted beyond what you can bear, and to shield you from the plundering exploits of the powers of this present time. He holds you close to his heart, to love you and care for you, and to keep you safe from all harm. He knows your human failings, and yet He is gracious and merciful, ready to forgive. He is calling you to come back to Him, searching for you and calling you by name. He is calling you to repentance so that He may carry you home in His loving arms and celebrate your return with a grand party. Now that you're home with

---

[24] 2 Samuel chapter 11.

your Heavenly Father, take some time to hang out with Him. Dwell in His presence. Talk to Him. Listen to Him. Celebrate His presence.

Day by day God will reveal himself to you and you will come to know His heart; you'll get to know Him. You'll gain a greater sense of His presence. His purpose and plan for you will be opened to you. God Almighty dwells with you and He is ever present with you no matter where you go.

Q & A Chapter 9: Knowing God's Presence

1. In a crazy, busy world, how is it possible to know God's presence?

2. What are the benefits of having an awareness of God's living, active presence every day?

3. Describe God's watchfulness over you.

Your Mission Journal Notes:

10

Obedient by Nature, Forgiven in Christ

"Forgiveness comes easier than permission" was an often-heard statement from my boss, Tim. His second most well-worn saying was, "Shoot first and ask questions later." He was a true Texan with a Lone Ranger mind set. He knew best what to do in a decisive moment and his boss would just have to forgive him. The company values were thrown out the door and he would just shoot from the hip, Wild West style. It only took a few years before forgiveness ran its course and he was told, "This town ain't big enough for the two of us."

Tim's company had foundational vision, goals, and values. In a similar way, God has established order in the kingdom of heaven. Within God's realm, instead of shooting from the hip, it is better to intend to work in agreement with God's order of things. The way of the world is to say, "Forgiveness is easier than obedience." God's way is for His righteousness, at work in us, to give us hearts that purposefully pursue righteous deeds for His glory. And yet God knows our weaknesses and is quick to forgive us and restore us when we fall.

Hearts that pursue purposeful obedience are in harmony with God's perfect creation. In fact, our righteous deeds bring us into agreement with the perfect order that God established as He created the heavens and earth. When we fail, God's forgiveness beautifully restores the work of His righteousness in us and brings us back to a path of obedience.[25]

Because of our human weaknesses, we tend to give forgiveness a front row seat and assign obedience to the back row. As Christians,

---

[25] Isaiah 32:17

we're immersed in teaching about forgiveness. We know forgiveness inside out and backwards. We've examined forgiveness from every angle — maybe we're looking for loopholes. We've got the doctrine of forgiveness down pat. Done deal! We're good to go.

Let's invite "obedience" to join "forgiveness" in the front row, beginning with this Scripture: "...to obey is better than sacrifice" (1 Samuel 15:22). We know that God is quick to forgive. We see God's forgiveness as work when King David came to God, broken over his sin with Bathsheba, to confess his transgression by saying, "I have sinned against the Lord." In that very moment, the prophet Nathan proclaimed God's forgiveness to David: "Now the Lord has put away your sin; you shall not die."[26]

What we minimize and too often forget is the immense price paid for our forgiveness, and not just for forgiveness, but also for our very lives. It came at a cost so high that it may be too much for the human mind to comprehend. All the earthly treasures of all the nations could compensate for the sacrifice that was made for our forgiveness. "...And without the shedding of blood there is no forgiveness of sins" (Hebrews 9:22). The prophets foretold of the price to be paid for our sins: "Just as there were many who were astonished at him — so marred was his appearance, beyond human semblance, and his form beyond that of mortals ..." (Isaiah 53:14). In other words, Jesus was beaten so badly that He was hardly recognizable as a man.

Sin invaded God's perfect order of creation as recorded in Genesis 3:6, and just a few verses later we read of the first blood shed to cover the shame of that sin: "And the Lord God made garments of skins for the man and for his wife, and clothed them." This was a temporary fix, so to speak. It was, in fact, a shadow and a promise of a greater remedy to come. When the Old Testament system of worship was established for the children of Israel, sacrificial blood was required to cover their sin. This foreshadowed the true sacrifice for sins that would completely wash away even the stain of sin.

---

[26] Read on in 2 Samuel and see the horrific consequences King David paid for his moment of pleasure and his murderous attempt to cover-up his sin. He was completely forgiven and cleansed of his sin, but for the peace of his kingdom, the consequences were severe.

Our Lord Jesus Christ gave the ultimate sacrifice through the shedding of His own blood. And we cannot even calculate the price he paid. We can watch the movie *Passion of the Christ* while munching popcorn, with ice-cold Pepsi in hand, and we'll get just a little sense of the price He paid; but we only see the tip of the iceberg, so to speak.

Will you drive the nails into His hands and feet again and again by intentionally turning away from obedience? The writer of Hebrews teaches us that when we persist in deliberate sin, presuming again and again upon God's abundant grace and forgiveness, we are the ones who will suffer great loss:

> *"For it is impossible to restore again to repentance those who have once been enlightened, and have tasted the heavenly gift, and have shared in the Holy Spirit, and have tasted the goodness of the word of God and the powers of the age to come, and then have fallen away, since on their own they are crucifying again the Son of God and are holding him up to contempt." (Hebrews 6:4).*

Read this Scripture again and again until you see it. When we get stuck in the rut of deliberate, knowing-we're-wrong kind of disobedience, intending to depend upon the blood sacrifice of our Lord Jesus for forgiveness and cleansing, we are dead wrong. This kind of rebellious attitude is like a cancer that eats away at our faith. The deliberate sin and wicked acts we do because of our willing ignorance of what God desires of us is tragically wrong, because we are taking a hammer in our fist and pounding the nails into his hands and feet again and again and again, holding the Holy Name of Jesus up to contempt before a lost and dying world.

Sunday morning confessions of faith, reciting the Lord's prayer over and over, communion every Sunday, and having the pastor proclaim Christ's forgiveness will do us no good if we *intend* to go our own way again and again. If we live our lives in willing ignorance, we thereby subject our Living Savior's holy name to repeated contempt.

It gets personal here. The writer of Hebrews writes: "...it is impossible to restore again to repentance... those who have fallen away." God's patience in my life is beyond comprehension. I know beyond the shadow of a doubt that I have presumed upon God's grace and forgiveness to the point that He ought to have tossed me away because of the mess I made of myself, because of the mess I made of my life more than once, more than twice, more than three times — countless times. God had every reason to throw me aside because I brought shame to His holy name. But He did not.

Tears of joy well up in my eyes as I think of his patience with me, for He has carried me through all the trouble I have made for myself. He has reached down to me and accomplished the mission impossible — bringing me to repentance, forgiving me, cleansing me and restoring me to a position of grace in Christ. God has accomplished the impossible in me by His power and might to save my most wayward soul.

This obedience isn't a matter of "you must, you shall, and you will." In ancient cultures it was typical that when a boy turned ten or twelve he would no longer be under his mother's wing, but would graduate to being apprenticed in his father's trade. Imagine a ten-year-old boy on his first day as an apprentice. He would watch his dad like a hawk and imitate his every move. He would learn to talk to the customers in the same manner as dad, and wear a carpenter's hat just like dad. You would see him trying to walk like his dad. He would put on a tool belt like his dad.

Why does he do this? Because he loves and admires his dad and he's thrilled to be so close to him. It's a joyful privilege to be near him. Because of the love we have for our heavenly Father, we imitate Him in how we speak, walk, and do. This love is the righteousness of Jesus Christ at work in our hearts, causing deeds of righteousness to overflow.

"Obedience is better than sacrifice!" This statement makes the way clear for us to walk hand in hand with our loving Shepherd. But how can we do this? Here's one possible way that could change your life. In the morning of every day, ask your Shepherd to lead you; in other words, commit your steps to follow the Lord. From the rising of the sun, intend that your actions and your words will be in agreement with God's order of things, and in harmony with God's loving commands. Yes, determine to follow the precepts of your heavenly Father, committing your steps unto the Lord. And then as the sun goes down, look back on the path you have followed, confess where your feet have slipped and receive forgiveness and cleansing. Take an inventory, looking back on the path you have taken, the words you spoke, the deals you made, the work your hands have accomplished, and confess your shortcomings before a Holy God. What you're doing is intending to be obedient and then calling on God for mercy when you are not.

A passive approach would be to say, "God is sovereign, so He will make sure I go where I'm supposed to go and end up where I'm supposed to be. It's not mine to worry about." With that kind of attitude, we're trying to fill the role of puppet, having little or no responsibility for our own actions. Yes, God is sovereign over all the heavens and earth, and yet, His righteousness at work in our hearts effects righteousness in us. Because of His righteousness in us, we obey in relationship with Him, not because He manipulates us with strings.

This is my amplified paraphrase of 1 Samuel 15:22: "To obey is better than continuing in deliberate or willingly ignorant sins that once again drive the nails into the hands and feet of our Lord Jesus and bring contempt upon His Holy Name." This is not to advocate obedience to a code, law, edict or some new standard. This is a love-driven obedience, an obedience that results from of His goodness at work in our hearts.

Another danger of persisting in deliberate, intentional sin is that very often we become addicted to that sin. "An evil man is held captive by his own sins; they are ropes that catch and hold him" (Proverbs 5:22, NLT). Continue with verse 23: "They die for lack of discipline, and because of their great folly they are lost." The Apostle Peter confirms this truth, writing, "...for people are slaves to whatever masters them" (2 Peter 2:19). These are perfect descriptions of addiction, but addiction is not the final word. God's mercy has the final word. The cross of Jesus Christ finished the matter once for all time. What often begins with a lack of self-discipline, what starts in a moment of self-indulgent weakness, may turn into addiction. But oh, what a blessed hope we have, for our Lord Jesus Christ holds the key that releases us from this prison of our own making, from the chains in which we have bound ourselves. He is the Alpha and the Omega, the beginning and end of all things.

Hold out your hand to receive the key that unlocks your chains.

Now, if you are ready, ask yourself this question: "Do I *intend* to obey, or do I *intend* to be forgiven?" They are polar opposites, so to speak. They are the difference between darkness and the Light. There is a Grand Canyon sized chasm between the two. On one side the righteousness of Jesus Christ changes our hearts and effects righteousness deeds in us, and on the other side we have a pretentious, legalistic obedience. "But thanks be to God, that you who were once slaves of sin have become obedient from the heart..." (Romans 6:17 ESV).

Be encouraged — intend to walk in obedience, according to the righteousness of Christ and according to God's established order. Allow the Holy Spirit to appoint your steps. Ask for the mind of Christ, and imitate Christ Jesus, submitting to the Spirit of Jesus. Seek for your heart of hearts to be filled to overflowing with the Word of God by the power and work of the Holy Spirit. When you fail in this, confess it and you will receive abundant forgiveness.

Mission impossible? Totally possible in Christ. [27]

Q & A Chapter 10: Obedient by Nature, Forgiven in Christ

1. How is obedience so much a part of living in agreement with God's created order?

---

[27] Additional study Scriptures: 1 John 2:1—2, James 2:22, 1 Corinthians 13:5, Colossians 1:24.

2. What does it mean that to "obey is better than sacrifice?"

3. Write about God's forgiveness and mercy in your own life.

Your Mission Journal Notes:

11

Giving Homage to our King

I'm blessed with a grandson who lives close enough to come over and enjoy our backyard. We do all kinds of fun and silly things like collecting cones from the cypress trees and saving them in a pile. We chase lizards, sword fight, role-play Peter Pan and Captain Hook. We even go fishing for flying fish, if you can imagine that. Sometimes he wants me to be Mr. Smee (slight resemblance). In the garden area we have old buckets turned over where we play king of the mountain. When one of us is standing on the biggest bucket — he is king until toppled by some treacherous deed.

In our American culture, king of the mountain may be our first impression of kingship. Typically we are clueless about the concepts of kingdoms and kings. Yet we serve a God who is King above all kings. He is Lord above all Lords and His desire is to reveal Himself to us in all His splendor and majesty. As we come to know Him, our love will grow and hearts for the kingdom will pour out homage to our king.

In this chapter, we'll answer the question: What is the nature of a sovereign? We'll see the bitter consequences of turning away from God our King. And then we'll discuss the beauty, majesty and glory of our Sovereign Lord and God's desire for us to know Him. From there we will go on to see the value of the spiritual discipline of giving a portion of our blessings back to God above. In fact, it is for our good.

The news tells us about the Queen of England, the King of Saudi Arabia and the monarch of Jordon. But the English monarch is not a true sovereign, the Saudi king is unknown to us and the Hashemite Kingdom of Jordan seems rather obscure. The best image we have of a king is likely from Hollywood movies like *King Arthur and the Knights of the Round Table.*

Kingship and the reality of God our King is like a thread of truth woven through the whole of Scripture. A king is a sovereign ruler within his vast domain. Everything in his kingdom belongs to him. He determines what is right and what is wrong, he is highest judge, he hears the people's petitions, he imparts favors, he defends his citizens, he provides for his subjects, and he receives tribute.

Adam rejected God as King, loving the gift more than the Giver. Abel gave homage to his King while his brother Cain rejected God as King. Noah obeyed his King and saved a remnant from God's just wrath. Abraham came into covenant with God as his King and gave a king's tithe to Melchizidek.[28] Jacob acclaimed God as King.

> *"Then Jacob made a vow, saying, 'If God will be with me and will keep me in this way that I go, and will give me bread to eat and clothing to wear, so that I come again to my father's house in peace, then the Lord shall be my God, and this stone, which I have set up for a pillar, shall be God's house. And of all that you give me I will give a full tenth to you.'" (Genesis 28:20)*

The nation of Israel rejected God as King, demanding that Samuel give them a human king instead. "But the people refused to obey the voice of Samuel. And they said, 'No! But there shall be a king over us, that we also may be like all the nations, and that our king may judge us and go out before us and fight our battles'" (1 Samuel 8:19-20). God told the prophet Samuel, "they have rejected me from being king over them" (1 Samuel 8:7).

Israel's people rejected God as King again in Malachi's day. The prophet confronted them saying, "Return to me, and I will return to you, says the Lord of hosts. But you say, 'How shall we return? ' Will

---

[28] Hebrews chapter 7 gives an account of who Melchizidek was. "...and to him Abraham apportioned a tenth part of everything. He is first, by translation of his name, king of righteousness, and then he is also king of Salem, that is, king of peace. He is without father or mother or genealogy, having neither beginning of days nor end of life, but resembling the Son of God he continues a priest forever."

man rob God? Yet you are robbing me. But you say, 'How have we robbed you? ' In your tithes and contributions" (Malachi 3:7-8). The people argued with the prophet Malachi, "What do you mean, we've robbed God." They were counting mint leaves in their gardens to give precisely one-tenth of them to the Lord. They counted their coins right down to the last penny to make sure they didn't miss one for their offering. It's likely their deeds were well within the bounds of legality; but their hearts were in another kingdom.

Is there any doubt that the religious leaders in the years Jesus walked among us rejected God as King? They scorned and crucified Jesus, Emmanuel, God with us. They forcefully seized Jesus and took Him before Pilot and incited the crowd to scream, "Away with him! Crucify, crucify!"

We too may want to argue the point. "How have we stolen from God, our King?" Our minds race through the list of stuff we do. "I go to church, I take communion, I speak with boldness as I confess with the congregation, I sing praise songs with great enthusiasm, I pray and read my Bible, I attend Wednesday Bible Studies, I teach a Sunday school class, I write a check to the church every week, I wear a gold cross around my neck, I do the lunch prayer at my club meetings; what more could anyone ask? Isn't that enough — what do you want from me?" With a deep, frustrated sigh we say, "I don't have anything left to give. I'm exhausted."

Take a deep breath and when your head quits spinning, take a real inventory — an account of yourself. I'm urging you to do a check up on the condition of your heart. In all this stuff that you're doing, in the busy business of the church, is God, Creator of all heaven and earth, your King?

If He is not your King, all this stuff you do is of little consequence. It may be good, it may be right, it may be helpful, it may seem necessary; but it is of little value to the eternal kingdom of heaven. Give it up and imitate our Lord Jesus Christ.

How is giving homage to our King a part of spiritual discipline? How is it that taking a portion of what God has given you involves the disciplines of faith? My own human weakness gives witness to a failing that is common to man. My own struggles are little different than yours. When we get our paychecks, an insurance settlement, an inheritance or any other kind of income, before it is auto-deposited in the bank, it's spent. Our credit card is maxed because we have too many "I needs" and way too many "I wants." The family car has 120 thousand miles on it and "I want" to take a family vacation to the Oregon coast. Little Missy needs braces and Johnny needs soccer uniforms. And they just introduced a new cell phone. The list goes on and the monthly payments go up.

This is the discipline of being a godly steward of the blessings God has poured out upon us, whether lesser or greater. Godly management of our assets is a part of what we are called to do. Our job as managers of Kingdom assets is to practice self-discipline as we deal with them. First of all, we ought to be good handlers of our gifts, talents and financial assets in order to offer up to God a portion of what He has given us as a means of acknowledging that all we have belongs to Him. Next, we handle our gifts, talents and earthly assets in the best way possible to provide for our families. We must also manage them in a way that is beneficial to our local church, to our community and our family. All of this requires good management and wise stewardship.

I'm not advocating a legalistic system of calculating your weekly/monthly income, times ten-percent equals the check you write to the church. In fact, love cannot be measured or calculated in percentages. Homage is not a mathematical equation. And yet, what we do with our wallets is often a reflection of what is in our hearts.[29] What I'm encouraging is a heart attitude that worships God as King, and acknowledges God as King in all that He has blessed us to receive. In doing this, the Spirit will lead and guide you in all that is right and good as you give back, returning to Him a portion of His blessings. You can be confident in all you offer before God because you are acknowledging Him as your Lord and King. As you practice this spiritual discipline, you will be given greater responsibilities in God's kingdom. Start where you are and with what you are able to do and expect to grow in your acts of homage as you mature in your faith.

---

[29] The Law is not irrelevant today. In fact, the Law is now written in the believer's heart (Romans 2:15, Jeremiah 31:33).

Be encouraged to be a prudent and godly overseer so that you may give homage to your King, the King above all kings, Lord above all lords, in a way that is true and right — from the depths of your heart of hearts, motivated in love for your Heavenly Father.

Q & A Chapter 11: Giving Homage to our King

1. In everything you do, is God, who is Creator of all heaven and earth, your King?

2. How does our stewardship of God's blessings reflect our true heart?

3. How will you give homage to your King?

Your Mission Journal Notes:

12

Under Authority

The decade of the Sixties changed our American culture dramatically; or more accurately, in the Sixties, existing cultural undercurrents rushed to the surface. We left our hearts in San Francisco and embraced the idea that "all you need is love." Before the decade came to an end we were all singing along with Ol' Blue Eyes, crooning out the words of his newest hit, "My way." We knew each word by heart and sang along, "I planned each charted course. Each careful step along the byway. And more, much more than this, I did it my way." This is the all-American way. We pull ourselves up by our own bootstraps. We're mavericks. We grit our teeth and head off on our own to make a trail where no man has ever gone before. We have a deep-seated Wild West mentality, and we are like that proverbial man riding out of town on his horse as the blazing sun pierces the horizon. He leaves behind everything, anything that would hold him down and keep him from being his own man — a free spirit.

You've seen this All American style maverick in the car next to you at a stoplight? He's that boomer generation guy with the pony tail, sitting in his classic red Camaro with the eight-track stereo cranked, singing out of tune at the top of his lungs, "Regrets, I've had a few. But then again, too few to mention. I did what I had to do." He's not so much a Sinatra fan as he is his own man, a rebel. He a product of his generation, singing, "I did it my way."

God's Word gives us a better way.

He established order, and when God's order is abandoned, chaos is the result. There is comfort, strength and value in coming under the authority of Christ and thereby stepping into God's perfect order.

With the very first words of Scripture, "In the beginning," God reveals His very nature as a God of order. He ordered the stars, the planets, the galaxies and he brought order out of chaos upon this tiny planet called earth. He created everything with an infinitely wise and logical order. He made the earthworm that converts organic matter into natural compost, the seed that reproduces after its kind, the rain that waters the earth, seed time and harvest time, the sun that rises and sets; and He commanded the man whom He created to subdue the earth and fill it with God's bounty. In all this we see God's order.

God has ordained governments and established order within them, for the good of every tribe, nation, people and tongue. Our Creator has blessed both the just and unjust among mankind, from ditch digger to rocket scientist, with natural talents for the good of all people. We can see the glory of God's established order in everything from subatomic particles to the stars and galaxies in the heavens above. How awesome is our Creator God who orders all of creation, keeping it from imploding into nothing! "If he should take back his spirit to himself, and gather to himself his breath, all flesh would perish together, and all mortals return to dust" (Job 34:14). "He himself is before all things, and in him all things hold together" (Colossians 1:17).

In everything God has established, there is order. It all makes perfect sense. God established a system of justice to provide order for the tribes of Israel. Our Lord God Almighty established order in how His people worship Him. Especially in the family, God established the most basic, foundational order of all. Apart from God's order, there is disintegration and chaos.

As we see the marvelous, miraculous nature of God's established order in all that He has created, wouldn't it make sense to cooperate with the established order, live within that order and "submit" ourselves within His time-proven order?

In our American culture, "submit" might as well be lumped together with offensive four-letter expletives. We just don't do the "submit" thing – we do it our way. And "submit" is certainly not a politically correct word. Yet, from my personal experience I can tell you – I did it my way for too many years and to this day I'm living with the regrets. Yes, I'm forgiven, cleansed and being healed of this sickness called sin; but when I look back I have twinges of regret. I am thankful that God has changed my perspective, and I can now look forward with great hope in Christ because He is restoring me within His order.

The Sixties dramatically changed American culture, but the God of the heavens and earth has not changed. It took me a while, but I had to learn that my way is not God's order of things. In fact, when it comes right down to it, my way is at best silly and too often very self-destructive.

Throughout all of creation, from the moment God said, "Let there be light," we witness God's order being established, "and God saw that it was good" (Genesis 1:10). God made light and gave it dominion over darkness. God created the sea and dry land, setting a boundary the sea could not cross. At His command the earth brought forth vegetation and trees of every kind, for mankind to nurture, care for and enjoy. God made the sun and the moon and gave one to rule over the day and another to rule over the night. Then God made a partner for Adam to help him lovingly watch over Creation. In all of this, it is immediately apparent that God established order. Not a hierarchy. Not a chain of command, but an order of things for our good.

It's an incredible understatement to say that it is good for us to submit to our Creator's order of things. Without this order, the earth would collapse into the very chaotic, formless void from which God created it. Apart from God's order, families disintegrate and fragment. Deprived of godly order, nations are destroyed. "A just king gives stability to his nation, but one who demands bribes destroys it" (Proverbs 29:4). Lacking God's established order, churches are thrown into bitter rivalries and turf wars. When we neglect godly order, we allow our domain to be relegated to chaos like a trash heap. When we reject God's created order and God's charge to mankind,[30] we allow the earth to fall into neglect and ruin.

Rarely do we find Christians who understand God's established order, especially His order of authority. Yet, when Christians refuse to submit to God's order we become powerless mavericks who must blaze

---

[30] "Be fruitful and multiply, and fill the earth and subdue it" (Genesis 1:28).

our own trail, and it is a pitiful trail of destruction we leave behind us when we do it our way.

Have you ever built a tall castle out of children's building blocks and then pulled one block from the bottom corner? It's likely the whole structure collapsed. When you want to officially become part of your local church, you desire something very good. In doing this, you place yourself and your family under the authority of the church's spiritual leadership, who are under the authority of Christ, who is under God's ultimate authority; and God's good order of things is fulfilled. Anything less than this is like pulling the corner support block from under the building.

You may be thinking, "Place myself and my family under *their* authority? You don't know what's happened to me in the past." You're right, I don't know. But I do know the abuses I've suffered along with other dear friends of mine. If you have a desire to become a local church member, but you just can't trust pastoral authority or the elders' authority — you have some trust issues and in all likelihood they are legitimate. This is my suggestion. Take some time before making this commitment, search your heart, fast and pray. Continue to fast and pray (See chapter on "Fasting"), and wait until you get a clear answer. No doubt, you will get the answer in time. It's worth the time to be sure you are following God's plan for you.

What does God's order look like in the Kingdom of Heaven? God's people minister and serve in submission to the elders of the church. In submission, they have the power and authority to do what God has called them to do. The elders lovingly serve in submission to pastors or bishops and by doing so minister in the strength and power of the Spirit. The pastors and bishops serve under the authority of Christ, the head of the church, and under Jesus' authority, minister with great purpose. The Holy Spirit ministers under the authority of the Father and the Son, emanating from the Heavenly Father and the Son. Jesus Christ our Savior is seated at the right hand of the Father, ministering to the church under the authority of the Father.

When any part of this order gets out of order, the result is chaos. When pastors, elders or deacons circumvent order, the congregation suffers. When God's people reject order, the church becomes disorderly.

Disorder results in God's leaders and His people becoming weak and ineffective as they minister within the church. When the apostle Paul instructs the church regarding order, he is not saying that a church has to have an order of service printed in the bulletin every Sunday. He is saying so much more than "Don't let people be disruptive." His teaching is a call to God's established kingdom order, because only within this order, will people and leaders serve under authority: "...but all things should be done decently and in order" (1 Corinthians 14:39).

Living in God's established order, being under authority, is most important in the ministries of spiritual gifts. The gifts of the Spirit are in essence the backbone of Christian service and ministries. The gifts of ministry[31] are central to Jesus' ministry in the world today and the essence of fulfilling the Great Commission. Apart from the Spirit given and empowered gifts, the church is only a little better than your local service club, which is a great organization but without eternal purpose. Take a look at God's order when applied to spiritual gifts. God sent Jesus to be "God with us" and everything He did was under His Father's authority. After Jesus returned to heaven He sent His Holy Spirit who gifts and empowers God's people to go, under His authority, and make disciples of all nations, just as Jesus commanded.

Let's dig further into what it means to be under God's authority and living according to His perfect order. When you read through the Gospels you will see that Jesus served under a clear order of authority, healing the sick, raising the dead, casting out evil spirits, and breaking five loaves and two fish to feed five-thousand families. All of what He did happened because He submitted to Father God's order of authority. Jesus did what He saw the Father doing, spoke what He heard the Father speaking, and reached out to those the Father was reaching out to. The Roman centurion who came to Jesus to heal his daughter was one of the few that understood this order of authority, because he too was under authority (Romans 8:5).

Now, in the age of the church, we are Jesus' hand extended to a lost and dying world. He has ascended to the right hand of the Father

---

[31] The spiritual gifts are not reserved for the work of bishops, priests, vicars, pastors, elders, and deacons. When you come to saving faith you are included in the priesthood of believers, and spiritual gifts are available to you, as the Spirit desires.

where He is praying for us and preparing a place for us to dwell with Him for all eternity. Before He ascended to heaven he told his disciples, "Nevertheless I tell you the truth: it is to your advantage that I go away, for if I do not go away, the Advocate will not come to you; but if I go, I will send him to you" (John 16:7).

Jesus ascended to the Father and sent the Holy Spirit as Advocate and Comforter, but so much more than this. The Holy Spirit is God's active presence in the world today, but more specifically He inhabits the church[32] that is in the world. The Holy Spirit indwells us, gifts us and empowers the priesthood of believers who are now His hand extended. We are light that dissipates the darkness. We are called to minister the resurrected Christ to those who are bound in chains of sin; the desperate, the troubled and the discouraged people around us. We are called to be God's visible, living, active presence in the world today. But as soldiers of the cross, we serve under authority.

Here is an illustration of this truth.[33] If you sent a ten-year-old boy into his dad's workshop on his own to make a toy sail boat, what would he come up with? Maybe a block of scrap wood with bent nail pounded in it for a mast and a rag for a sail. The same boy, under dad's loving, authoritative direction could make a beautifully shaped sailboat with a dowel for a mast, red and white paint and a sail with riggings. And the breeze will carry the boat to the other side of the pond on its first voyage.

Now we can picture why it's so important to be under authority; that is, to submit ourselves under God's order of authority. Like our Lord Jesus Christ who submitted to God the Father's authority, we are called to submit ourselves under Christ's authority in order to accomplish what is of lasting, eternal value. The Holy Spirit is sent by the authority of the Father and the Son. And we are sent as ambassadors, as His hand extended, under the authority of Christ

---

[32] This means the church universal and individual members that make up the church.
[33] It is good to keep in mind that most illustrations like this fall short of giving a complete picture of the truth it demonstrates. This illustration doesn't show the difference between human strength and the strength of the Lord at work through us as we serve and minister. It also fails to show that the end result of serving under authority is eternal and not temporal.

Jesus, by the power of the Holy Spirit, to do God's work in the world today. We are appointed to manifest God's living, active presence in the world today, in the Holy Spirit, under the authority of Christ and by the authority of Christ. Within God's order of authority, the work we are called to do becomes eternally effective and doing Great Commission work becomes mission possible.

Q & A Chapter 12: Under Authority

1. Describe God's order of authority.

2. Why is it so important to submit by placing ourselves under God's authority?

3. How does being under authority relate to the ministries and service of spiritual gifts within the church?

Your Mission Journal Notes:

13

Deeds Overflowing from the Heart

Laura gasped as she glanced at the time on her cell phone. She was already late and still in her gardening clothes. "Oh, well!" she sighed, talking to the gardenias she just planted. "Jill said it was a garden reception. Come as you are." Laura pulled off her gloves, threw down the trowel, ran in the house, grabbed her backpack and car keys, jumped in her Ford Taurus and raced off to the other side of town. She would be late, but she didn't want to miss Joel and Jasper's wedding reception. She had always wanted to dance with Joel, and this might be her last chance.

"Just my luck," she moaned. The only parking spot was on the far side of the parking lot. It was a good thing she had her tennis shoes on because she sprinted across the pavement to the city park's wedding garden. The sun was ready to hide behind a cloud when she stopped inside the rose covered archway, arrayed with fragrant red rose buds. Her face flushed, matching the roses, but her mad dash wasn't the cause. Everyone was dressed to the hilt. The guys were wearing suits and ties and the gals were in the most fashionable, colorful and feminine party dresses.

"Just wait 'til I find Jill," she hissed under her breath.

Before she could take another step, two men in black suits approached her. "Excuse me, but this is a private wedding. May I see your invitation?"

Laura stammered, "Oh, ah, well you see, um, my friend Jill Hampton told me it was come as you are and I forgot my invitation at home."

A football lineman sized guy bent over and got in Laura's face, and she could smell the wine on his breath. "It's obvious you didn't read the invitation. You have to leave." And then he motioned with his burly hand to the garden gate she had entered through. Both of them followed her out. She could see them in her rearview mirror, still watching as she drove out of the parking lot.

We who are in Christ are invited to the Bridegroom's wedding supper. Yet we must come prepared. In Jesus' parable of the ten bridesmaids recorded in Matthew chapter 25, we learn that preparations for the Bridegroom's wedding banquet are not transferrable. We learn in these next verses the importance of the bride making herself ready:

> *"'Let us rejoice and exult and give him the glory, for the marriage of the Lamb has come, and his bride has made herself ready; to her it has been granted to be clothed with fine linen, bright and pure — for the fine linen is the righteous deeds of the saints. And the angel said to me, "Write this: 'Blessed are those who are invited to the marriage supper of the Lamb.'"* (Revelation 19:7-9)

> *"But when the king came in to see the guests, he noticed a man there who was not wearing a wedding robe, and he said to him, 'Friend, how did you get in here without a wedding robe?' And he was speechless. Then the king said to the attendants, 'Bind him hand and foot, and throw him into the outer darkness, where there will be weeping and gnashing of teeth.' For many are called, but few are chosen.'"* (Matthew 22:11)

As it turns out, Laura got off easy.

Some may wonder if "deeds overflowing from the heart" is just another earn-your-salvation doctrine, but clearly it is not. First, it's good to remember that our own good works, deeds done in our own strength and by means of our God given natural gifts and talents, are likened to filthy rags. With great clarity the Scriptures refer to our works done in the strength of the flesh, apart from the Spirit, as "wood, hay and stubble," which burn up when tested by fire.

"For no one can lay any foundation other than the one that has been laid; that foundation is Jesus Christ. Now if anyone builds on the foundation with gold, silver, precious stones, wood, hay, straw — the work of each builder will become visible, for the Day will disclose it, because it will be revealed with fire, and the fire will test what sort of work each has done. If what has been built on the foundation survives, the builder will receive a reward. If the work is burned up, the builder will suffer loss; the builder will be saved, but only as through fire." (1 Corinthians 3:11-15)

At the wedding supper of the Lamb of God, the bride of Christ is "... granted to be clothed with fine linen, bright and pure — for the fine linen is the righteous deeds of the saints" (Revelation 19:8). The NIV interprets it, "...the righteous acts of the saints." The robe given to the saints who have been ushered into the wedding banquet is made of fine linen, the cloth of a priestly garment, and she is granted to be clothed with linen garments which are the righteous deeds done in preparation for the coming Bridegroom. It is as if the robe is woven of pure white linen fibers that are deeds of Spirit — the righteous work of the saints. We see this same principle when God instructed the tribes of Israel who gathered each year for the festival of harvest: "No one shall appear before me empty-handed" (Exodus 23:15).

The best way to explain this principle to the Star Trek generation is to say that we are speaking of two different realms or realities. The first and most familiar is the visible reality that we see with our human eyes. The other is the spiritual realm that is unseen. In the unseen realm are two kingdoms, the Kingdom of Light and the kingdom of darkness. Now we can begin to see the differences in what we do by human strength (in the visible reality) and what we do by means of the Kingdom of Light. Both can be good, but what we do in the strength, power and gifts of the Holy Spirit is of eternal value.

The apostle Paul gives us an interesting example. "If I fought wild beasts in Ephesus with no more than human hopes, what have I gained? If the dead are not raised, "Let us eat and drink, for tomorrow we die" (1 Corinthians 15:32). Paul is speaking of the resurrection power of Christ. Without an eternal purpose, we can say, "If I have done_____ (fill in the blank) with no more than human hopes, I'll just give up the battle and go party."

We begin to see here a clear demarcation between deeds done "my way," using our God given natural gifts, and righteous deeds, done by means of the gifting and empowering work of the Holy Spirit that are only made possible by the resurrection power of Christ. Righteous deeds and spiritual ministries are not done by *human* strength, but in the strength and power of the Spirit of Jesus. Our acts of service can be distinguished between the natural and spiritual, between flesh and spirit, and between common and holy. There is day and night difference between them. They are light-years apart. The difference is serving and ministering in God confidence, or in self-confidence.

Imagine showing up like Laura, at a wedding reception where the guys are wearing tuxedos and suits with ties, all spit and polish. Then you notice the ladies are all wearing the most beautiful gowns, lace and finery. You let out a big "Oops" because you showed up in your soiled gardening clothes with dirt under your fingernails. In the Bridegroom's wedding banquet, the guests are given fine linen wedding garments, which are the righteous deeds done by the gifting and empowering work of the Holy Spirit — not by our own means. If you show up in back yard work duds, i.e. only having deeds that are by the work of your own hands, you'll be thrown out of the banquet.

Now for the Good News! Our Lord Jesus credits his righteousness to you and me. In other words, we get credit for the good He has done as if we did it ourselves. But His work of righteousness given to me is just the beginning. In the refining[34] work He does in every Christian, His righteousness increasingly overflows in godly deeds, servant ministries, and acts of righteousness — manifested by the empowering work of the Holy Spirit in and through us, to do the work He has prepared for us in Christ Jesus.

Let's unfold this picture of righteousness to get a better perspective of it. When we are baptized into Christ, He attributes His

---

[34] The Bible calls this sanctification, which is the work of the Holy Spirit to work on us until we become more and more like Jesus.

righteousness to us. This righteousness is positional in that we are given the righteousness of Christ when we are "in Christ." And when we are in Him, the righteousness of Christ permeates us and covers us. His righteousness is not given to us as our own, but in Christ we get credit for it. It's not like He makes this big deposit in our personal bank account and we now own it. Instead, we now have the right to draw on His bank account because we are adopted members of His family. It isn't like we draw wages we've earned and receive a bonus for good performance; it's His righteousness, freely credited to us. This is like one rail of a railroad track.

On the parallel track we find that the righteousness of Christ is not a matter of Christ having done all the righteous deeds and that's all there is to it. This is a beautiful truth to grasp hold of. Because you are now the righteousness of God in Jesus Christ, you can now do what He is doing, say what he is saying, and go where He is going. You are able to do these things because His righteousness is manifested in you, empowering you in deeds of righteousness. His power at work in you in this way is proof positive of the power of the resurrected Christ at work through you.

The apostle Paul makes this clear in his letter to the believers in Rome: "Through him we received grace and apostleship to call all the Gentiles to the obedience that comes from faith for his name's sake" (Romans 1:5 NIV). Did you catch the key phrase in this verse? "Obedience that comes from faith." Through the finished work of Christ Jesus on the cross, we have been set free from the curse of the law. We no longer obey because it's the law, but our faith in Jesus Christ compels us and is the root cause of our obedience. All that we do is, or ought to be, the result of faith—for His name sake. This is the second rail of the righteousness of Christ at work in us.

A deed done by means of the Spirit and in resurrection power is like planting a seed in your garden. Without hope of a harvest you wouldn't go to all the trouble. And yet, even while you're stuck in this visible, earthly reality it is possible to step into the reality of the Kingdom of Heaven and by the power and strength of the Spirit, plant "seeds" that will produce a harvest in the Kingdom of Light. It's like planting a garden in Death Valley and having it pop up and flourish in the beautiful San Joaquin Valley.

When you do the work of the Kingdom of Light, as you minister and serve, you do not do so with human words of wisdom, that is, in the strength of the visible realm. Paul is a living example of this truth.

> *"For I decided to know nothing among you except Jesus Christ, and him crucified. And I came to you in weakness and in fear and in much trembling. My speech and my proclamation were not with plausible words of wisdom, but with a demonstration of the Spirit and of power, so that your faith might rest not on human wisdom but on the power of God." (1 Corinthians 2:2-5)*

Now you're all dressed up in the beautiful white garment you are able to minister and serve just as Jesus would if He were wearing your sandals. You are prepared, adorned with precious jewels, ready to do all that God has prepared for you to do. On your own you would come as you are in your soiled garden clothes, but you are not on your own – you have been given Jesus robe of righteousness. On your own, your works of service and ministry have no eternal value, but you come in weakness, offering yourself now clothed in righteousness, and what you do is treasure for all eternity.

Hear the call of wisdom and He will put His robe on you as you work in His garden until the return of the Bridegroom on that great day. This is the effect of righteousness in you.

Q & A Chapter 13: Deeds Overflowing from the Heart

1. What is "wood, hay, and stubble?"

2. Describe the two realities.

3. What are the first and second rails of the righteousness of Jesus Christ?

Your Mission Journal Notes:

14

Welcoming the Ministries of the Holy Spirit

In the gloom of night, I cowered.
But not in darkness shrouded from light.
My eyes were dim, impenetrable shadows cast upon my soul.
The warmth of light shined out for me, but
shackles of iron held me in the gloom.
At the slightest pinpoint of light, fear rose up in me like a flood.
What I do not know, what I could not see, I feared.
Cringing in the shadows I shrank back.
Fear had me in its steely grasp and would not release me.
Tears for my bitter estate streaked down
my face and I brushed them away.
But then a gentle voice pierced the gloom, "Do you want to see?"
"See?" My voice strained with alarm.
"W-well, wh-what w-would I see?"
"The Light of the World," and with those
gentle words, he touched me.
"Yes, yes, I want to see," the words fell from
my mouth and I couldn't stop them.
In a moment the warmth of his touch spread over my eyes.
My eyes burned and tingled as if coming to life for the first time.
"Go wash and be clean." His gentle words penetrated my dark soul.
I smiled with joy, reaching out for my
friend, knowing I would soon see.

⌘

Like the blind man, we fear what we don't know. We cannot welcome what we do not see. And how can we take hold of what we do not comprehend? This is the state of the church in much of the Western world today. We don't know what we don't know. We lack elementary knowledge of God and we do not take hold of the Spirit of Jesus, our Comforter, our Advocate, because of ignorant, servile fear.[35] We are bound with the chains of ignorance.

As Jesus ascended into heaven to sit at the right hand of the Father, he said, "...it is to your advantage that I go away, for if I do not go away, the Advocate will not come to you; but if I go, I will send him to you" (John 16:7). God has at all times and in every age manifested Himself, having a sure and trustworthy witness in the earth. In the age of the church He manifests Himself by His Holy Spirit, the Spirit of Jesus. The active presence of the Holy Spirit gives witness of our Living Redeemer, our Lord and Savior, Jesus Christ. The presence of the Spirit of Jesus is as real and active as the presence of Immanuel, God with Us, who walked among us, taught us, fed us miracle bread and fish, healed our sick, raised the dead, and suffered to die in our place, for our sins.

The Holy Spirit's living and active presence is of great benefit to us, the church, and we must receive the fullness of His manifest presence. The Holy Spirit accomplishes all that He desires in and through us, empowering His people to manifest the saving power of God. The Scriptures reveal to us how God's Kingdom comes, and His will is done on earth as it is in heaven. Let's go beyond the foundational topics of the faith and dig into the meat of the Word. Get out your steak knives and prepare to enjoy.

Where does the Holy Spirit dwell today? How does the Spirit of Jesus make Himself known in the earth today? "Or do you not know that your body is a temple of the Holy Spirit within you, which you have from God, and that you are not your own? For you were bought with a price; therefore glorify God in your body" (1 Corinthians 6:19).

---

[35] Servile fear is best defined as: "Fear of paying the full price or penalty for your offenses, especially those imposed upon you by a Just, Holy, and Righteous God.

We who are in Christ are called to be the manifestation of God's living presence in the world today. Jesus' words are perfect and clear: "You are the light of the world" (Matthew 5:14). This is only possible in the power of the Holy Spirit and by the work of the Spirit of Jesus in us. Yet because of ignorance, we back away to hide in a dark corner, fearing the Light of the Spirit.

The Holy Spirit does not take over our bodies, moving us about like robots. The Spirit does not control us like dummies on strings. We won't be compelled to do things we don't want to do. We won't say things that we refuse to speak. Rolling in the aisles, falling down like we're dead, crying uncontrollably, laughing out of control – we will not do anything we don't want to do. When the Holy Spirit ministers through us by means of spiritual gifts, it is possible because of His empowering work. He gives us control over the manifestations of spiritual gifts (1 Corinthians 14:32-33).

It becomes clear to us in the book of Acts that the early Christians, the disciples and Apostles were adamant in their desire to be witnesses to all people that their Lord Jesus Christ was the Resurrected Christ, their Living Redeemer, present and active in the world. They were Jesus' hand extended to a lost and dying world. Early Christians manifested His living presence to all they would touch, to all who would hear their testimony.

We need God's living, active presence. His presence was crucial for early Christians, and He is just as important in this American, post-Christian culture. We are called to manifest all that He is because we are called by His name. We are commissioned to be witnesses of His power and might to save, and to reflect His light to drive back the darkness. As we minister and administer the truth of the Gospel and when the Good News is believed and received, signs and wonders are sure to follow. Love and peace will reign supreme. These signs confirm and prove that the whole truth of Scripture has been taught, received and believed.

The Holy Spirit is referred to as the "seven-fold Spirit."[36] You will find references to the sevenfold ministries of the Holy Spirit, the seven

---

[36] Isaiah 11:2.

lamps of fire and the sevenfold nature of the Spirit of Jesus. Like each person of the Trinity, the Holy Spirit has many names. The purpose of each of these names is to reveal to us the nature and purpose of the Holy Spirit. Who is the Holy Spirit? What is His plan? Let's examine each building stone engraved with the Spirit's name.

The Holy Spirit is the Spirit of wisdom,[37] the Spirit of life,[38] the Spirit of joy,[39] the Spirit of fire,[40] the Spirit of truth,[41] the Spirit of cleansing fire,[42] of holiness,[43] of power,[44] of love[45] and the Spirit of revelation.[46]

The Holy Spirit is the giver of all good gifts to all who will receive.[47] The Spirit empowers all believers in works of ministry in the church.[48] He is Comforter,[49] Counselor,[50] Advocate,[51] and Teacher.[52] The Holy Spirit regenerates,[53] sanctifies,[54] disciplines[55] and indwells God's people.[56] The Spirit of Jesus is the assurance of our salvation.[57] He does a mighty work in us, convincing and convicting us of our sin before a Holy God.[58] He chastens us,[59] strengthens us and guides us.[60] The Spirit

---

[37] Exodus 28:3, Ex 31:1—4, Deuteronomy 34:9, Isaiah 11:2—3, 1 John 2:27, James 1:5.
[38] Genesis 1:2, Psalms 104:30, Job 26:13, Job 33:4, John 3:5, John 3:8.
[39] 1 Thessalonians 1:6.
[40] Isaiah 4:4, Malachi 3:1—2, Luke 3:16.
[41] John 16:13.
[42] Matthew 3:11, Isaiah 6:6—7.
[43] Ps 51:11, Matthew 5:45, Romans 1:4, Romans 8:1.
[44] Luke 4:18, Luke 4:14, Luke 24:49, Acts 1:5 & 8, Acts 2:4, Romans 12:6, Hebrews 4:13.
[45] Romans. 15:30, 1 John 4:7 & 16, Romans 15:30, Romans 5:5, Galatians 5:22, Matthew 5:46, 1 Peter 1:22.
[46] Ephesians 1:17, 1 Corinthians 2:10, Ephesians 3:5, John 16:14—15.
[47] 1 Corinthians 12:4—11.
[48] Luke 4:14 & 18, 24:49, Romans 5:19, Acts 1:8, 10:38, 19:6, Ephesians 4:12.
[49] John 14:16 & 26, Acts 9:31, Ephesians 4:30, John 14: 15—17, & 25—26.
[50] John 14:16, John 15:25, John 16:7.
[51] Ephesians 2: 18.
[52] John 14:26, 1 John 2:27, 1 Corinthians 2:13.
[53] John 3:5—8, 2 Corinthians 3:18, Titus 3:5.
[54] Romans 15:16, 1 Corinthians 6:11, 2 Thessalonians 2:13, 1 Peter 1:2.
[55] Hebrews 12:5—6.
[56] Romans 8:9 & 11; 1 Corinthians 3:16, 2 Timothy 1:14, John 14:17.
[57] Romans 8:16, Ephesians 1:11—14, 1 John 4:13, 1 John 5:6, 2 Corinthians 1:22.
[58] Genesis 6:3, John 16:8,
[59] Revelation 3:19, 1 Corinthians 11:32, Titus 3:5.
[60] John 16:13, Romans 8:14, Acts 15:8, Galatians 5:18,

grants access to the Father and helps us when we pray.[61] He is the One who unifies us as a body of believers in Christ.[62] He is the Spirit of love and He seals all who are in the faith, keeping us from the righteous wrath of God.[63]

The ministries of the Holy Spirit are like a multi-faceted diamond, refracting His light in every possible dimension. There is no language on earth that can fully describe or reveal the fullness and beauty of the Holy Spirit sent by our Lord Jesus. There are no libraries big enough to contain all the books that would describe the fullness, scope and ministries of the Holy Spirit who emanates from the Father and the Son. And yet, in all His glory, the Spirit comes to dwell in us so that our Lord Jesus may be glorified in all the earth. As the Holy Spirit's living, active presence is manifested in us, the Kingdom of Light spreads its radiance, dissipating the darkness – "Thy kingdom come, thy will be done on earth as it is in heaven" (Matthew 6:10). The ministries of the Spirit are God's power at work in us to fulfill His Great Commission.

By faith, ask for and receive His precious gifts held out to you in Jesus' open and nail-scarred hand. He paid a great price so that you may receive these precious kingdom treasures. It is good that you desire all God's good gifts; all you need to do is ask for them. It's simple to say, "Just ask." But my encouragement to you is to earnestly seek; knock on every door where the Spirit leads you. Prayerfully ask, search, and ask again until you receive these great and wondrous gifts of the Spirit. Ask, believe and receive.

Q & A Chapter 14: Welcoming the Ministries of the Holy Spirit

1.   How does God manifest Himself in the age of the church?

---

[61] Jude 1:20, Romans 8:26, Ephesians 2:18.
[62] Ephesians 2:14—18, 4:3.
[63] Ephesians 1:13; 4:30, 2 Corinthians 1:22, Ephesians 4:30.

Cho Larson

2. Where does the Holy Spirit dwell today?

3. Describe the nature and work of the Holy Spirit.

Your Mission Journal Notes:

15

Prayerful, Interceding, Worshipful, and Thankful

"All I can do is pray."

"There's only one thing left to do — pray."

We've all said it in one way or another. We often talk like this when things get tough. When we face trials and get frustrated, we get on our knees out of desperation. It's common to feel like life is an endless pushing, pulling, pounding, and shoving at obstacles that won't budge. Our faces are tight; we're bruised, tired, and just plain fed up with it. Sure, we've been praying little prayers through each challenge we face, but now we have to get serious because we've tried everything and nothing else works.

We're absolutely right to work and pray, to toil and talk to God. It's a good plan to prayerfully press forward, calling on the name of the Lord as we do what we are able to do. As we grow in our walk with the Lord, we begin to do this as a natural response to what is thrown at us. The Scripture encourages us to "devote [our]selves to prayer, being watchful and thankful" (Colossians 4:2).

Yet, when I hear people say, "All I can do now is pray," I get a sense that they think prayer is a long shot, a last resort. It's a last ditch effort. It's as if they are thinking, "I've tried everything else so I guess I'll try prayer." But they're underestimating the power they have in what Jesus taught us to do.

You could fill an entire library with the books and articles that have been written on prayer, especially word-by-word, phrase-by-phrase teachings of the "Lord's Prayer." And certainly, we cannot grow in prayer and intercession until we fully understand the Lord's Prayer, not as a formula but a foundation for prayer. Because so much has been written, this chapter is not an exhaustive study on prayer, but a useful overview and a reminder of the blessings in the habits of prayer. As you enter into these disciplines of prayer, you will learn to enter the gates of thanksgiving. You'll discover what to avoid as hindrances to your prayers. You will see the importance of being persistent. You will come to receive the Holy Spirit's help as you pray, knowing what to ask for and presenting your case before the Lord. And finally, you will be blessed to know that all your prayers are valued and treasured.

Prayer is like a journey. Not a busy business trip or hectic family vacation, but more like a peaceful ascent, one step at a time, to the very throne of Grace. It is certainly like a celebrative parade as the Psalmist wrote: "The Lord is God, and he has made his light shine upon us. With boughs in hand, join in the festal procession up to the horns of the altar" (Psalms 118:27 NIV). It's a procession because prayer is not something we do alone. Even if we're praying by ourselves in our closet, we come together in the Spirit, before the Father, in the Name of our Lord Jesus and in agreement with our brothers and sisters in the Lord. The festal procession captures us in the flow as we approach our Lord God Almighty. Wouldn't it be awesome to have someone come before God's people to pray, doing cartwheels just as King David did when bringing the Arc of the Lord was brought into the city? Now that's a festal procession.

God, in his grace and mercy, comes down to us with His gift of salvation. He meets us at our point of need and lifts us out of the muck and mire of the gutter, and He cleans us up by means of the blood of the Lamb and sets our feet on the Rock, Christ Jesus. With our feet on the Rock, in worship and prayer, we now ascend to the throne of Grace to offer homage and to present our petitions before a Holy God.

The Psalmist reveals to us a most beautiful and blessed entrance into prayer: "Open for me the gates of righteousness; I will enter and give thanks to the Lord. This is the gate of the Lord through which the righteous may enter. I will give you thanks, for you answered me; you have become my salvation" (Psalms 118:19-21).

As you read the above Scripture, do you begin to feel a refreshing, cool breeze? Entering this gate of prayer by means of thanksgiving reminds me of the time we visited Benson, Arizona. It was a typical high desert day with clear blue skies and a blazing hot sun. We put up with the heat because we wanted to tour Kartchner Caverns. When our guide finally opened the last door to the caves, a cooling mist greeted us. There was a collective and thankful "Ahhh!" from our tour group.

These are the gates I'm inviting you to enter – the gates of righteousness. Go through these gates to be refreshed. Enter with thanksgiving to find peace, comfort, joy and strength. Step into this garden of delight, and come boldly before the Almighty God, Creator of all heaven and earth, to offer up your thanksgiving and praise, and to receive all that our Lord God has for you.

Do you want to have a powerful effect on the world around you? Do you desire to be His light to those around you? Here is God's promise to encourage you: Pray. "The prayer of a righteous person is powerful and effective" (James 5:16).[64] The KJV has a great translation of this same verse: "The effectual fervent prayer of a righteous man availeth much."

Hindrances to Answered Prayer

"You may ask me for anything in my name, and I will do it" (John 14:14). Think about it. Do you really believe this? Your experience may tell you otherwise. All of us have prayerfully pleaded with the Lord and He has not done what we asked. So is there something we're not doing? Maybe we need to pray until our knees are red and sore. Maybe we aren't earnest enough in our prayers. Is it possible that we haven't done a good job of "presenting our case" before the Lord? We ask the pastor to pray for us. We tell our story when our Bible Study group asks for prayer requests. We call the church prayer chain asking them to intercede for us. But where is the answer?

We find many examples in Scripture of unanswered prayer. God would not listen to Balaam who was paid to prophesy against Israel.

---

[64] If you're asking, "I'm not righteous, so what comes of my prayers?" Remember, you are the righteousness of God in Jesus Christ. You come before God in the righteousness of Jesus Christ, and God answers according to His righteousness.

Job cried out to God but He was silent for a time. The tribes of Israel wept before the Lord and God turned a deaf ear because of their unrepentant hearts. Our Lord Jesus fell on his face to the ground and prayed, "My Father, if it is possible, may this cup be taken from me. Yet not as I will, but as you will" (Matthew 26:39).

As we search the Scriptures we begin to see the whole picture, for certainly a single Scripture doesn't stand by itself for us to build upon. We build brick by brick, Scripture upon Scripture, until the whole truth is within our grasp.

Without a doubt, our prayers can be hindered. We can, by our own doing, act in ways that cause our prayers to not to be heard. The heavens become like brass. Here's just one example: "Husbands, in the same way, show consideration for your wives in your life together, paying honor to the woman as the weaker sex, since they too are also heirs of the gracious gift of life – so that nothing may hinder your prayers" (1 Peter 3:7). This Scripture ought to fill men with the fear of God, causing us to take stock of the way we live with our wives. Here is another way for your prayers to go unanswered: "If you close your ear to the cry of the poor, you will cry out and not be heard" (Proverbs 21:13).

God's people are warned of this possibility: "The sky over your head shall be bronze, and the earth under you iron" (Deuteronomy 28: 23). When the Heavens are so hard that our prayers bounce back, it is often of our own doing. We have no one but ourselves to blame. This is simply the result of sin, the hardness of our hearts, rebellion, selfish ambitions, and being ruled by our flesh. "Surely the arm of the Lord is not too short to save, nor his ear too dull to hear. But your iniquities have separated you from your God; your sins have hidden his face from you, so that he will not hear" (Isaiah 59:1-2). Beyond a doubt, our sin does separate us from God who hears.

If we do **not** do what the Bible instructs us to do — love mercy and justice, for example – why should God answer us when we ask Him for justice and mercy? "He has told you, O man, what is good; and what does the Lord require of you but to do justice, and to love kindness, and to walk humbly with your God" (Micah 6:8 ESV). If we do not intend to do what Scripture instructs us to do, our prayers become meaningless.

They go no further than the sound of our voice. The prophet Zechariah makes this point clear: "'When I called, they did not listen; so when they called, I would not listen,' says the Lord Almighty" (7:13). When your Lord is knocking on your door wanting to speak to you, answer the door, invite Him in and hear what He has to say.[65]

Does this mean that all unanswered prayer is the result of sin? Not in the least. But I cringe when I hear the trite saying: "God always answers prayer. Sometimes He says, 'yes.' Sometimes He says 'No.' And sometimes God says, 'Wait.'" The Scripture refutes this clichéd statement. The apostle Paul, who walked as Jesus walked, wrote to the churches: "As surely as God is faithful, our word to you has not been 'Yes and No.' For the Son of God, Jesus Christ, whom we proclaimed among you, Silvanus and Timothy and I, was not 'Yes and No'; but in him it is always 'Yes.'" (2 Corinthians 1:18-19). God is a God of "yes." And we must dwell in the kingdom of God — the kingdom of "Yes."[66]

There are few references in Scripture where God says "no." The most prevalent examples are when Jesus prayed, "My Father, if it is possible, let this cup pass from me; yet not what I want but what you want" (Matthew 29:39); and when God told the apostle Paul "no" three times when he asked God to remove the "thorn" in his flesh (2 Corinthians 12:7). In saying "no," God fulfilled a greater purpose. We also see that God told the tribes of Israel "no" when they tried to enter the Promised Land after first refusing to cross the Jordon. This "no" came as a consequence of their rebellious unbelief (Numbers 14:30). But even in our weak and fallible condition, because of God's forgiveness and mercy, we find great hope in this Scripture. "If I had cherished sin in my heart, the Lord would not have listened; but God has surely listened and has heard my prayer. Praise be to

---

[65] This is a good example of the need for the spiritual gift of prophecy in the church; giving His people the privilege of hearing Him speak in the moment to address a present need.
[66] It is so important that we do not teach based on our own experience. This "yes," "no," "wait" cliché is not from the Bible but from people's experience. Experience is not the arbiter of truth. Jesus revealed the kingdom of "Yes" when a leper came to Him. "Jesus reached out his hand and touched the man. 'I am willing,' he said. 'Be clean'" (Matthew 8:3).

God, who has not rejected my prayer or withheld his love from me" (Psalms 66:18-20).

Persistence in Prayer

From an early age, our youngest son asked for a dog. He wanted a dog so badly that there were certainly days that it was all he thought about. But mom's answer was always the same: "We don't have a fence so we can't have a dog."

He didn't give up. At Sunday school he asked his friends to pray with him that he could get a dog. When the adults gathered at home for Bible studies he would come out at prayer time and ask people to pray that he could get a dog. Any time someone asked for prayer requests, he put in his appeal for a dog. During family prayer, he prayed to have dog. During bedtime prayers he asked for a dog.

This went on for a few years until he was ten years old and his mom and I became engaged. Almost within minutes of hearing the announcement of our engagement, he asked me, "Can you build a fence?" Together we built a chain-link fence around the back yard and he finally had what was needed for a dog. Immediately he dug through the ads in the Phoenix newspaper until he found what he wanted – a four year old female beagle.

After years of persistence in prayer and help with interceding as people joined him in his request, our son got his answer. When he put a leash on her and took her to the car, she was smiling. (She was especially happy because when we stopped for lunch she jumped into the back of the car and ate a whole bag of fresh bagels.)

Being persistent doesn't mean that you always have to pray in a certain way; praying on your knees, hours long prayer sessions, praying in any particular manner, or praying in King James English. Your external style does not give you an edge for God to hear your prayers. Instead, it is prayer from the depths of your heart and soul that is cherished. It's good to bow our heads in prayer if the heart is also bowed before the Lord. It is excellent to lift our hands to the Lord in prayer if our spirit is lifted up unto the Lord. Bending our knees before the Lord is an outstanding way to pray if from our innermost being, in reverence and awe, we are submitted before a Holy God. But external form without inner submission is of no use and doesn't add anything to being fervent or persistent in prayer. Apart from a right heart, prayers are little more than a legalistic act and a nice performance.

The Holy Spirit's Help

Do you ever get stuck, not knowing how to pray for someone? Have you started to pray and then realized that you're clueless regarding the person's greatest need? When you begin to pray, do you feel inadequate for the purpose? You may desperately need to pray for your sick child but you don't know how best to pray.[67] Be encouraged; we're not on our own when it comes to prayer.

> *"Likewise the Spirit helps us in our weakness; for we do not know how to pray as we ought, but that very Spirit intercedes with sighs too deep for words. And God, who searches the heart, knows what is the mind of the Spirit, because the Spirit intercedes for the saints according to the will of God."*
> (Romans 8:26-27)

What an incredibly rich and beautiful Scripture. In the weakness of our mortal bodies and minds, we do not know how to pray according to the heart of the Father, agreeing with the desire of the Spirit as we pray. What does the "Spirit intercedes with sighs too deep for words mean?" Other translations use the word "groanings."

What do you do when you're hurting? You sigh. Have you ever been around someone who is suffering? They sigh a lot. They groan when the pain is intense. The Holy Spirit takes on our suffering as

---

[67] It is common for us fallible humans to feel inadequate when praying. But there is no need to make prayer difficult, especially when you're doing a 911 kind of prayer. Remember that there are times when the best and most honest prayer is "Help! God help me." He will hear you and answer.

His own and brings our distress before the Father, interceding on our behalf with great sighs and groans. This is the work of the Spirit on our behalf; but it is not only a matter of the Holy Spirit advocating for us in some far off distant place in the heavens, in a mysterious place shrouded in darkness. The Holy Spirit has taken up residence in God's people of faith and there will be times the Holy Spirit's groaning will well up inside of you and pour out of you in prayerful intercessions with sighs and groans offered up to the Father.

In the same way, the Holy Spirit will help you to know how to pray. Ask for His help and He will give it to you in abundance. The Spirit of Jesus will give you the words to pray, whether in your native language, another earthly language, in the tongues of angels or in sighs and groans from the depths of your spirit. Yes, you may find there are times when no earthly language can adequately express the burden of your heart, and in that moment, the Holy Spirit will help you to pray, if you are willing.

A Spirit-inspired prayer will always be prayed according to the will of God, and be in harmony with the desire of His heart. The Holy Spirit is praying and you are praying, together in total agreement according to the purpose and plan of the Father. It's as if you are yoked together in prayer, with the Holy Spirit pressing forward under the shadow of the Almighty to move mountains and straighten out crooked pathways, to make straight the way of the Lord.

Prayer Burdens

One of the greatest delights you can be a part of is when you are given the gift of a prayer burden. This special blessing is given to you when God takes a desire of His heart and places it in your heart. As God's prayer burden fills your heart and you begin to pray, you will know more and more of the desires of God's heart. To know the heart of God in a matter is the most precious and joyous occasion and you will soon see that not only are His burdens light, they are a delight. These burdens will make your feet dance and your voice sing with joy.

When praying according to the burden the Holy Spirit puts in your heart, you will be praying according to the desire of God's heart and you know beyond the shadow of a doubt that He will answer your prayer in His time. You will be praying in agreement with the purpose and plan that God has ordained. You can pray with great confidence, knowing that you are in partnership with God Almighty as if praying hand in hand with our Lord Jesus Christ. In this kind of prayer you are pulling together with the hosts of heaven to make the way straight for all that God has proclaimed to come into being.

Why would God need you to pray in agreement with Him when He is Sovereign over all the earth? He didn't need our advice when He created all the heavens and earth. He didn't need our know-how when giving each and every creature its natural instincts and unique characteristics. He didn't inquire of us how much a grown elephant should weigh. And yet God brought the animals to Adam to name them: "So out of the ground the Lord God formed every animal of the field and every bird of the air, and brought them to the man to see what he would call them; and whatever the man called every living creature, that was its name." (Genesis 2:19).

It is the very nature of God to work hand in hand with His people to accomplish all that He desires. We are His children, the sheep of His pasture and His desire is to extend His hand into the world through His people.

We find many Biblical examples of this. John the Baptist made the way straight for Jesus the Messiah. King David prayed prophetic prayers proclaiming the coming Yeshua Hamashiach. Isaiah prophesied the King who would come to rule in righteousness. God put it on Elijah's heart to pray that no rain would fall on the lands of Israel for three years.[68]

Here is an opportunity to dig into God's Word on your own, and with the Holy Spirit's help, to see these truths first hand. Daniel is a great example of praying the heart of God according to a prayer burden placed on his heart. Read Daniel chapter 9. This is a record of Daniel's repentant prayers and intercessions on behalf of God's people.

---

[68] (1 Kings 17 & 18, James 5:17)

In verse four, Daniel makes reference to seventy years of exile because of the sins of God's chosen nation. The seventy years was prophesied by the prophet Jeremiah many years before and recorded on a scroll. Read Jeremiah 29:4-14. Especially note verses ten and eleven. This is the heart of God. In this you may see the very nature of our Heavenly Father. Daniel came to know the heart of God in this matter as he read Jeremiah's worthy words. By the power of these words the Lord placed a burden on his heart to pray according to the promise of God.

If God has spoken into being, through the words of His chosen prophet, an event that is to happen in the near or distant future, why does He want or need us to pray in agreement with Him in the matter? I haven't come to a complete answer to this question, but what I do know is that God chooses to bring us together with Him, yoked together to accomplish His purpose and plan.

It's like a dad saying to his son, "Hey, give me a hand here," when in fact dad really doesn't need his son's help. The dad's purpose is to teach his son the joy of a job well done, to help him learn the trade or just to build his son's confidence. God's desire is to include us in what He is doing among mankind, and that may involve making us a part of the process, too. Just as important, God's desire is to accomplish His will, purpose and plan through His servants — you and me.

You have heard the phrase, "Moving the hand of God." It's a reference to God's desire to do more than just involve us in His purpose and plan. God's desire is for us to ask Him to act on our behalf, for our good and for the good of those around us. It is His desire for us to come before Him with our petitions, asking for the desire of our heart — often the desire He has placed in our heart.

Seek with all your heart to know God's heart. Dwell in the Father's council, walk with Him, talk and listen to Him, and enjoy sweet fellowship in Him. Lend a hand in the work you see Him doing. Speak what you hear Him saying. Go where you see Him going. In time, in a moment only He knows, He will put on your heart the burden of His heart.

The reason: your motivation is clear. When you complete the work God has ordained for you to do, His name is glorified. Especially when that work is on our knees — His name is glorified.

Ask Anything in My Name

Mary Jo Packard[69] was so excited as she looked forward to her sixteenth birthday. At last, she would take her driver's test and get a license to drive. Months ago she had asked her dad for a car; after all, her dad was the head of the Packard Motor Car Company. The one she wanted was tan and white with a flip down top. She imagined herself driving to the lake with her friends, their hats blowing in the wind, singing "Swinging on a Star" as they motored along the tree lined lanes. Her request was granted because, after all, her dad was Mr. Packard. His name was synonymous with fine, quality automobiles.

Serena Leilia Lenova was busily planning her wedding day with Mom and her best friend at her side. It would be a big wedding at a posh resort with spacious manicured lawns and trimmed hedges surrounded by majestic sycamore trees. Over two hundred guests were expected to witness them being united as husband and wife. There was one special request she made of her dad and it meant so much to her. Her dad was a developer who built homes and planned communities all over the state. He had a reputation for being the best in the trade. Serena asked him to build a custom home on a lot the new couple had picked out with a view of the lake and mountains. She received exactly what she'd asked for; after all, her dad was the one and only Mr. Lenova, the exclusive developer of Bridgeport Estates.

In each of these fictional stories, the girls asked their father for what his name was known for. In the Scriptures, we find almost two hundred references to "My Name," and by this we know that His *Name* is of utmost importance. Jesus encourages us in this: "I will do whatever you ask *in my name*, so that the Father may be glorified in the Son. If in my name you ask me for anything, I will do it" (John 14:13-14, italics added).

Why does Jesus say, "Ask anything in my name," as opposed to saying, "Ask anything of me?" Is there a difference between His Name and the person of Christ? The truth is, His Name reveals the person

---

[69] Mary Jo Packard and Serena Leilia Lenova are fictional characters used for the purpose of illustration. The Packard Motor Company was real, established in the year 1900.

of Christ. It is in His Name that God reveals to us His nature, and the desires of His heart.

The Name of our Lord Jesus is holy. His Name is mighty in all the earth, and at the sound of His Name, enemies scatter. At the sight of His battle flag, declaring His Name, those who are called by His Name are drawn to Him.

Beyond a doubt, His name reveals the nature of the triune God. We know God by His complete and proper name, Father, Son and Holy Spirit. Jesus is the perfect manifestation of the Father. The Holy Spirit proceeds from the Father and the Son. The beauty and splendor of the Holy Trinity is revealed in the Name of Father, Son and Holy Spirit. In this Name, according to what His Name reveals to us, because of what we know God to be, and because of His Name, we pray in accordance to His Name. In other words, to pray in His Name would be to pray in concert, in harmony or in agreement with His character, mind, purpose and plan.

Here is a beautiful example of praying in His Name, "Yahweh **Yireh**" (my best pronunciation of Yireh is Yeah-Rah). "So Abraham called that place The LORD Will Provide" (Genesis 22:14, NIV). This is His Name. In Genesis 22, God provides a substitute to die in Isaac's place. As we read through Scripture, we see God's name, "Provider" of our daily bread, and certainly everything that we need. In this Name, God reveals his desire and nature as Provider to His people and all of His creation. He purposes to provide. His desire is to supply, especially for those who call on His Name, but also for all, man and beast alike. Because this is revealed to you, you can pray in great faith and confidence, asking God to provide according to His will, purpose and plan for you – according to His name.

There are many more names that reveal the nature of God:[70] God my Shield, God my Defender, God my Fortress, God my Righteousness just to name a few. As you search to know the Names of God, you'll find spectacular dimensions illuminating God's nature, continuing on into timeless and infinite beauty.

Pray in His Holy Name.

---

[70] A more complete list Names for God, Christ Jesus and the Holy Spirit may be found in the book "Kingdom Treasures." A list may also be found in Nave's Topical Bible.

Common Sense Prayers

There is an old saying in the Middle East that goes like this: "Trust God and tie up your camel." The amplified paraphrase of this saying could be: "Do what wisdom and common sense compel you to do and trust God in all that you do." Nehemiah knew this truth better than most. "So we prayed to our God, and set a guard as a protection against them day and night" (Nehemiah 4:9).

The Scriptures are clear, stating what God desires of us. None of us is a special case, able to do what nobody else gets to do. Why would we prayerfully ask about something that God has already told us not to do? A blatant example of this principle would be to pray about sleeping with the neighbor's[71] wife when God has already directed you on this matter? "So is he who sleeps with his neighbor's wife; no one who touches her will go unpunished" (Proverbs 6:29). There is no need to pray about what God's Word has already spoken to. I've used a rather graphic example, but this is a truth that applies to many of the commands and imperatives of Scripture.

So what's the point of praying about what you know is wrong? You'll only be praying to yourself and your "self" will always bless what your flesh wants to do. You're prayer may be very nice and sincere, but the heavens will be like brass and it will bounce right back at you. Maybe we should call this a yo-yo prayer. We can easily deceive ourselves because of the deceit in our hearts and we easily convince ourselves, rationalizing that God has indeed blessed us with permission to sin. Another great deception is to think, "God is sovereign. If He doesn't want me to do this, He will stop me. He'll close the doors so I can't go there." But God has already disclosed to you His will and His plan for you in the Bible. By His Word He has already closed the door, but you're banging it down with your self-centered, doubled up fist. The truth is, you will go where you want to go, and do what you want to do completely on your own by virtue of your own rebellious heart.

---

[71] Jesus made it clear in the parable of the Good Samaritan that our neighbors are not just the people living in the house next to us.

Read, study, explore and know the Scriptures so that you have a grasp of what God desires of you. If you are determined to go against what God has called you to do, don't attempt to pray yourself into doing it by imagining that God has given you the go ahead. Instead, pray that He will keep your feet from slipping off His narrow pathway. Pray that He will convince you and convict you of sin.

When you have been a yo-yo and slipped from the path and then finally come to your senses, call out to the Good Shepherd to come untangle you from the mess, to graciously forgive and cleanse you, and to bring you back into the fold. He is gracious, merciful and always faithful to forgive your sins and to clean you from all unrighteousness. The natural consequences of your sin may take much longer to untangle, but even in that, our Lord God is your great hope and ever-present help.

Present Your Case Before the Lord

Bring the Lord to remembrance. "Put me in remembrance: let us plead together" (Isaiah 43:26, KJV). Here we find the Hebrew word, רַכָז zakar, which means, to remember or call to mind. But did God forget? Does he need to be reminded? Not in the least. Recently my wife and I went to a dance at the Community Center. We enjoyed an evening of being close, swinging to the music, and exchanging that "look of love" as we danced together. It was a special and memorable evening for us. My wife enjoys bringing this evening to my memory. Does that mean I forgot about it and need to be reminded? No, not in the least. She brings it to memory so we can enjoy, once again, the special blessings of being together for a very fun evening that strengthened the bond of our love.

In Isaiah 43:26 we are encouraged to remind God. "Put me in remembrance." This is to be done in times of prayer, intercession, and pleading our case before a Holy God. We are encouraged to remind God of what He has done in the past. We are to present them as a legal precedent to build our case. Again, God didn't forget. In reminding Him, we don't gain power over Him because we remembered and He didn't. We are strengthening the bond of faith and love.

Why is it that God encourages us to remind Him? I know that I need to be reminded of His goodness, His mercies, His forgiveness and His cleansing. Yet God encourages us to come boldly before His throne of grace, to stand at His footstool in His council chambers and to thoughtfully, thoroughly present our case before Him — because He is a Holy and Righteous Judge of all the heavens and all the earth. As Jacob was returning home, his brother Esau approached with 400 armed men. In great fear Jacob pleaded his case before God, reminding him of His promise:

> *"I am unworthy of all the kindness and faithfulness you have shown your servant. I had only my staff when I crossed this Jordan, but now I have become two groups [two camps]. Save me, I pray, from the hand of my brother Esau, for I am afraid he will come and attack me, and also the mothers with their children. But you have said, 'I will surely make you prosper and will make your descendants like the sand of the sea, which cannot be counted.'" (Genesis 32:10-11)*

Jacob pleaded his case before God and accomplished two things. First, he came into God's council and was strengthened in his faith. Second, he called out to the God he served and was assured that the God of his fathers was walking forward with him in the way God had commanded.

The remembrance chases away fear and fortifies our bond of love. The reminder is like glue in a relationship that builds on a common connection. These precious memories are like tying a knot in a bow of the ribbon on a special gift.

Your Prayers are Treasured

The morning sun pierced through the small gap in the curtains, shining a beam of light on Anita's face. She awoke with a start and glanced at the clock. 6:15. She threw back the covers, stretched and laughed to herself. This was a very special day — her wedding day.

She opened the curtains to brighten the room and whispered excited prayers for God to watch over them during this special event. Then she sat cross-legged by the cedar chest at the foot of her bed to look through her treasures. She looked at her senior annual where Joshua had scribbled his first expression of affection, "I ♡ U, Josh." He was a man of few words.

She checked the dried flowers, holding them one by one to her lips and nose to see if the fragrance lingered. It always surprised her that she could remember each fragrance from their special occasions: the senior prom, the engagement flower, the "I'm sorry" flowers, and the "just-because-I-love-you" flowers and the bouquets he had sent to her while she was away at university. She rubbed the plastic gumball ring that he'd given her in seventh grade. She hugged the fuzzy stuffed lamb he'd won for her at the fair. Then she put on the green hat he'd worn on their first shared trick-or-treat adventure. Josh had been Robin Hood to her Maid Marian. Anita inhaled the aroma of cedar as she stroked the tea linen Josh's mom had given her. So old fashioned with its white lace and brocade, but a precious family heirloom. She held up to the morning light the special lingerie she'd bought for their first night together; no one but her best friend Sheri had ever seen it.

Then a knock on her door brought her back to reality. Mom cheerfully sang out, "Time for breakfast, dear." Anita closed the lid on the cedar chest as the door opened a crack. "Oh, I see you're awake. I have coffee ready for you." The smell of coffee and bacon poured in through the door, and she jumped to her feet.

Whether child, adult, or well-aged, we all have treasures that we collect, preserving them as special memories to hold onto. Mine are stored on a bookshelf and on my desk. They're within reach for my grandkids to pick up and examine. At times they'll say, "Tell me the story about this one, Papa." They've heard the stories before and love to hear them again and again. I always laugh with the delight of having them sit on my lap, telling them the stories that give life to my special treasures.

Did you know that our Heavenly Father has treasures that He keeps in a special place? Can you even imagine what God treasures and holds dear? Our Heavenly Father tells us what He treasures: "When he had taken the scroll, the four living creatures and the twenty- four elders fell before the Lamb, each holding a harp and golden bowls full of incense, which are the prayers of the saints" (Revelation 5:8).

How beautiful and lovely. Picture it in your mind's eye. The prayers of the saints, your prayers, are stored up in golden bowls, like incense. Our prayers are like a beautiful fragrance to the Lord, and He treasures them, holding them dear in bowls of gold in heaven above. In this I see a beautiful picture of the blessings of prayer. Our individual, personal requests of the Lord are stored in bowls made of the purest gold. Even your short and desperate one word prayers and your earnest and heart wrenching hours-long prayers are all treasured. What great assurance we see that our God Almighty values our petitions, intercessions, requests and prayers.

The spiritual discipline of prayer keeps our weaknesses in check and connects us to the very heart of God. Prayer becomes more than a ritual; it becomes personal. Prayer becomes more than a conversation; it becomes a covenantal act. Our prayers are frequent, constant, casual, persistent, fervent, and intense; yet all of them are stored up as a great treasure.

Our God is the God of "Yes."

Q & A Chapter 15: Prayerful, Interceding, Worshipful, and Thankful

1. What are the benefits of offering thankful prayers of thanksgiving?

2. How can prayers be hindered?

3. What is a prayer burden and what are the blessings that come with it?

4. What did Jesus mean when He said, "Ask anything in my name?"

Your Mission Journal Notes:

16

Living the Scriptures

Krista and Jonathan had birthdays on the same day. June 10th was a bright, sunny day, perfect weather for a birthday party with all their friends. It was a double celebration because it was the start of summer vacation. Krista and Jonathon had each asked for a puppy for their birthdays; but that's where the similarities ended. In fact, they had never even met.

Along with a puppy, Krista and Jonathan were each given a book called *The Care and Feeding of Your Dog*. Her puppy chewed on her hand playfully as Krista thumbed through the book to find the most important part about feeding her Spaniel mix. Then she put the book aside until she mastered that part of pet care. Next she went to the exercise section and then to the grooming chapter, mastering the concepts in each chapter before going on to the next.

Jonathan took his pure bred Border collie home, turned her out into the fenced back yard, and plopped on his bed to pour over his book. He absorbed every chapter in the same way that he tackled his studies, which made him an "A" student. Before long he started sounding like a dog expert, quoting important facts from the book. His parent's friends patted him on the back, telling him he was such a good pet owner because of all his knowledge.

It wasn't long before Jonathan came to the attention of the local kennel club because of his dog knowledge and his charismatic sharing of dog trivia. The club voted unanimously to invite him to give a short speech at their annual dog show and awards banquet. Dressed in a new jacket and tie, Jonathan gave a splendid lecture filled with anecdotes.

He got a standing ovation, even though he went over his time. His boyish face flushed as he bowed.

When his family was finally able to break away from all the handshakes and pats on the back, they were shocked to find flashing lights and police cars blocking their SUV. They had left the dog in the car with the windows down an inch, and it had died in the heat.

Upon examining the dog, the veterinarian's diagnosis was that if the dog had been healthy and well nourished, it might have survived. But it was not strong enough to endure the heat, even on a moderately warm day. The pet doctor made his point by pulling loose clumps of matted hair from the dog's coat, holding it up for them to see.

Krista wasn't invited to the kennel club meeting. But that was okay. She was busy giving Trixie a bath, giving her a doggie chew to clean her teeth, brushing out her shiny coat, and checking her floppy Spaniel ears like the book said.

Krista and Jonathan demonstrate a sharp contrast between knowing and doing. If you're like Jonathan, a Bible may grace your book shelf, you may pack a thick Study Bible under your arm when you go to church, you listen carefully when the Scriptures are read every Sunday, you dig into your Bible when you have time, you have some great Scriptures committed to memory, but the Word does not rule your life, it does not influence everything you do, it does not bring you to Christ, and as a result, your spirit and soul are vulnerable and weak. Those who do what the Book says become spiritually healthy and well nourished.

Jesus confronted the religious leaders over the same issue in his time.

> *"And the Father who sent me has himself testified on my behalf. You have never heard his voice or seen his form, and you do not have his word abiding in you, because you do not believe him whom he has sent. You search the scriptures because you think that in them you have eternal life; and it is they that testify on my behalf. Yet you refuse to come to me to have life. I do not accept glory from human beings. But I know that you do not have the love of God in you. I have come in my*

Father's name, and you do not accept me; if another comes in
his own name, you will accept him. How can you believe when
you accept glory from one another and do not seek the glory
that comes from the one who alone is God?" (John 5:38-44)

Note the most incriminating part of these verses: <u>*"You search*</u>
<u>*the scriptures because you think that in them you have eternal life..."*</u>
Teachers of the law, the Pharisees and Sadducees, and every
Jewish boy who wanted to become a man committed the Scriptures
to memory. They diligently studied the Scriptures. They discussed the
Scriptures at great length and searched out the words of Scripture.
They listened intently to their rabbis as they taught, to catch every
nuance of meaning from the inspired Word from the scrolls. But that's
as far as it went. This problem wasn't new in Jesus' day. King David
wrote a warning to the people of his day. "But to the wicked God says:
'What right have you to recite my statutes, or take my covenant on
your lips? For you hate discipline, and you cast my words behind you'"
(Psalms 50:16-17).

In fact, Jonathan had no right to be spouting out all kinds of dog
knowledge and trivia because he would not accept the responsibility
that came with the knowledge. He was a fraud, deceiving the kennel
club while his dog was dying in the car. Is it possible to diligently
search the Scriptures, to completely know the Scriptures or even to
memorize them entirely but, in fact, not have the Word in you? You
say you believe it, but your actions prove your words to be nothing but
meaningless chatter. Jesus makes this point clear. "He replied, 'Blessed
rather are those who hear the word of God and obey it'" (Luke 5:28).
If you don't do what you hear, you are building a house that won't
stand. "And everyone who hears these words of mine and does not
act on them will be like a foolish man who built his house on sand"
(Matthew 7:26).

The prophet Jeremiah also confronted this hypocrisy. "How can
you say, 'We are wise, and the law of the Lord is with us,' when, in fact,
the false pen of the scribes has made it into a lie" (Jeremiah 8:8).

When you go to a restaurant the server will offer a menu. On it is
written what the restaurant offers. Now, if you memorized the menu

and examined the words and phrases of their unique cuisine, and then discussed with your friends at great length exactly what they meant by the word "sautéed," and what kind of pan they used and at what temperature they stir-fried the vegetables, then in essence, you have come to know the menu better than the server.

But in the end, if you did not give the server your order and partake of the beautifully presented cuisine, the menu is of no use to you. Now consider this. You may be holding a "spiritual menu," called the Holy Bible right in your hands. You may well have memorized whole chapters in the Bible. In your home Bible study groups you expound at great length on the deeper meaning of Scripture. But if you don't do what it says, you have nothing but words on the page.

Many of Jesus' disciples deserted Him when He taught that they must partake of His body and His blood (John chapter 6). They refused what was on the "menu" and walked away. The Holy Bible's "menu" is simple, revealing to us the only One who is true and real, and that is Jesus Christ. If you're reading, studying, searching and examining the Scriptures, and all the commentary notes as well, but refuse to partake of what is offered, your bowl is empty. Your pursuits are nothing but an empty, lifeless, religious exercise.

We must listen to the distinct instructions: "Do not quench the Spirit. Do not treat prophecies with contempt but test them all; hold on to what is good, reject every kind of evil" (1 Thessalonians 5:20-21, NIV). The Apostle Paul gives a clear and present charge for churches that is still in effect to this very day. It has not been rescinded. "So, my friends, be eager to prophesy, and do not forbid speaking in tongues; but all things should be done decently and in order" (1 Corinthians 14:39-40). These are two examples of spiritual gifts (adornments for the bride of Christ) that are often rejected. We have blazed Scriptures into our memory and read them over and over in our Bible study classes. On Sunday morning someone reads from the Bible, "But you are a chosen race, a royal priesthood, a holy nation, God's own people, in order that you may proclaim the mighty acts of him who called you out of darkness into his marvelous light" (1 Peter 2:9). What this Scriptures says is that all Christians are called to serve and minister, fulfilling our special parts in proclaiming

God's mighty acts. But instead, we are content to sit in church as spectators.

A good friend of mine was a regular in my adult Bible study on "Spiritual Giving." One day he came up to me after class and said, "I don't know why I'm taking your class. I don't do what I know I'm supposed to do as it is. Why should I learn more of what I won't do?" At least he was honest about his bad attitude. That's a good place to start but a horrible place to be stuck.

Too often churches choose not to teach some truths of the Scripture. We relegate them to a time long past, claiming that they are no longer necessary because we have the complete canon of Scripture and no longer require these precious gifts. Our teachers handle the Word falsely, either twisting the truth to their own liking or adjusting their doctrines and theology to match their own experience. In turning away from the whole truth of Scripture, in choosing only what we like, rejecting the rest, we create a buffet style god according to our own preferences that can neither hear, nor see, nor speak. This god we have created by the work of our own hands is no better than wood or stone.

We read the book of Acts and witness the confirming signs and wonders that followed the true proclamations of the Gospel message. We watch from afar as they received the Good News with joy and embraced the truth as it was proclaimed. These signs and wonders, performed by the Apostles and disciples, were the hand of the Holy Spirit, extended to prove that a true message was proclaimed and that the truth of the message was received and believed. Signs and wonders confirm that the Scriptures have been preached and taught in truth and received in truth, without being twisted or edited to our liking. Yet we say that these signs and wonders by the hand of God are no longer needed because we have the complete written Scriptures.[72] Again, the question is; will we find our security in the fact that we have the complete canon of Scriptures, or will we live the whole

---

[72] Please understand that there is no word to be added to Scripture, no word that will contradict scripture, and no word of prophecy that will conflict with God's written Word. When God speaks spontaneously, in the moment, through those who have the spiritual gift of prophecy, His Word is being applied in the moment and addressing a present need in the gathering of believers.

Scriptures according to truth? Will we twist God's holy words to suit our pet doctrines, or will we allow the Holy Spirit to teach us truth? These are hard questions that deserve an answer.

We may memorize Scriptures in its entirety, we may have our doctrines and theology down pat, we may read through the Bible every year, and hear the Scriptures read every Sunday morning, but if we don't rightly teach the Scriptures (2 Timothy 2:15) and then do what it says, the dog will die in the car. We must understand that it is the worst kind of hypocrisy to claim the Lord's Holy name as the Author of our message and then twist His Word to suit our personal preferences. Indeed, if you don't live the Scriptures according to truth, you have nothing but wood, hay, and stubble and it will not stand the test of fire.

Jesus faced down the destructiveness of this hypocrisy: "I know that you are Abraham's descendants. Yet you are looking for a way to kill me, because you have no room for my word" (John 8:37). The Jewish leaders claimed Abraham as father and Jehovah as God, but they rejected Jesus, who is God. The truth was not in them and they were defeating themselves.

In the earliest years of the Christian church, they confronted the threat of those who twisted the Scriptures. They claimed the Scriptures instructed Gentile Christians to be circumcised. They said, "Unless you are circumcised according to the custom of Moses, you cannot be saved" (Acts 15:1). They were adjusting the truth according to their own philosophies and cherished doctrines, and they were not teaching truth. They were quoting Scriptures to prove their point, but their point missed the true mark of truth.

This is a great failing of the church today. When Scriptures are dismissed, like 1 Peter 2:9 regarding the priesthood of the believer, it is debilitating and destructive. When we reject any part of Scripture, the church suffers spiritual poverty. This great shortcoming saps strength and power from the church, putting out the Holy Spirit's fire. All of us suffer harm when we don't do what we know is right and good.

And yet, even when we are not faithful to God's Word, we have the greatest hope in Jesus Christ who is always faithful. He knows our weaknesses and our human failings. He knows the temptations that attempt to take us down. Remember this truth and it will save your life: "If we confess our sins, he is faithful and just to forgive us our sins, and to cleanse us from all unrighteousness. If we say that we have not sinned, we make him a liar, and his word is not in us" (1 John 1:9-10).

Grieve over your sin, confess your sin, turn from this great sin, be honest about your failings before a Holy God and trust Him to cleanse and make you whole once again. He will lift you up to set your feet on the solid Rock. He will renew and restore you and confer on you a Kingdom. "And just as my Father has granted me a Kingdom, I now grant you the right to eat and drink at my table in my Kingdom"[73] (Luke 22:29-30 NLT).

Yes, Lord. Amen.

Q & A Chapter 16: Living the Scriptures

1. Describe the difference between Jonathan's and Krista's applications of their dog care knowledge.

2. What is the consequence of picking and choosing what we like and don't like?

3. How is it possible to live the Scriptures in the real world?

Your Mission Journal Notes:

---

[73] This is certainly a reference to communion, and yet it is so much more.

17

Fasting is Feasting

How can this be good? My stomach is growling and it's way past my dinnertime. I can't think of anything but this empty churning in my belly, and my head is dizzy from hunger. Why do we have to talk about fasting anyway? Is it really that important? Does it actually make a difference in a Christian's daily life? Isn't this just some obscure, obsolete religious practice? Get real, okay?! This is for monks who cloister themselves in a remote mountain monastery, milk their goats by hand (and smell like goats), brew their own beer and don't have to deal with reality, right?

I must confess, I'm a typical American Christian and I've never been strong on fasting. I've resisted the concept and avoided it as much as possible. I've had more questions about fasting than you'll find on your standard SAT test, and few answers. It's always been a major challenge for me. I've talked to my Christian brothers about it and I get a brush off like, "Get real, bro. You know I'm hypoglycemic." Bottom line: We're going to learn this together, because I, too, have much to learn about this spiritual discipline. As we explore this topic, we will see that fasting is not what many people think — starving ourselves to get what we want or need from God. We'll discover ways to fast that fit our personal needs and differences. In fasting we enter a spiritual reality, but we must never ignore the needs of this human body.

A complete definition isn't practically possible, but we must attempt one. Fasting is denying the flesh and refusing to strengthen our "self" in order to draw near to a holy God. Also, in denying the flesh, we become stronger to resist temptations of the flesh. Fasting is more than a day or so of self-denial. Fasting ought to become a lifestyle, a habit, an attitude of heart that focuses the eyes of our spirit heavenward, centering our attention on strengthening those around us and furthering God's kingdom in all the earth. We fast from those things that strengthen the flesh.[74] When we fast, we confirm our faith that declares, "Man does not live by bread alone." We may fast from food, praying to know the Bread of Heaven above all, nourishing us in soul and spirit. We could agree with our spouse to fast from sexual relations for a short time to focus on prayer and interceding before God. A fast may be giving up something we regularly enjoy and donating the money to a godly cause so that we may know God Who Provides. We can fast of our favorite tunes, praying to enter into the awesome joy of praising a Holy, Almighty God. Another fast might be giving up time spent in our favorite hobby, sport, or leisure activities for a time, to pray and to give that time to a godly cause in order to know God's blessings and strength in our service to the saints.

There are more ways to fast. A good fast may be from "spirits" (wine, beer, liquor) to pray and more fully know the Holy Spirit, to receive a refreshing measure of the Spirit of Jesus. Prayerfully fasting from sweets may remind you of the refreshing sweetness of our Lord and Savior. You can forgo your morning coffee buzz and pray for an extra jolt of the empowering work of the Holy Spirit. Skipping your comfort tea while praying for the comfort of the Holy Spirit might be an excellent way to fast. Your fast could well be getting away from the pressure of being the one who must "make it happen" in the corporate world, taking a time for quiet solitude to prayerfully remember that the world continues in its orbit without you. A good fast may be daylight fasting, from sunrise to sunset — accompanied with prayers and intercessions throughout the day. (This will be easy for our friends who spend the winter in Fairbanks, Alaska.)

You may choose a Nazirite fast which would be similar to the vow found in Numbers 6:3-7. This would be a fast from any of the fruit of the vine, meaning wine, fermented drink, grape juice, grapes or raisins, for the purpose of strengthening the bond between yourself

---

[74] When we refer to the "flesh," this is a reference to our physical body, our "earth suit," and its natural desires.

and the True Vine. You might also consider the part of a Nazirite vow that includes not shaving or cutting your hair during the fast. Again, there are no rules chiseled in stone for this kind of fast. Fasting while only having unleavened Matzo bread, water and prayer may be an excellent cleansing fast — not for your body, but for your spirit and soul.

Some choose a Daniel fast, refraining from rich foods, meats and wine (Daniel 10:3). Again, there are no rules or laws for Christian fasting. You are not required to spend forty days in the wilderness, fasting like Jesus did before beginning your ministry. This is a spiritual discipline that is between you and the Lord, as the Holy Spirit leads you. There are no step-by-step formulas for fasting to give you predetermined results. Each one of us is a unique and special "vessel" and each may fast in a way best suited to the way God has made us.

In essence, what is fasting like? Fasting embraces prayer like a bear hug. Fasting joins together with purposeful meditation on God's Word like lovers walking hand in hand. A fast may be like prayerfully stepping back from the limelight, so the Light of Life may be exalted. A fast is like feasting before the Lord. God becomes to us what we deny ourselves in a fast. If you are in a food fast, He nourishes you. If you are fasting from spirits, He refreshes you in His Holy Spirit. When you fast of your favorite tunes, He is your new song.

If you've been around church very long, you know about potlucks, but have you ever heard of a community fast? Coming together to feast before the Lord is a powerful way to bind us together in Christ. Yet how much more powerful it would be for our leaders and the whole church to fast before the Lord?

It is important to know what a fast is not. There is no cut and dried, chiseled in stone, legalistic system. Fasting is not something you absolutely must do to gain a higher level of spirituality. It's between you and the Lord, and your fast may be done in the way you choose. It is not a pass or fail test of your spirituality or of your faith in Christ. It's not a "Lone Ranger" thing, because you fast in the presence of our Lord Jesus who is constantly with you, nourishing your soul and spirit. Denying "self" in a fast is not a cure all. It's not a formula for getting your prayers heard and answered. Fasting is not a religious ritual. Fasting is not a weight loss program. It's a spiritual discipline. And beware of getting legalistic about fasting. During a fast, if your family is celebrating a birthday, share a piece of cake and then resume your fast.

A fast, done by the leading of the Spirit, and according to godly wisdom, does not harm your health, for the Lord "will strengthen your frame" (Isaiah 58:11). Doing a two-day or even a forty-day fast does not give you bragging rights. Fasting does not elevate you to a higher spiritual level among your Christian brothers and sisters.

Jesus chastised the Pharisees for their legally perfect fasting, when they were at the same time evicting widows and orphans who were late on their rent. They went about town with their hair disheveled and their face unwashed so people would know they were fasting, and at the same time they were withholding financial help they owed their parents (Mark 7:11). Their fast was a sham—an empty, self-serving, self-glorifying con job.

This is my story about how a "fast" began to transform my mind. It was the beginning of a long process that changed my heart. This happened a few years after God called me out of darkness, adopted me into His family of faith and gave me a new name. I was living in Northwestern Washington State on a small farm near the banks of the Nooksack River. I worked as a sales representative for the industrial division of a sporting goods conglomerate, and my territory extended from the Canadian border in the north all the way to Southern Oregon. I logged a lot of highway miles.

It was winter and the roads were hazardous, making travel slow on my business trip to the Portland area, where our manufacturing plant was located. Because I was running late, I decided to drive a little longer that evening and stay over at Troutdale, Oregon. My first client in the morning would be a short drive away. Waking up at 5 am, I looked outside to see my yellow Chevy buried under five feet of drifted snow. I wasn't going anywhere.

As was my habit, I took time to be quiet before the Lord, to pray, read my Bible and get my spirit prepared for the day. During my quiet time I sensed God's call to fast and pray. I got dressed and checked out the parking lot at the truck stop adjacent to my hotel. It was wall-to-wall 18-wheelers, buried in snow. Next I checked out the restaurant and found that they were concerned because they couldn't get food deliveries and their workers couldn't get to work. Interstate 84 was closed for the duration.

"Okay, God. This really *is* a good time to fast and pray." What took me so long to get it? Truly, God brought me into circumstances where I had to stop all my rushing about and draw near to Him, be quiet and listen. Finally, I did just that.

Over the next four days, I prayed, searched the Scriptures, talked to my Heavenly Father, prayed in the Spirit, meditated on God's Word, and cleaned out my ears to listen. God began a remarkable work in me at that time. It was the beginning of a long road that has brought me to where I am today, with a few hazardous detours of my own making. In this time of fasting He poured into me a fresh, empowering work of His Holy Spirit. It was like He turned one power switch on, and over the years, as I've studied, searched and dug deep into the Scriptures – as I've prayed, interceded, and sought the Lord, the second switch is being turned on in order to be powered up to do the work He has ordained for me.

In that snowed-in time of fasting and prayer, God began to reveal to me His intention and what He has prepared for me to do in this life. He ramped up His process of molding and making me into a useful vessel in His kingdom, to accomplish all He has planned for me. In every sense, this was a kind of cocooning fast, secluding myself to pray and seek the Lord God Almighty.[75]

I wish I could say that from that time on I walked on the straight and narrow without slipping. But my feet slipped. At times I chose to follow my own way and feed my own weaknesses. Yet God was faithful even when I was not. God saw me through, working in me to mold me for the good work He prepared for me before I was even born.

---

[75] For those of you who want to hear the rest of the story: Finally, late in the third day, the snowplows opened the freeway, followed by trucks from the food suppliers, but the parking lot was still solid, deep snow. We formed a human chain from the freeway to the restaurant, passing cases of food hand to hand. The next day we finally got out of there after the parking lot was plowed.

To be clear, it was not an external experience[76] that transformed me; but it certainly got my attention and began a fresh work of the Holy Spirit in my heart, a process of transformation in my life that is still going on today.

The prophet Joel called God's people to a fast. "Sanctify a fast, call a solemn assembly." He began by warning of God's judgment, calling the people to repentance, and imploring them to mourn over their sin. Then as God's spokesman he called out, "Declare a fast." He entreated the people, "Gather the elders and all the inhabitants of the land to the house of the Lord your God, and cry out to the Lord and all the inhabitants of the land to the house of the Lord your God, and cry out to the Lord" (Joel 1:14). We, too, are called to forsake our rebellious ways, to abandon our dependence upon the work of our own hands, to leave behind the wellspring we have dug for ourselves, and to return to the Spring of Living Water.

Many times throughout the Scriptures a fast is declared, and the people come before the Lord in humble repentance; they turn from their sin and God is faithful to forgive.[77] Our heavenly Father renews and refreshes His beloved ones. In response to their humble, repentant fast, God speaks through His prophet Joel once again. True to His word, God shows His people mercy, forgives them of their sin, washes them clean and proclaims a blessing upon them, and He restores the years their sin has eaten. "I will repay you for the years that the swarming locust has eaten, the hopper, the destroyer, and

---

[76] Many in the church today denigrate any kind of spiritual experience, possibly fearing that this would distract them from the centrality of Christ and the cross. Quite the opposite is true. In fact, a good test of any such experience is this: Does it bring your attention back to Christ, His redemptive work on the cross and the Resurrected Christ? This is my council. Don't seek or yearn for spiritual experiences, and don't glamorize such events in your life. Overemphasis of external manifestations too often degenerates into a form of legalism and elitism. True ecstatic experiences come in God's time to fulfill what He desires of us. Check out your Bible from Genesis to Revelation, from Abraham to the Apostle John and you will see clearly that spiritual, ecstatic experiences, while not common every day occurrences, are too numerous to discount. Check out the stories of leaders throughout the history of the historic, orthodox Christian faith and you will see that such experiences happen throughout the history of the New Testament church to this very day. God has not changed.
[77] 2 Samuel 1:12, Joel 2:12, Joel 2:15-16.

the cutter, my great army, which I sent against you" (Joel 2:25). "I am sending you grain, new wine and oil, enough to satisfy you fully; never again will I make you an object of scorn to the nations" (Joel 2:19 NIV). What a gracious, merciful, and faithful God we serve, for in place of judgment He sends "grain" that nourishes the soul. He offers "new wine" to strengthen the spirit. He sends the oil of His Holy Spirit, anointing oil for the wounds of His people. The Good Shepherd binds up the wounds of the sheep and pours healing oil upon them.

Here are some simple tips for implementing a fast: If you're doing a total food fast, the first meal or two you miss are difficult to get through.[78] Try to keep busy to take your attention off your stomach. Pray while taking a hike, going for a long walk, digging in the garden or doing your spring-cleaning. Always drink water and don't allow yourself to get dehydrated. If you start to get so grouchy that no one wants to be around you, it's time to stop your fast and try again at another time. Or try another way of fasting.

Don't wait for the Lord to get you "snowed in" before you agree to fast and seek the Lord. Don't hesitate. Don't hold back. Today is the time for us to mourn over our sins, turn from our sins, turn our faces heavenward, lift our hands to a Holy God and declare a holy fast. In a time of repentant fasting, we lay a good foundation for our Lord and God to build upon, to heal, restore and strengthen. In our newfound strength we will earnestly exalt Him and worship Him in spirit and in truth. Lord, glorify Your Holy Name in all the earth.

My understanding of fasting is not yet complete. My exercise of this spiritual discipline may be flawed. But that's okay. I don't have to get it perfect before getting started. With practice, my understanding will grow and mature.

Join the feast that strengthens your soul and spirit and choose a fast that suits who you are and meets your personal needs. Deny yourself and draw near to a Holy God. Of all the disciplines of the

---

[78] Before starting a total food fast, check with your doctor to be sure you're healthy enough to do so.

Christian faith, this is the one that offers the greatest benefits, because when we get close to God, our lives change dramatically.

Will you join with me in a holy ~~fast~~; feast?

Q & A Chapter 17: Fasting is Feasting

1. Is fasting a worthwhile Christian discipline for modern day Christians?

2. What are the different ways Christians can fast?

3. How is it that fasting is a feast?

Your Mission Journal Notes:

18

Hearts at Rest

Take a deep breath. Grab a cup of coffee or make some tea, and take a break. Close your eyes, breathe, and let the world go by without you for just a minute. Doesn't it feel good to let go? There's nothing better than a Sunday afternoon nap after taking the kids to church, then Happy Meals and baseball in the park. Ah, yes! It's a perfect respite to prepare you for a busy week.

But this kind of Sunday rest is just a bite-sized sample of the "rest" God has prepared for you. It's like a grain from a mountain of salt. A Sunday respite is like putting your toes in the water before you dive in headfirst. Yet this is a rest you can step into now, thereby entering rest in greater and greater measure until you get to that final, eternal rest in the living presence of a Holy God. The writer of Hebrews encourages us with these words: "Let us, therefore, make every effort to enter that rest" (Hebrews 4:11). Yes, *effort* is allowed and even necessary.

Rest is the grand finale of all God created. God likened Israel's promised land to a land of rest. God promises rest for our souls. "For I have given rest to the weary and joy to the sorrowing" (Jeremiah 31:25). In rest, we are blessed now and for all eternity.

Search the Scriptures with me and we'll figure out why we're so resistant to entering into our Heavenly Father's rest. We'll come to see the source of our rest, which leads us to understand that rest is not something we earn. We will enter into God's rest through Jesus Christ who is the Gateway. Rest will become familiar and recognizable to all who desire to enter.

Some people might respond to the premise that they should rest more by saying, "Of course I think about rest - meditation, I think they call it – when I'm commuting to work. Unless, of course, there's a traffic jam and I have the radio on for the traffic report. And how can I meditate when someone cuts me off? Then again I get interrupted when my cell phone goes off as I'm trying to switch lanes. Maybe there's a 'meditation' app for my smart phone. That would help get me focused."

You may agree that rest is important and your eyes may be searching for the road sign that says, "Next Exit Rest." You scan the skyline for some clue to how to get there. Where is the gate through which we enter this blessed rest?[79] How do we escape this rat race? How do we find our way out of the Urban Jungle? Or is escaping what it's all about?

Americans aren't good at rest. We work hard and play hard and take a pill to sleep hard. Even in retirement we have so much to do we don't know how we got everything done when we did the 9 to 5 thing. Like the rest of the world, American Christians have also been caught up in this insanity. We're driven by a cultural need to succeed and to have all the trappings of success. We want a career, a nice home with a landscaped yard and a hot tub. We need the latest fashions, the cool shoes, birthday parties for our kids and their friends at the pizza place, the car with the latest whistles and bells, the new cell phone with the bigger screen and fantastic apps, and the shopping list goes on while the credit card balance goes up. We're forced to work even when we're sick, because we have to write a check to pay the mortgage, make the car payment, feed the kids and pay the credit card bill — or at least the minimum payment.

On Sunday mornings, you punch the alarm clock, groan, and turn over to throw your arm across your wife's dozing body and whole house sleeps in; even the dog and cat. Now that's rest. Right? But in reality it's total fatigue. It's an all out drained-to-the-bottom-of-the-cup, nothing-left-to-give exhaustion. You rub your eyes and doze off again with a twinge of guilt — you really need to take the kids to church. And then the zzzz's take over until you have to take Billy to his afternoon soccer game. You throw on your sweats and make a quick dash for an espresso and some fast food and zip across town,

---

[79] Psalms 118:20, "This is the gate of the Lord; the righteous shall enter through it."

but you have to make another detour because in your rush, you forgot the bottled water. Finally, you're there and you slide into a parking space. You lock the van with your key fob while making a mad dash across the parking lot with the kids in tow because the game starts in one minute.

So where do you find this promised rest? Is it just an idealistic illusion? You can't remember a Sunday morning sermon about it — but maybe you slept through it. If there were a book about rest, it would probably put you to sleep too. Is it even realistic in this crazy world we've made for ourselves? Is there any chance to carve out a minute of rest? A power nap, maybe, but true rest? Give me a break and get real. Even on vacation, there are too many things to do, too many places to go and you have to take the kids to visit Grandma and Grandpa. We come home from our trips exhausted. Rest just isn't realistic. Right?

The writer of Hebrews encourages us to "make every effort to enter that rest." But this is for when Jesus returns in that great day sometime in the future, isn't it? It's somewhere up there in the clouds. It's pie in the sky in that sweet by and by, right? It seems so remote, somewhere out of reach in the heavens. When my head stops spinning for just a second or two and I can forget my to do list, I'll take a minute to think about it.

Stop! Listen. Be quiet. This insanity must end. I have to let this craziness go. I'm pushing hard on the brake pedal like I'm avoiding a crash but the brakes refuse to work. I feel powerless and the car is speeding toward a brick wall. I need to dial heaven's 9-1-1 right now. Stop!

This is of critical importance. "For thus said the Lord God, the Holy One of Israel: In returning and rest you shall be saved; in quietness and in trust shall be your strength" (Isaiah 30:15).

This is a great mystery, the mystery of the Gospel as revealed in Jesus Christ. Entering God's promised rest is not something you can earn; yet it is not without effort on your part. There are no strings attached to your feet to make you take this step, and you do not have the strength on your own to step out, but step out you must.

God gave the children of Israel freedom from the bondage of slavery in Egypt, but they had to obey His call, pack up, and follow

Moses into an unknown wilderness. The Great I AM led them through the desert to the Promised Land, but they had to step into the waters of the Jordan River before He parted the waters for them.

But where are we going? What does it look like? Is it a figurative land of milk and honey? Taking a nap on Sunday afternoon does not fit into the definition of God's promised rest. Resting from your labors gives you a thumbnail glimpse of God's eternal rest, but it is certainly not the fullness of it. Now look at the other side of the coin. Being crazy busy with things you have to do every day may be detracting you from God's rest, but His promised rest is not the opposite of being crazy busy.

Hebrews chapters 3 and 4 contain clear and powerful instructions to enter God's rest and a warning against refusing. Read through these chapters and you will see that faith and obedience are like hand and glove. To enter is obedience, to refuse is unbelief and disobedience.

Each of us must decide to release this crazy, busy world and our fate in it, including our personal success and reputation among our circle of friends and associates, into the loving, caring hands of our Heavenly Father. This is not a decision for inaction, but a conscious choice that you will act, fully dependent upon God Almighty for the outcome of all we put our hands to.

But how do we get to this "rest that God has established for us since creation"?[80] Jesus Christ is the way into God's rest. Peace overwhelms me! He is the key to our eternal rest. He is the gateway through which we may enter. He has made a way to the Tree of Life, for He is the Tree of Life. In so many ways His words teach us, illustrating His offer of rest. "Come unto me…"

But what is this rest He calls us to enter? Is it heaven? Is it a spiritual state of mind? Is it a meditative level of being? It is so much more. It is like the most precious and costly diamond you have ever heard of. The cut facets of the diamond catch the light and reflect a prism, a blaze of light that is multi-dimensional and incomparable in beauty. God's promised rest has so many dimensions. There is no language on earth sufficient to describe in full this unfathomable

[80] Matthew 25:34

mystery of God's rest. Brush stroke upon brush stroke, layer by layer, we are painting the best picture possible of God's rest.

In God's rest we are freed from the burden of guilt and it is removed from our shoulders.[81] The Father's rest empowers, renews and restores His children.[82] The Almighty's promised rest is strength to those who are called by His Name.[83] In His perfect rest we cast away all anxieties, cares and troubles.[84] As we are saturated in His gift of rest we know Him, see Him, and hear Him as never before possible.[85] Bathed in rest that He has prepared for His adopted sons and daughters, we find freedom even as we are caught up in the pressures and conflicts of this world, in the frustrations of daily life and in loneliness that attempts to overpower us.[86]

As we enter into rest, the loving nature of God is revealed to us.[87] His promised rest refocuses our attentions and redirects the attitudes of our heart.[88] Within this great and glorious rest we receive, in all gratefulness, the abundance God has given us — enjoying it, reveling in it, being saturated in it.[89] In His rest we escape from the need to build ourselves up.[90] God's rest makes a way to courageously face our deepest fears.[91] In rest we flee the snare of self-importance.[92] In entering this perfect rest we find true treasure, and our own unique value in Him.[93] Rest teaches us to give up control of the result, entrusting the outcome to Him.[94] God's perfect rest sets us free from striving for more of the things of this world that are nothing but "wood, hay and stubble."[95]

---

[81] Matthew 11:30
[82] 2 Corinthians 12:9
[83] Psalms 84:5
[84] 1 Peter 5:7
[85] Psalms 62:5—6
[86] Matthew 11:28—29
[87] 1 Corinthians 2:9—10
[88] Hebrews 4:12
[89] Psalms 84:6 –7
[90] Psalms 3:3
[91] Psalms 32:8—10
[92] Philippians 2:3
[93] Philippians 3:15—16, Philippians 4:8—9
[94] 2 Corinthians 5:7
[95] Galatians 5:1

This glorious gift of rest resets our priorities to value what is of eternal worth.[96]

Is "rest" just another word for salvation? Is this great promise just another way of expressing that we get to go to heaven when we die if we're born again? Salvation and the new heavens and new earth are certainly two dimensions of God's rest that we may enter, but there is so much more. In the book of Revelation, the Apostle John paints a picture for us, offering a glimpse into what God promised. "For the Lamb at the center of the throne will be their shepherd; he will lead them to springs of living water. And God will wipe away every tear from their eyes" (Isaiah 25:8).

This is sounding better all the time. What happens to us as we enter God's rest? It is nothing short of miraculous. This may be a small step, but resting in the Lord teaches us that life doesn't depend upon us. Very quickly we see that the world goes on, whether or not we're on board. We are doing things we couldn't possibly do ourselves, in our own strength. We find complete rest for our souls as we join our spirit with His Spirit. We find a satisfying love for our Lord and Savior that is complete and solid like a Rock.

The invitation is extended to you. This marvelous rest is ready today for you to enter. You cannot earn your way through the narrow gate into rest, yet you must act. Hear Jesus, the Good Shepherd, calling. His eyes search across the wilderness and beyond the horizon. He cups his hands to his mouth and calls out your name. Over and over he calls to you by name. He has left the herd behind in His search for you. Will you answer His call? Will you enter His eternal rest?

Take a look at how vital this rest is to your Heavenly Father. After six days of creating all the heavens and the earth God rested. In this rest, in His finished work, the Creator God made room for us to rest with Him, or rather, in Him. What an incredible God we serve. Just think of it. God rested and in His rest was more than enough room for all who God foreknew, a people from every tribe, nation, people and tongue, who would be called by His Holy Name. There is room enough

---

[96] 2 Corinthians 4:18

for all His adopted sons and daughters to be included in this great inheritance He calls REST.

By faith, we find assurance of what we cannot now see, and we can take that step forward to enter His perfect rest. This rest is available to all who earnestly seek Him. A place is prepared for any who will cry out for mercy. For those of contrite heart, there is room enough. Jesus called to all who would hear, "Come unto me, all you who are weary and burdened, and I will give you rest."

Your understanding has been building so you can see the gateway to rest. It's like you have been building brick by brick. Now we are ready for the Capstone who is Jesus Christ our Lord and Savior (Psalms 118:22). He is our rest.

Let go of the burdens that entrap you. Abandon what imprisons you. Jesus has paid a great ransom for your very soul, to release you from slavery to sin and death. Will you open your eyes to see His precious sacrifice made for you and enter into His freedom and rest? You will find strength in rest; you will be unburdened in God's rest. As you rest in Him, your eyes and understanding will be opened to see God clearly. In rest you'll find a great freedom from the pressures of the world. In all the insanity, troubles and chaos happening around you, you'll find rest, knowing you're in the loving hands of your Heavenly Father. Let out that big sigh that's been building up in you and let the Good Shepherd hold you close to His heart.

Today is the day. My invitation to you is to believe this great and precious promise and to receive all that He holds out to you in His open hands. He is calling out your name. "Come to me, and I will give you rest."

Q & A Chapter 18: Hearts at Rest

1. Why are we encouraged to enter God's rest today?

2. How do we enter into God's rest?

3. Describe your understanding of God's rest.

Your Mission Journal Notes:

19

Waiting upon the Lord

"Hurry up and wait." That's one of the first things I learned in Army basic training. We would "double-time" to the mess hall, only to wait in line for chow to be served. We had to double-time to sick call and wait for our names to be called. We were required to double-time to morning formations, and wait for the First Sargent to show his snarling face. The drill sergeant would yell, "Double-time, huh!" And off we would go, our boots stomping in the rhythm of perfect formation to await our morning drills and assignments.

Waiting is my least favorite thing to do, almost a pet peeve. Don't put me on "hold." I'll drum my fingers, tap my pencil, doodle, find places that need to be scratched — anything to keep my mind off of waiting. And then there's the doctor's office. Without some germ infested, dog-eared, months old *National Geographic* lying around, I couldn't sit and wait. I'll pace. I'll wander about. Look out the windows to watch people. I'll do almost anything to avoid waiting. But it is good for me to learn to wait upon the Lord,[97] because in this I become attached to my Lord Jesus and we become intertwined.

"Even youths will faint and be weary, and the young will fall exhausted; but those who wait for the Lord shall renew their strength, they shall mount up with wings like eagles, they shall run and not be weary, they shall walk and not faint" (Isaiah 40:30-31). Now wait just a minute — hold on there! Wait so I can run? Wait so I can fly like an eagle? Aren't those conflicting activities? I like to run and I would love to go hang gliding, but what does waiting have to do with that?

[97] Psalms 130:5

First we need to understand what "waiting" means. The original Hebrew word in this verse has a clear connotation of being bound together with the Lord like strands of a rope braided together. I picture it like this. Three strands of cord, one each for the Father, Son and Holy Spirit woven together with my strand and we become one cord, strong and unbreakable. This is waiting on the Lord. It is seeking, searching, and straining our eyes to see our God and King on high.

King David's story is a picture of amazing faith. He was anointed as a youth to be king of the tribes of Israel, and yet it was almost a decade before he took the throne. Even when the opportunity came to him to take King Saul's life and become king, David waited upon the Lord. He continued to bind himself to the Lord in preparation to be king.

The Apostle Paul, one of the best-educated men in ancient Palestine, waited as he was taught about the Lord until finally Barnabus brought him to the church at Antioch so they could minister together.[98] Moses, who was called by the Lord to deliver Israel, tried to start on his own by killing an Egyptian who was abusing a fellow Hebrew.[99] It didn't work out as he planned, and he fled into the wilderness to wait upon the Lord in preparation to lead the tribes of Israel out of bondage in Egypt. Elijah waited a long while beside a brook called Wadi Cherith, being fed by the ravens.[100] (I don't know if they had road kill in those days, but for me, it would be very hard to wait and eat what the ravens brought.)

Abraham was promised descendants as numerous as the stars of the sky, and then he waited, and waited, and waited until God gave him one son, even though he and Sarah were too old, beyond the age when they could have children. Jesus' disciples were instructed to wait in Jerusalem "until you have been clothed with power from on high" (Luke 24:49). Jonah waited in the shade of a bush that shot up just to cover him, and then waited in the hot sun after a worm came and ate away the bush. King Saul was instructed to wait for Samuel to sacrifice to the Lord before going into battle. He waited seven days

---

[98] Galatians 2:1 "Fourteen years later..."
[99] Exodus 2:11—12
[100] 1 Kings 17:3—5

and then gave up waiting. Not waiting cost him his kingdom. (You can read about this in 1 Samuel 13.)

It is good to wait upon the Lord, to be bound to Him. I've witnessed what happens when God gives a man or woman a call and they immediately jump into the work given them without a time of waiting on the Lord. They don't stop to allow the Lord to prepare them for the work He has ordained. The result is the chaos and confusion that comes from trying to force this new work into being. It's like a baby born before his or her time.

Consider a giant oak that is chosen to become a beautiful banquet table for the king's palatial dining room. The plans are drawn and the master craftsman looks them over and says, "This is good." Then the tree must be cut down, sawn into rough lumber, and kiln dried. Waiting, waiting and more waiting. Only the master craftsman can see the beauty that will result by the work of his hands. The rough lumber is cut to plan and shaped with saw and router. The craftsman makes oak dowels to peg together each segment. Finally the assembly begins and the work takes shape as the banquet table waits to fulfill its purpose. Then the wood is planed and sanded, first with rough sandpaper, then medium and then the finest, until the master craftsman rubs his hand over it and says, "It is good."

He seals the wood and then he begins with the fine oils that will bring out the beauty and color of the grain. He rubs and rubs each part until the beauty of the wood shines out. Waiting and waiting, the banquet table waits to begin its work. Again and again the craftsman rubs finishing oil into the wood until he can finally say, "It is finished." Only then can the table begin to serve its purpose.

Will you wait on the Lord so you may serve in the work God has prepared for you? Even before you were known to exist, before you were conceived, God had a purpose and plan for your life. A Kingdom purpose and a Kingdom plan. And then, from the moment you came to be, our Heavenly Father began to shape you and mold you and bring out the beauty in you so that you could fulfill His purpose for you.

You may be thinking, "You don't know about the horrible, traumatic things that happened to me." No, I don't. But I know about the awful, hurtful things that happened to me, especially as a child, and I trust that

God used it all for good, to mold me, shape me, and make me into a useful vessel to fulfill His purpose and plan for me. What was intended for evil, God has turned into good, to accomplish all that He has ordained — to accomplish all that He has spoken into being. Even as Christ Jesus overcomes the evil done to me, I become strong to minister God's grace and healing to others who will overcome the evil done to them.

God's plan isn't like the Army, requiring us to hurry up and wait. It's more like he's telling us stop all our crazy busyness, take time to rest in the Lord, be molded, and get fully prepared to do what God has planned for us to do. Stop, pause, wait, stay still, bind yourself to the Lord, and wait for Him to finish His good work in you. Wait and He will gift and empower you according to His plan for you.

Now you are ready to begin doing what God has ordained for you to accomplish. Go in the strength, power and anointing of the Spirit of Jesus.

Q & A Chapter 19: Waiting upon the Lord

1. What does it mean to "wait" upon the Lord?

2. What is the purpose of waiting on the Lord?

3. Will you wait upon the Lord to fulfill His purpose and plan for you?

Your Mission Journal Notes:

20

The Heart of a Servant

I have been privileged to know many good and godly people who have a servant's heart. You'll find their names on the top of the sign-up sheet for the church potluck. They're the ones who look around for the ignored people at gatherings. They're the people who are first to notice a sad face and offer a caring hug and a prayer. A new family at church gets their first meet and greet from them. A young couple in the grocery store, agonizing over whether to buy the large or small oatmeal, because it has to last all week and they only have five dollars left, gets a helping hand from these good people who happen to notice their plight. A new co-worker gets to know these godly people when the electricity at home is about to be shut off.

And yet, the servant's heart is not motivated by must-do, you-shall-do, or even a to-do list. A servant isn't driven by a need to be needed, or by a compulsion to fix things. It's the effect of the righteousness of Christ at work in them. It's the Spirit of a Holy God who is at work through these willing servants, manifesting His vital, living and active presence to pierce the darkness. These kingdom hearts are the hand of Christ extended to a hurting world, ministering His loving compassion and His healing touch.

The best way to get a picture of a kingdom heart is to hear some stories about them. The following stories are true, but the names have been changed and the stories have been altered slightly so they are not too easily recognized.

Before John and Sarah made their way up the steps to the church, they noticed a young man who was sitting on his backpack in the grass. His tent and every earthly possession were tied together in a bundle. His face was smudged and his hair was long, unruly and unwashed. His clothes were worn, torn and in need of some scrubbing. He was wet from the rain, and I'm sure you can imagine that he didn't smell very good either. He reminded them of Pigpen from *Peanuts* with a cloud of dust hanging over his head.

John and Sarah had never met him before. They didn't know where he came from, or to whom he was related. They didn't know if he had a police record and they couldn't have known if there was a warrant for his arrest. As John extended his hand, the young man would only respond in a quiet voice, "I'm Justin." But after church they took him to their favorite restaurant for lunch and then brought him home, not the least bit worried if he might stain the back seat in the car. Once at home, he was antsy and uncomfortable inside, so they encouraged him to stay out of the drenching downpour and pitch his tent in the dry, warm loft of the barn.

After a couple days, Justin took his first shower in a long time. After a few weeks he got a shave and a haircut and bought some second hand clothes and new shoes. Gradually, he came to trust his hosts and his story came to light. He was on the outs with his dad, who was a wealthy businessman, but very stubborn and bull headed towards his son. Justin had left in anger and rebellion, and rage toward his dad consumed him. He was unable to get himself together and make a life of his own, because he needed to be the opposite of his dad in everything.

Before John and Sarah met Justin, he had been camping at the edge of a strawberry field, working as a migrant picker and eating strawberries to fill his stomach. After several weeks of telling his story bit by bit, being listened to and accepted, and receiving wise words of council, his heart changed and decided to take a bus home and reconcile with his dad — come what may. He didn't know what kind of reception he would get, but he knew he needed to go back and face reality; he could no longer allow bitterness to destroy him.

Sheila was a stay-at-home mom, church volunteer and wife to a disabled husband who worked, as best he could, as a repair technician for a Christian broadcaster. Unexpected bills were piling up and she felt pressed to find a job to help make money. A temporary job became available working for Bill and Ruth at a small import/export company and she jumped at the opportunity. The job suited her perfectly and she was quick to learn the job. But after just a couple weeks she got a call that her dad, who lived back in the Midwest, was failing rapidly and had been given only a few days to live. She had no money, and there wasn't time enough to drive back to her hometown. Holding back her tears, she told her Bill and Ruth she had to take a trip but didn't know how she would get there or when she would be back.

The next morning, she raced down the road, late for work. Sheila rushed through the door and came face to face with the boss. She was shocked when her boss smiled and gave her a check. Not a severance check, but enough to cover an open ticket for a round trip flight to her hometown, where she could be with her family in their time of grieving and loss. It wasn't a loan. She wouldn't have to work it off, a little out of every paycheck. It was a gift. There was no need to say "thank you." Her tears of joy told the whole story of her gratefulness.

Neither Bill nor Ruth ever told anyone about the gift of generosity. It was enough that God was able to use them in a very special time of need.

Chad and Wendi's hearts broke as they heard the story of a teenage girl who was being harassed and verbally abused by her stepfather. After talking with the stepdad and mom, they agreed that their home would provide a needed break from the pressure of a home in turmoil. Over several months, Tiandra was able to unwind from the tension and become herself. Her grades improved, and she began to talk more. With Wendi's encouragement, she was finally able to enjoy being a girl and doing girly things, like experimenting with make-up and doing her long, dark hair in different styles. She was flourishing physically and spiritually in this new and comfortable atmosphere.

Chad and Wendi fed her, took her to school, bought her clothes and took her with them to church. In an atmosphere of safety, she was becoming a positive and adventuresome person who enjoyed getting together with her friends, even inviting them to her new home.

Then the threats started. Chad and Wendi tried to ignore the stepdad when he demanded Tiandra move back home; after all, her mom knew it still wasn't safe. Then the stepdad deceived his wife, giving her "pain medication" that induced a compliant state of mind. He started rumors about Wendi, totally false, but plausible to an unsuspecting person on the receiving end of gossip.

The looks Wendi got at church and in the grocery store clearly showed the damage from the rumors. But still Chad and Wendi hung in there for the good of the child. Finally, Tiandra's mom agreed, under duress, to join her husband in demanding that their daughter move back home. It tore Chad and Wendi's hearts out, but now they had to let her go. They stood together on the front porch, crying and waving as they watched Tiandra drive away with her parents, their car disappearing down the long driveway. They had no choice, because child protective services, after interviewing the parents, agreed that it was a safe home for the child.

A couple months later, they got a call saying that Tiandra and her mom had escaped the abuse and were making a break for it. Chad and Wendi got to see them off at the bus station, helping them on their way to safety. As they watched the bus drive away, they both agreed that it had been worth all the heartache and that they would do it all over again.

In these stories you can see the hearts of these servants. They didn't do these things because they had to. What they did blossomed as naturally as a tree that grows fruit in season. They were resilient and tough in doing these difficult things by the strength of the Lord. Apart from the effect of the righteousness of Christ at work in them, none of these deeds would have been possible, let alone have made an eternal difference.

It is necessary, because of our human failings, to offer a word of wisdom for those who have a servant's heart. Because there are so many demands on the church, leaders are constantly scouting for workers. They can identify a servant's heart from a mile away, and they will encourage you take up the mantle of service in the church — at times with more work than is wise and profitable.[101] To those being recruited, remember that being asked to teach Sunday school is not always God "calling" you to step into that ministry. You must prayerfully consider each task you are asked to do and depend upon the Holy Spirit for direction.

Too often, I've watched as talented, giving Christians say "yes" to everything they are asked to do. Before long they are neglecting their first call to fellowship with their Heavenly Father, and their call to love and care for their own family. They're so busy in church that they neglect their time of private prayer and worship, their Abba time. It's easy to justify this by telling themselves, "I'll be praying, praising and singing in church so I can skip talking to God on my own this morning." But then when they get to church they're so busy with their assigned tasks that they are not able to attend the morning worship gathering to receive from the ministries that strengthen them in the Lord.

Remember to apply godly wisdom when church leaders ask you to serve. There is a time for "Yes," and there is a time to say "No." Nurture the heart of a servant that God has given you, and be wise in all that you would put your hand to do. Give the glory to God because all that you do results from the righteousness of Jesus Christ at work in you. God's holy name is exalted because of the work He is doing through your willing hand.

---

[101] A good leadership practice to follow is this; when calling people to ministries in the church, prayerfully consider those who you will ask, taking the time to fast and pray before contacting them. When talking to them, present the task clearly and completely so they can see the whole picture. Then tell them why you are asking them in particular. Review the training available to help them prepare for this ministry. Explain whom they will be working with and who will be there to back them up. Don't allow them to give you an immediate answer, but encourage them to prayerfully consider what you've asked them to do. Give them a definite date that you'll be calling them back for their answer. When they agree to serve in a ministry, even if it's as janitor, bring them before the church for the elders to pray for them and lay hands on them to impart the necessary spiritual gift to them, asking the Holy Spirit to gift and empower them in their new ministry.

"Do not lag in zeal, be ardent in spirit, serve the Lord. Rejoice in hope, be patient in suffering, persevere in prayer. Contribute to the needs of the saints; extend hospitality to strangers" (Romans 12:11-13).

This is the heart of a servant.

Q & A Chapter 20: The Heart of a Servant

1. Describe the heart of a servant.

2. How do you know when to say "yes" and when to say "no?"

3. After counting the cost, are you willing to pay the price of servanthood?

Your Mission Journal Notes:

21

Nurturing Children and Grandchildren

One afternoon my grandson came to visit while I was busy at my desk. No matter what I'm doing he likes to hang out with me, so he was rummaging about in my office. Quite often, when I don't give him the attention he wants, he'll climb up and sit on top of my desk to check out my model sailing ship with all its sails and lines. But today he went to the shelves of my bookcase and one by one brought my favorite objects to ask me, "Tell me the story about this one, Papa."

He's heard the stories before, but he wanted to hear them again. The familiar stories connected him to me and to years gone by. Stories are like roots that go deep into the soil, giving him a firm footing. I told him about the lathed wood paperweight I made in high school wood shop. When he handed me the picture of my mom and dad, I told him about Pastor Larson and my fun loving mom. He was beginning to value those things that I value. His roots were growing deeper and intertwining with my roots.

This is a joyful mission God has given to every parent and grandparent, uncle and aunt: to tell the children of the godly foundation of their lives, and to show them the Rock on which you have built. Children benefit greatly when they hear about a parent's failings and how God's forgiveness and mercy overcame the weakness. We are also given responsibility to offer our children and grandchildren a living example of godliness by rooting out our hidden faults.

Can you name the greatest missionaries of all time? Can you identify the ones who have brought the most souls into the kingdom of heaven? Was it Billy Graham, Billy Sunday, John Wesley, John Wycliffe or the apostle Paul? The answer will surprise you, because it is none of the above. Beyond the shadow of a doubt, they are Mothers. Mom has been the greatest soul winner throughout the ages. She exerts the greatest influence over the lives of young children. You can take the kids to church and Sunday school every week, but if mom doesn't believe the Good News and pass it on to her kids, it won't take root. You can have your baby baptized or dedicated, but if you don't believe the Gospel, live according to truth, or speak of your faith in front of them, they will not be grounded in the faith.

Based on this truth, William Ross Wallace stated, "The hand that rocks the cradle is the hand that rules the world."[102] We can also say with great confidence that "the hand that rocks the cradle is that hand that sways the church." Consider the influence Martin Luther's mother had on the church. Only a few recall her first name. Who among us knows more than little tidbits of her life? Yet her hand upon the cradle rocked the church to its foundation.

What will your children and grandchildren find on your bookshelves to ask you about? When your children or grandchildren's roots intertwine with yours, will they be ensnared or strengthened? You have to know that children specialize in snooping and eventually they will find your secret hiding places. The place you stash your favorite butterscotch candy. The dark corner where you hide that magazine. In reality, there are no secrets. There is nothing hidden away. And when the truth is exposed for all to see, will you hang your head in shame? You will grieve if your sin manifests itself in your child.

A parent's hidden sin is a serious issue. The theory is certainly true that a mom or dad's secret sin will most likely manifest itself in one of your children, even though they don't know about what you're doing on the sly. The bottom line is this. We are no more successful than Adam and Eve at covering up our sin. They tried fig leaves. We are like them and attempt our own "fig leaf" cover-ups — but it didn't work then and it doesn't work now.

Here is the good news — the greatest news of all time. Confess your sin to God and a trusted, wise and godly confessor who will hold you

---

[102] Source: Wikipedia: August 19, 2015. The poem was first published in 1865 under the title "What Rules the World.",

accountable. "If we confess our sins, he who is faithful and just will forgive us our sins and cleanse us from all unrighteousness. If we say that we have not sinned, we make him a liar, and his word is not in us" (1 John 1:9-10).

What a great hope we have in Christ. He hears the cry of our hearts as they break because of our sin. Our Lord Jesus forgives us of our sin and restores us to a rightful relationship with the Father. But he is not finished. He washes us and cleanses us of even the stain of sin. He restores our soul. He heals the broken heart.

Be honest with your children about your past. Not graphically honest, but a healing kind of honest. Let them know how you have suffered as you endured the consequences of your sin. Tell them of God's love, mercy, forgiveness and healing. Share your faith with them as you're going out the door, as you're riding in the car, as you're enjoying a sunset at the beach. In everything you do, pass on to your children and grandchildren an inheritance of faith. "Teach them to your children, talking about them when you are at home and when you are away, when you lie down and when you rise" (Deuteronomy 11:19).

What an awesome God we serve. He is worthy of our praise, of all glory and honor. May His Name be glorified in all the earth.

Q & A Chapter 21: Nurturing Children and Grandchildren

1. Can you name the greatest soul winners of all time?

2. Describe the joyful responsibility of being a missionary to your children and grandchildren.

3. What legacy will you leave with your children and grandchildren?

Your Mission Journal Notes:

22

Sword Skills

Recently we joined the crowds at a community event in a local park where scads of kids were having the time of their lives playing with swords made of cardboard and duct tape. Men dressed up in medieval costumes with shiny silver helmets had modeled swordplay for the crowd and the kids were now playing their roles with enthusiasm.

My own history with sword fighting is a rather sordid tale. Doing battle with my new metal file in Junior High shop class earned me my first "hacks." The rule was simple: Don't use tools for toys. We broke the rule and earned swats on the seats of our pants. The shop instructor had a very well-polished four-inch wide board perfectly designed to do its work as we grabbed our ankles.[103] We didn't break that rule again and I gained a new respect for my teacher.

I remember that many times in Vacation Bible School, I was challenged to memorize this Scripture: "Take the helmet of salvation, and the sword of the Spirit, which is the word of God" (Ephesians 6:17). Of course, all of us boys would start to duel with our imaginary swords while the teacher was working up a sweat trying to teach us something.

Sword skills are for all Christians, not just Sunday school kids. What is the "sword of the Spirit" all about and how do we use it? This vital offensive weapon is given to us for effective spiritual warfare; let us prepare for battle.

Paul wrote, "No temptation has overtaken you that is not common to man. God is faithful, and he will not let you be tempted beyond your

---

[103] I'm pleased that schools no longer allow corporal punishment.

ability, but with the temptation he will also provide the way of escape, that you may be able to endure it" (1 Corinthians 10:13 ESV). Each of us has weaknesses. Each one of us has a failing of one kind or another. Every one of us has habitual things we struggle to overcome. What you struggle against, the sins you work so hard to gain victory over, all of these you have in common with the people who you rub elbows with every day. You're not alone in this because you have help from above and brothers and sisters who love and support you.

Even more than this, you have spiritual weapons, God's weapons, to fend off these temptations. Note in the Scripture above: "...but with temptation he will also provide the way of escape." In Christ you have been given the "sword of the Spirit, which is the word of God" as one powerful means to ward off your greatest temptations. We are given this sword for the purpose of defeating the temptations that try to overcome us. This sword will defend us when we come too close to the edge, where sin would take us in its grasp.

How does this work? We can't run around with a Bible in our hands, swinging it in the air or banging ourselves on the head every time some temptation comes our way. That's ridiculous, even though I can imagine some people trying this without much success. The first step is to recognize and admit our failings and the sin we often get pulled into because of the weaknesses of our flesh. These may be generational sins that have been in our family for centuries. It could well be guilt that you've struggled with since you suffered traumatically as a child — guilt that is not your own. The roots of our sin are many, and yet they are not insurmountable; they are overcome in Christ.

I've heard it said that God delivers you from your enemies, but not from your friends. There is truth in this, because if you've befriended your sin, if you're comfortable in it, you're likely to be stuck in the muck for a while. If you're grieving over your sin, hating it each time it raises its ugly head, you're on the winning side of the battle.

So recognize your sins and your weaknesses. This can be a challenge if you've lived with your sin for a long time. Confess your sin and your powerlessness over these sins and the Holy Spirit will step in to help. Now search the Scriptures for what it says about your failings. If it helps, get a pocket-sized notebook and write your common weaknesses on one side. On the other page, write the Scriptures that speak to your sin. (Not condemning words but overcoming and strengthening Scriptures.)

In our American culture we are inundated with graphic images. Billboards, advertisements, magazines, commercials, everywhere we look we're assaulted with images that feed our selfish desires. The way people dress provides opportunities to feast the eyes. A day at the beach can be too much for you. But the solution is not to force other people to cover themselves from head to toe. Even if you could accomplish that, there would still be no change in your heart. A person's cover up may help us to be legally obedient, but our eyes would not be redeemed and our hearts would still be in the wrong place. The cover up only provides an inadequate and temporary fix.

Your sin may be the "lust of the eye," that is, looking too long at what you shouldn't be looking at and allowing yourself thoughts and emotions that in the end are destructive. In this, as in all temptations, you have a great hope. This sin is common to man. Even one of the most righteous men who walked on earth had to deal with this sin. Job made an agreement with his eyes: "I made a covenant with my eyes not to look lustfully at a young woman" (Job 31:1 NIV).

Use Job as an example. Make a covenant with your eyes and when you're tempted, speak the Scripture you've prepared (unsheathe your sword) and go to work on this temptation with the cutting edge of the sword. Simply bring to mind, "I have made a covenant with my eyes," and then ask for God's strength to act according to your covenant. God does more than just give you strength; He is strength living in you.

Abraham's weakness was to tell self-protective lies, saying that his wife was his sister. Jacob's sin was to deceive his father by saying, "I am Esau your firstborn." And from Genesis to Revelation, the list goes on of God's people and their weaknesses, their failings, and their sins. Why is Scripture so openly honest about the heroes of our faith and their great failings? Because God's very nature is to redeem us from these sins. He is the final answer to our wrongdoing, and He has given us great weapons to fight against the temptations that confront us every day of our lives.

All sin is an affront to a Holy God. It is a violation of the covenant to which we have pledged ourselves. We do well to remember that in our depravity, we provide victory for the kingdom of darkness. But God has provided a way, with weapons of the Spirit that are empowered by the Spirit, to do battle against the tug of temptation.

Armor up. Take up the sword of the Spirit, which is the Word of God, and do battle in the Name of the Lord against the kingdom of darkness.

We are all "custom wired" by our Creator, every one of us is a specially made edition and wonderfully unique. Some people, because of the way they are wired, easily turn the repeating of a Scripture in a difficult or tempting situation into a self-defeating obsession. Repetition of a specific verse can become self-condemning and agitating.[104]

For those who are of this nature, it is best to simply remember that they can entrust their situation into the hands of a loving, caring and all-powerful God. "Cast all your anxiety on him, because he cares for you" (1 Peter 5:7). Our Heavenly Father will tenderly carry you through the present darkness. It may help to picture the Good Shepherd holding you close to His heart to bring you to pleasant pastures. Prayerfully work this through, asking the Holy Spirit to light your pathway to keep temptations from overwhelming you. God has made a way and He will lead you on His pathway — a pathway of abundant life.

When temptation drags us too close to a sin, but not yet over the edge, we find ourselves in a precarious situation. We may not legally be in sin when standing at the precipice, but we are in danger of going over the edge. If we are content to walk along at the edge of the cliff, declaring ourselves to be okay because we haven't yet fallen, we place ourselves on dangerous ground in the unmerciful kingdom of darkness. This is a time to take out your Scripture sword and do battle.

---

[104] If this is you it's because God has made you the way you are for a specific purpose. It may well be that you need to be the way you are in order to accomplish God's purpose and plan for which He has made you. God has not made anyone else like you because the task prepared for you from ages past is unique, and only you can do it because of the special way God has made you to be.

If I excuse my close-to-the-edge moments, not hating it when I'm too close to what would be sin, I will eventually find myself testing the edge to see how far I can go and still be legal. I become like the toddler who has been told not to go into the street. But then he steps with his toes over the edge of the curb and looks around to see if anyone notices. When he hears mom call out, "Jimmy, I said to stay out of the street," he can rightfully say, "I not." But we all know Jimmy's heart is in the street where the big kids are playing soccer. In reality, when we live by the law this is the effect of the law. The "don'ts" turn into little tests of the limits, and then further tests of the newfound limits, until we finally go over the edge. The outside of the cup is shiny clean, but the inside is a stinking mess.

The reality of a kingdom heart is revealed when temptation draws us too close to sin, and in this we see our need of Christ. If you're standing with your toes over the edge of the curb, ask yourself, "Where is my heart?" Use your Scripture sword to fend off the assault. If you're standing too close to the edge ask, "What longings fill my heart?" Test your heart with God's Word and remember: "Choose this day which kingdom you will serve" (Joshua 24:14-15). In the strength of the Lord, we take out our sword and attack what comes against us.

Recognize, admit and confess your weaknesses and then be strengthened to defend against temptations. Take out your sword, which is the Word of God, and do battle against the kingdom of darkness and advance the kingdom of light. Run away from those too-close moments where we stand at sins threshold. Practice your sword skills and always be prepared to do battle.

Q & A Chapter 22: Sword Skills

1. How will you use your sword to win the battle?

2. Why is it so important to recognize and admit our weaknesses?

3. What is your greatest weakness? What special Scriptures will help you fight against it?

Your Mission Journal Notes:

23

Prayerfully Strengthening our Leaders

An age-old Sunday afternoon tradition of the church may be referred to as "roasting the pastor." This happens when church people get together over lunch at their favorite restaurant and talk about how bad the sermon was and how the pastor's wife isn't very friendly and their kids act up during Sunday school. It doesn't matter that "roast pastor" is not on the menu.

This is one church tradition worth breaking.

So many times I've heard people lament over the failures of leadership in the church; but the truth is, there is no failure of leadership that does not stain all of us. We must all own it, for we are one in Christ. There is no compartmentalization in Christ, so we can't point fingers and say, "It's all his fault." Look at what the blame game accomplished when Adam said, "The woman whom you gave to be with me, she gave me fruit from the tree, and I ate." Blaming someone else didn't work for Adam and it doesn't work for us when we come before a Holy God.

When leadership fails, look in the mirror, because it is a reflection of you. I'm not pointing fingers at you and I'm not blaming you, but I'm asking you to accept responsibility, not individually, but as a part of the Body of Christ.

Daniel was one of the most righteous men to ever walk among his people. No fault could be found with him, yet he came before God confessing the sins of his people. He was called to repent and recorded this for our benefit:

> "I prayed to the Lord my God and made confession, saying, 'Ah, Lord, great and awesome God, keeping covenant and steadfast

love with those who love you and keep your commandments,
we have sinned and done wrong, acted wickedly and rebelled,
turning aside from your commandments and ordinances. We
have not listened to your servants the prophets, who spoke in
your name to our kings, our princes, and our ancestors, and
to all the people of the land."' (Daniel 9:4-6)

The sin of the tribes of Israel stained all who were called God's chosen people and Daniel repented as he said, "We have sinned."

I remember it as clearly as if it were yesterday when the Holy Spirit convicted me of this truth. I was standing with a group of well-seasoned Christian men, and for some reason I was listening to our conversation as if I was an observer. We talked at length about what was wrong with the church. We didn't mention names, but spoke generally — and what we said was basically true. But the question came over me like a flood: "Why are you talking and not praying?"

Discussing the challenges of the church doesn't change anything. Kicking around the problems we face as a church will not reverse our course. Agreeing about how bad things are rarely spurs us to godly action. The solution is always with the Head of the Church, our Lord, Jesus Christ. In Him the course can be reversed. He is the One who stirs our hearts to action. He calls us to humble repentance, for without coming to Him with contrite hearts in broken repentance, the best we can do is to kick the ball down the road to the next generation.

This is my encouragement to you. When you are with godly friends talking about the challenges we face as a church, invite them to get together to fast and pray about the problems that concern them. Pray for the leaders of your church for God to strengthen and encourage them. Pray for all those who serve in your local fellowship. Earnestly intercede for the people in your congregation, asking for them to turn, repent, and seek the Lord with all their hearts, souls and spirits. Together, repent of the sins of the church and prayerfully implore our Lord to strengthen us to turn away from our complacency and to change our hearts.

This is our calling. Will you answer the call?

Q & A Chapter 23: Prayerfully Strengthening our Leaders

1. How is a failure of leadership a reflection on you?

2. Whom does the stain of one person's sin affect?

3. What will you do to strengthen the leaders in your church?

Your Mission Journal Notes:

24

All to Him I Owe

His calloused hands shook as he gripped the quill pen in hand, the feather fairly fanning his red face. Thom Enrick Willis was certainly signing his life away. He blinked away the tears as he looked at the date at the top of the page. June 8, 1649. He was proud that he knew his numbers and he had practiced hard so he could sign his name just right.

"When does the ship leave," he asked with his hand poised over the "X" at the bottom of the page.

"She be sailing with the new moon," the gentleman pointed, urging him to sign.

"How many years work for my passage?" Thom squinted, trying to make sense of the script on the coarse, grey paper through the water in his eyes.

"Seven years for passage and seven for your debt. Fourteen years you'll be working for Sir Walton Charleston Banister of New York. He is a fine gentleman and shall treat you well if you serve him proper." The man's forehead creased, and his eyes squinted through the thick spectacles resting on his princely nose. "Remember, he paid a good price for your passage." The man motioned again with his hand for him to sign.

Thom dipped the tip of the quill in the ink well and scratched his name on the paper. It was done. He started to smile, feeling a sense of freedom, but the reality of indenturing himself for his passage and his debt wiped the smile away. He clenched his teeth, thinking it was so wrong. He didn't deserve to be indentured to another man, like a slave.

It was the cobbler shop that had gotten him into trouble — borrowing money from his tutor in the trade to start out on his own.

His new shop had been an occasion to celebrate and his feet had felt like dancing as he had locked the door behind him, thinking about the morning when he would hang out his shingle and open for his first day of business. His excitement had been so overwhelming he could barely sleep a wink.

In the morning he had jogged through the narrow cobblestone streets, arriving at the shop just as the sunlight washed over the rooftops. He had laughed as he reached into his pocket for the key. The door had been broken and looked like a bull had run through it. As he had stepped inside he could see that everything was gone, all of his tools, his supplies, his equipment, all gone. Everything, that is, but his debt.

The memory of grief washed away and Thom's heart warmed as he thought of Sir Bannister who had paid his debt and the cost of his passage to the Colonies. "I must thank him for his generosity," Thom smiled. And certainly he would thank him in many ways throughout his time of service.

In the years that passed, Thom gained a few strands of grey among the auburn waves under his sweat stained leather hat. Often, as he counted the daily receipts, he would rehearse in his thoughts the long talk he had had with Sir Bannister in his eighth year of service. He thought about it so often that the words imprinted on his mind.

"It has gone well with you all these years Mr. Williston. I'm proud to say that your work has been most profitable for the both of us." As if on cue, one of the servants had brought a steaming pot of tea with fancy china on a silver tray.

Thom reached out to accept the tea offered him, but his shaking hand made the cup and saucer clatter. He had never been called into Sir Bannister's office for anything other than to receive a work list and instructions. He had always stood in his presence, never been asked to sit.

"Mr. Willis." Sir Bannister always referred to him with respect, which Thom appreciated. "You have worked for me eight years and three months."

"Yes, sir." Thom could barely choke out the words. He sipped at his hot tea to soothe his parched throat.

"I have been watching you very closely, Mr. Willis." Sir Bannister's face showed the start of a smile. "You are a skilled workman, good with your hands and you have strength of character. And you're one of the smartest men I know."

Thom stammered, "Wh-why thank you, s-sir."

"This is what I want to do for you. There is a shop in town that has been vacant for some time now. Good spot near the market and across from the bank." Sir Bannister hesitated. "Are you finished with your tea?"

"Why, yes sir. Quite finished." He set his half full cup on the saucer.

"Take a little stroll with me."

As they walked to town, Sir Bannister explained his plan, and in fact it was already set in place. "I'm setting you up in a shop of your own."

Thom was speechless. His mouth opened to speak, but the words stuck in his throat.

As they stepped into the shop, Thom's eyes widened. The smell of leather overwhelmed his senses. All the tools of the trade were right in front of him. More than he could have imagined. He could make shoes, yokes and harnesses for oxen and horses, saddles and satchels. Any leather goods a man could require. Tears welled up in his eyes as he felt the cold metal of the tools, he bowed his head, humbled by such generosity. His dream had come true; his hopes had been fulfilled. It was no longer an unrealistic fantasy.

That was years ago now. As Thom finished counting his receipts, a little tow-headed boy came bounding down the steps.

"Papa, can I go to the candy store?"

Thom looked at the clock on the wall. "Ask me again tomorrow Tommy, and I'll give you a penny for you and your sister. You need to save room for supper tonight." He took a deep breath. "I smell the soup cooking." His stomach growled at the thought of a big bowl of vegetable stew with biscuits. "Tell your mother I'll be up in five minutes." He sent Tommy off with a little pat on the bottom. Thom finished counting the coins and bank notes, writing down the final count in his ledger. And then he set aside Sir Bannister's portion in a pouch. He smiled as he thought about Sir Bannister's very predictable quip as he brought his share to the office each week. He was old, bent and hard of hearing now, but he never changed. "No need of that, Mr. Willis."

Thom always answered the same. "Everything I have belongs to you. I'm bringing this so that neither of us forgets that it is all yours." He watched as Sir Bannister smiled, a knowing smile.

"Well then, give it to the poor Stevens family. They have six hungry children." Sir Bannister talked quite loud now days.

"Already helped them. Told them it was from you." Thom chuckled to himself, thinking of the pot of stew they had shared with their guests and how eagerly the kids had dived in.

This story illustrates our total indebtedness to our Lord and Savior. Indeed, everything we have belongs to our Heavenly Father. Everything we earn belongs to Him. It's like His name is on the title to our cars. His Holy name is on the deed to our homes. His name is on the incorporation papers of our businesses as 100% owner, with us working as His assigned stewards and managers. Everything we gain belongs to Him because we are His bondservants and He has given to us all that He pleases, for His glory and for the honor of His Holy Name (see Deuteronomy 15:16).

Jesus paid the price of our sin debt. He has made a way for us to come into His rest, a "Promised Land" for all eternity. Indeed, we owe Him everything, for He has purchased us from our bondage and set our feet on the solid Rock, Christ Jesus. Yet He only asks for a portion of what we gain so we can acknowledge that all we have is His alone. Some Christians call this a tithe (Malachi 3:10). Others refer to giving this portion as giving offerings (1 Corinthians 16:2). Whatever you call it, you're giving a portion of your belongings or earnings in recognition of the debt you owe.

If your money always runs out before the end of the month, give some of your money to the Lord. If your budget is short of money to buy food for the family, give some of your food to someone who has a greater need. Your car may be on its last legs, so give your friend a ride to the store. The principle is simple. Your giving makes it perfectly clear that you are depending upon the Lord and not on your own resources to meet your needs. When we give, even in our time of need, in doing this we cast our cares upon the Lord and He cares for us in our time of need. "Cast all your anxiety on him, because he cares for you" (1 Peter 5:7).

> *"Is it not to share your bread with the hungry, and bring the homeless poor into your house; when you see the naked, to cover them, and not to hide yourself from your own kin? Then your light shall break forth like the dawn, and your healing shall spring up quickly; your vindicator shall go before you, the glory of the Lord shall be your rear guard. Then you shall call, and the Lord will answer; you shall cry for help, and he will say, Here I am." (Isaiah 58:7-9)*

Q & A Chapter 24: All to Him I Owe

1. What do you owe to your Lord and Savior?

2. What is the significance of giving back a portion of your blessings?

3. What are the benefits of generous stewardship?

Your Mission Journal Notes:

25

Disciples of Christ

Junior High is an awkward time for most kids. Those of us who were extra awkward were assigned to the third string basketball team. The problem with third string is that no one was willing to coach us and teach us the game. Without having given us the benefit of practice, they told us, "Okay you guys, it's your turn. Get out there and play." It must have been painful to watch us play because the grandstands emptied of everyone but our parents.

I remember my moment of fame as if it were yesterday. I was surprised when I ended up with the ball but managed to dribble down to the basket. A handful of parents were cheering me on. "Go, go, go." With no defenders in my way I had a clear shot. The ball went straight up next to the basket and then straight back down. My moment in the limelight ended scoreless.

Contrast my ragamuffin team with the Final Four teams. The NCAA teams are practiced, trained, and disciplined to work together. They are a joy to watch and they make a three-point shot look too easy. The team players have worked hard, individually and as a team. Their coach has pushed them, encouraged them, and trained until they became a winning team.

Christians are called to be a disciplined people. When we refuse to submit to the discipline of our brothers and sisters in Christ, we become like my third string team. Disciplines of the faith are countercultural and disdained in American society and yet they are necessary. Faith disciplines are a shepherding kind of discipline, gently going ahead of the flock and leading the way. Without discipleship, Christians become like my untrained, undisciplined, third-string basketball team.

Clearly, the Scriptures call us to practice the disciplines of the faith. "For the Spirit God gave us does not make us timid, but gives us power, love and self- discipline" (2 Timothy 1:7 NIV).

The book of Judges paints a frightening picture of what happens to people who are not disciplined. You could rightly say, "They were not taught to be team players." And they were certainly not disciplined in godly character. Their hearts were not set upon God their King, they were set upon the gods of other nations. The fruit of their undisciplined lives left the nation in chaos and upheaval. The consequences of living in community apart from the discipline of the Mosaic Law brought disaster upon disaster.

For any people who are not instructed, the consequences are serious. After the death of Joshua, who led the people into the Promised Land, the tribes of Israel went their own way. "They forsook the Lord, the God of their fathers" (Judges 2:12). The newest generation of Israelites were not taught about all God had done for the nation, and they found other Gods, and adopted a system ruled by self-determined values. They each decided what was right in his or her own eyes.

Because the new generation of Israelites was not taught, they forgot God who was their King, and sought after other gods and kings. As you become aware that this same reality exists in our day, the story of Judges will rip you to the heart. "In those days there was no king in Israel. Everyone did what was right in his own eyes" (Judges 17:6). This lament is repeated so we wouldn't miss the point. "In those days there was no king in Israel. Everyone did what was right in his own eyes" (Judges 21:25).

The Israelites were like my ragamuffin basketball team, a gangly bunch of kids running around, not knowing what to do or how to do it.

We live in a culture that encourages us to determine what is right for ourselves. There is no solid foundation. No rock solid values exist to guide us in this topsy-turvy world. We are left to decide on our own. Our society is like the parent who says, "I'm not going to teach my child about Christian values and Biblical principles because they must decide on their own what to believe." Doing this gives your child a foundation of sand, when they are crying out for a Solid Rock to build on.

When a society, a nation, or a church has no solid foundation on which they may build, they build on quicksand and they will sink into oblivion. They can't win because they haven't been given winning tools.

The message here is not directed just to those who disciple and teach, but also to all who are called by Jesus' Holy Name. Be self-disciplined as you master your faith in Jesus Christ. I'm also encouraging you to have a heart that is teachable and become a true disciple of Christ. Submit yourself to the teaching of wise and godly instructors who proclaim the Scriptures to feed and nourish you so you may grow in grace and knowledge and be useful instruments in the work of God's Kingdom.

The task of a disciple maker is a greater challenge than coaching a team. Teaching disciples how to live before a Holy God is not a matter of instructing about what to do or what not to do. Telling them, "Do this, don't do that," isn't effective long term. Teaching believers is a great joy as you see them work together as a well-practiced team. Coaching people in faithful disciplines reveals a Holy God to His people and shows them the beauty, the goodness, the glory, and the delights of a kingdom heart that is growing in grace and knowledge.

God has put his law into the hearts of those who are called by His Name as a foundation, a Rock solid footing for Him to build upon. "This is the covenant that I will make with them after those days, says the Lord: I will put my laws in their hearts, and I will write them on their minds" (Hebrews 10:16).

In our New Testament covenant with God, He writes His laws in our hearts. He goes even further and He also "writes them on their minds." Do you see the significance of this? The Spirit of Jesus writes God's law, His guiding principles, His life directing imperatives, His helps for daily living right on our hearts. But He is not finished providing His goodness to us. He also writes His law in our minds.

This is important. God doesn't do this by means of a "download." We are not born with a USB cable port to plug into the big computer in heaven to get a download in our hearts and minds. In reality, God's way is a major improvement over Wi-Fi. I'm compelled to say it again:

this is the work-out-your-salvation part.[105] This requires effort on our part. We must participate. God has given us His Word, the Scriptures, the Bible for us to learn what He requires of us. God has given us anointed pastors and teachers, to enlighten us to what God desires of us in our daily lives. They will teach us the Scriptures in which Jesus Christ is revealed as the Rock on which we must build.

The Holy Spirit indwells the believer, placing into our heart of hearts the law of God that guides us, lights our pathway, and keeps our feet from slipping. What the Spirit of Jesus places into our hearts must come together in agreement with God's Word that comes alive in our minds through study, meditation, searching, being taught, and thereby growing in the grace and knowledge of our Lord and Savior, Jesus Christ.

Becoming a disciple and being self-disciplined is essential for spiritual maturity. We suffer a great loss to growing up in Christ if we avoid being a disciple. When we make the effort to exercise ourselves in the disciplines of the historic, orthodox Christian faith, the church becomes a winning team, advancing the Kingdom of Heaven throughout all the earth. Growing the Kingdom, one soul at a time, is the true purpose of the disciplines of the Spirit, and we do well to practice these disciplines that strengthen us for the good of the whole body of Christ, which is God's people — the church.

Q & A Chapter 25: Disciples of Christ

1. Why is it important to submit to Christian disciplines?

2. What is the result when people decide on their own what is right or wrong?

---

[105] "Work out your own salvation with fear and trembling" (Philippians 2:12).

3. Explain the connection between Christian disciplines and the Bible's call to work our your salvation.

Your Mission Journal Notes:

26

Sanitizing the Cross of Jesus Christ

Early one morning, as I finished my oatmeal, I looked over the greeting cards from our good friends and relatives. One of them displayed a cross in exquisitely embossed white paper adorned with periwinkle blue flowers. I enjoyed the beauty of the card for a moment and then I felt the twinge of a dour reality stewing deep within.

I admit to personal feelings on this issue and I must confess one of my pet peeves. It's an issue that is all too common and I'm compelled to share what is burning in my heart.

The Lord Jesus died in my place, paying the penalty for my sins on a rugged, cruel Roman cross upon a desolate hill called Golgotha outside the gates of Jerusalem. He died as a sinner in my place because of my sin. His body was beaten and torn with whips so that you and I could be made whole in body, soul and spirit. The splintered wooden beams of the cross were stained with His blood that He shed to wash away my sins.

Our human instincts compel us to clean up this horrible picture just a bit. We've sterilized the Christmas manger scene, kicking out the dirty, smelly goats and replacing them with warm, fuzzy, manicured sheep. We replaced the animal droppings with clean yellow straw and put clean, colorful robes on the shepherds.

But is there any need to clean up the ghastly scenes of Jesus' crucifixion when there is such incredible beauty to be found in it? The splendor of it is found in the fruit of it, which is the resulting victory of the cross for all who will believe. In the passion of Christ, in His trial, His conviction, His being beaten and flogged beyond human recognition, having a mocking crown of thorns slapped onto His head, nails driven through His hands and feet, suffering a suffocating death while hanging on the cross, a soldier's spear pierced His side – in all this our natural eyes see an unimaginably horrifying scene. There is no beauty to be found in Jesus' trial and crucifixion[106] until finally the sunlight pierces the horizon on Sunday morning. The stone was rolled away to reveal that the tomb was empty and He is risen. And oh, what a glorious morning it is, for He is risen indeed so that we may serve a Risen Savior. Our Lord Jesus Christ is not just a wonderful image in the church's stained glass windows, nor is He a delightful concept for creating fuzzy feelings at Christmas time. He is a living Redeemer who, in His glorified body, walked among His followers for many days before ascending to the Father, where He actively intercedes on our behalf and where He is preparing a place for us to come and dwell with Him for all eternity. He has sent His Holy Spirit to us, who is actively present among His people to this very day.

The cross and the suffering of Jesus are grievous to me because I've come to see that He died because of the wrong I have done. The spender and beauty of Jesus' finished work on the cross overwhelms me with awe. It's disturbingly wonderful and a great joy to me. And the truth of the matter is that the power of the cross of Jesus Christ is neither enhanced nor diminished because someone covers a cross shaped object with precious metal. What disturbs me is the way the American church and Western culture often presents the cross.

This is what I call "sanitizing the cross," that is, making the cross acceptable to our culture, to make it palatable to society at large. Too often, the American church is tempted to present the cross of Jesus Christ as if it were a gold-plated ornament, as if this good news message is something other than a radical, revolutionary invasion upon man's vested interests within the boundaries he has attempted to establish for himself on God's created earth.

This gold-plated mindset is like thinking that if every Christian would drive a Mercedes or Bentley, more people would be attracted to Christ. If only our elders would start driving rugged new 4-wheel-drive, super-duty GMC Denali trucks with a rifle in the back window,

---

[106] Isaiah 53:2-6.

we would get more "real men" to come to church. If we could get the deacons and deaconesses to come roaring into the parking lot on shiny new Harleys, we could attract the biker crowd. And if the youth pastor would buy himself a new Corvette, we could attract more kids who are in the groove.

If we attempt to attract people to Christ by creating an affluent front, a rugged, manly image or any other special lifestyle, we only attract people who desire to be materially rich, ruggedly manly, Hog riders for Jesus, or just want to be with the "in crowd." They would come to church so God will give them a new luxury car or a better truck to take hunting.

If a church ran an extensive advertising campaign aimed at convincing the unchurched that Christians are normal people, the church may well attract people who are seeking "normal." A church that fills the stage with hipster types leading rock concert style worship may well attract people who are looking for a free rock concert.[107] A sermon that proclaims a feel-good, you're wonderful message will attract people who need to hear how great they can be. A Sunday morning message that promises health, wealth, and success for all will draw in people who want the best of the American lifestyle with a "Jesus" stamp of approval on it. Projecting a rock star image before the people may well bring in a lot of starry-eyed celebrity seekers or even rock star wannabees.

Did you notice that in each of these examples, the people are not drawn to Christ, but to something other than Christ? Each of the above approaches may fulfill a felt personal need in people, but it does not draw them to the cross of Christ. As ministers of the gospel, as a priesthood of believers, we must be, in a sense, invisible, not attracting

---

[107] For those who minister in a gathering of the church, my council is to be as invisible as possible. Don't draw attention to yourself. If most people in your church wear shorts and t-shirts to church — wear clean, modest and presentable shorts and t-shirts. If they wear suits and ties — learn how to knot your necktie and wear it. Don't attempt to project an image; don't stand out from the crowd. The apostle Paul teaches (1 Corinthians 9:19-23) when in Rome, don't stand out from the crowd. Be like a Roman in order to reach the Romans about Christ. If you have a gathering of hippie types, enjoy their sing along accompanied by an acoustic guitar. If you're worshipping with staid, establishment types, crank up the pipe organ and open up your hymnbook.

attention to ourselves to stand out from the crowd. When we do stand out from the crowd, too often it's like presenting a gold-plated cross to the people, and the people who come to hear the message will be attracted to exactly what we present. Bait and switch doesn't work in a Kingdom economy. We must lift up Jesus Christ. We are to proclaim Christ and Christ crucified. We are to reveal the resurrected, living, and present Christ to the people — and He will draw all men, women, children, and teens unto Himself. "And I, when I am lifted up from the earth, will draw all people to myself" (John 12:32).

This is the work to which we are called. We are to lift up Jesus Christ, the cross of Jesus Christ, the resurrected and ever-present Jesus Christ to a lost and dying world. We do well to meet a person at the point of their felt need, and lead them to Christ to meet that need. We minister in a manner that is culturally invisible. We must not attempt to be like the world, doing things the way the rest of the world does it, but to lift up Christ, and the Good Shepherd will bring them into His fold.

Driving a nice car, even a luxury car, is no sin. There is nothing wrong with a decked out hunting truck and camper if you've been blessed to afford it. A shiny new Harley isn't a bad thing in itself. Normal, if there is such a thing, is okay. A Saturday night concert at the church is a great event to present to the community, but none of these things are, in and of themselves, a means to draw people to Christ.

We do not speak peace, safety, and prosperity to a person who is caught up in sin. Instead we admonish them in love. We don't help them cover up their sin, but rather we call them to confession, repentance, and to the altar of grace. There is no need for our culturally relevant paradigms. We are not commissioned to gold plate the cross of Jesus Christ or to sanitize the message of the cross in order to make the gospel palatable to the culture at large. Instead, we are called to lift up Jesus Christ and the cross of Christ, pure and simple.

Jesus extended His loving, caring, forgiving hand to prostitutes, tax collectors, and rough-cut fishermen. The hurting people in Jesus' day didn't need a sanitized cross to redeem them, and they don't need it today. We, like Him, extend our hands to the people around us who are hurting and in need of loving, caring forgiveness.

There is no need to wash the blood from the cross of Jesus. Covering the blood stained cross with gold or silver is of no use because, in fact, the power of the cross is in the blood that Jesus shed so that you may be washed, cleansed, and made whole by the power of the blood. Let us present the Gospel according to truth and light, and Jesus Christ will draw people to himself; the Living Truth.

Q & A Chapter 26: Sanitizing the Cross of Jesus Christ

1. Describe the realities of Jesus' suffering on the cross.

2. Why are people often driven to clean up the image of the cross?

3. What is the true attraction of the cross of Jesus Christ?

Your Mission Journal Notes:

27

Immersed in Christ

Have you ever been totally immersed in something? Many years ago the Firestone Tire Company engineered a tire body nylon that they would saturate with liquid natural rubber. The finished product was trademarked as "Gum Dipped." A great expression evolved within the Firestone corporate culture to describe an employee who was totally immersed, completely trained, and an absolute company man. "He's gum dipped," they would say.

Discipleship is the means for Christians to become "gum dipped." Except, of course, that we are to be saturated in the light of Christ, not black gum rubber. The effect of His light is even greater than that of the rubber. Being soaked in God's Word, drenched in the truths of the kingdom of heaven, drinking in His Living Water until you overflow, feasting until stuffed full with the meat of the Word, and being sanctified by the power of the Word are all a part of how we are discipled by Christ.

Being a disciple is a significant part of the process of sanctification (that is, being conformed to the image of Christ). As your "vessel" becomes like Christ, it is possible for Jesus to manifest himself in you. Without submitting yourself as a disciple, you are in danger of adhering to Christ-less Christianity, a religion that is Christian in name only. You can wear your t-shirt with John 3:16 written on it and put a gold cross around your neck and get some Hebrew Scripture tattooed on your arm, but it's only surface stuff that covers up what is really underneath. If you call yourself a Christian but have no interest in being conformed to the image of Christ through discipleship, you are in danger of walking on a pathway of your own making, a broad and easy pathway that is all downhill.

Every Christian has a unique and special calling. God has ordained a specific work, a job that only you can accomplish. All who are Christians are called to be disciples taught by Jesus. Jesus, in His High Priest's prayer, says, "I glorified you on earth by finishing the work that you gave me to do" (John 17:4). In verse 18 Jesus prays, "As you have sent me into the world, so I have sent them into the world." Do you see the connection? When we submit ourselves to being taught by Jesus and then finally complete our mission, God is glorified.

Doesn't it overwhelm you with a sense of great satisfaction to know that you, insignificant you, can bring incredible glory to God's holy name simply by completing the work God has especially designed and uniquely planned for you?

How can you begin? How can you get started on this distinctive task God has especially intended just for you? I truly believe most of us are clueless about the work God has prepared for us. But we must know what it is before we can get started. "For we are what he has made us, created in Christ Jesus for good works, which God prepared beforehand to be our way of life" (Ephesians 2:10). Before you were conceived, before you drew your first breath and cried your first cry, God ordained a work for you to accomplish in your life on this planet He called earth.

Think of it this way. God wrote down in His good book in heaven, in permanent ink, what He desired for you to accomplish. Does God write with a pencil and a big eraser? Does He say, "Oh well! Scratch that. She blew it so let's go to plan B." I don't think so. He can restore the years your sin has wasted and then gift and empower you by His Holy Spirit to complete the task in the time you have left. He is more than able to accomplish through you all that He has purposed and planned for you. And yet effort is required on your part.

God uniquely prepared you to accomplish that task. He gave you the natural abilities and talents you need. He will also give you the spiritual gifts that you need. He gave you the personality necessary for this work. He gave you family to stand with you. He brought you into His church to strengthen and encourage you for this special task. But most of us don't know what we're called to do.

If we don't "get it," it's because we are not immersed in being a disciple of Christ. We cannot be entrusted with a unique and special calling that will bring glory and honor to His mighty name because we haven't been taught. Why would God make known to us a greater task, when we have neglected a lesser task? Consider what Jesus taught in the parable of the talents: "Well done, good and trustworthy slave; you have been trustworthy in a few things, I will put you in charge of many things; enter into the joy of your master" (Matthew 25:23).

First be immersed, be faithful as a disciple and God will prepare you to begin the work He has prepared for you since before you existed. You have been created a new creature in Christ Jesus for the purpose of accomplishing a good task on behalf of the kingdom of heaven and the church. Make the effort to become soaked in God's Word. Drink the Living Water until your vessel overflows. Feast until you're stuffed with the truth of the Scriptures. Be sanctified in Christ, that is, "gum-dipped" in our Savior's teachings. He will lift you up and set you on your way to accomplish your appointed mission impossible.

Today is a good day to begin submitting yourself to be a disciple of our Lord and Savior, Jesus Christ. Glorify His name.

Q & A Chapter 27: Immersed in Christ

1. How do we become saturated in Christ?

2. How is being immersed in Christ a part of sanctification?

3. Describe the connection between being immersed in Christ and accomplishing the work God has ordained for you to accomplish.

Your Mission Journal Notes:

28

God Watches Over You

A fruitful tree, set to grow in rich garden soil.
In fallow ground, was planted with sweat, blood and great toil.
This chosen garden, away from unyielding, forbidding stone,
Far from hardened and beaten path, the bush is fruitfully prone.
My Eden, secured from parched and cracked soil,
Protected from hazards, shielded from untoward roil,
Planted by springs of pure water to soak deep upon its roots,
Sweet sunshine floods round its leaves and its shoots,
With roots in the ground, pressing deep into the soil,
Established inch by inch into depths without toil.

Yet upon my return to inspect the fruits of my labor,
With stab of pain I see branches turned away, rejecting my favor,
Roots of the sapling instead to callous stone it did go.
Vigorous growth no longer nourished by the pure crystal flow,
Its sinews grown weak pushing out into parched ground,
Into shifting dry sands, for bare roots no strength is found.
Once sun kissed with warmth, growing fruit bright and plump,
Now scorched and withered, reduced to burning stump.
Refreshing water springs so clear, once caused it to flourish.
The fruit and leaves turn away, now appearing so garish.
I walked the trampled path, so hard under foot,
Trodden roots beaten and torn, made worthless by the boot.
With tears of grief I did water withered roots at my feet,
No strength to be found, devoid of life, only defeat.

I turn my back in despair,
The bush ravaged beyond all repair.
But with burst of light, trumpets sound to announce
New hope from above, refreshing words now pronounced!
From death to life, great hope I now see;
From withered tree, fresh buds come to be.
The fruit it does grow, so sweet and so fine.
A bounty to satisfy, my cup overflows, so divine –
The soul is restored, renewed and made right,
Resting assured, this vine now lives in the Light.
The roots once again entrenched to the very depths of His love,
Grief and sorrow washed away with new life from above,
Awash in peace and transplanted by the River,
Renewed in the Tree of Life, the true Giver.

Writing this section of the study stirs up great conflict for me because I know it hits close to home for so many Christians today. This could get personal because too many of us are looking everywhere for anything that satisfies and quenches our thirst for fulfillment. We announce with our words that we would defend to the death the name of our Lord and Savior, Jesus Christ, and yet we dabble in those seemingly fun things that the world offers, testing our true intent. I truly believe that many who call themselves "Christian," when tested, will remain true in their faith in spite of all threats; yet we undermine our loyalties when we seek to know what's ahead by using things that are an affront to His Holy Name. When we seek this foreknowledge from any other source than the Spirit of the Lord, we have already failed the test.

Recently, I saw an entry on Facebook by some dear friends who are leaders in a church. They posted about a game they were playing, roleplaying some dark world characters with various spiritual realities. While I didn't know much about the game, I was overwhelmed with grief after researching it and seeing the spiritual nature of the game and the roles they were acting out in order to participate in this form of amusement.

So many Americans have an eclectic kind of spirituality, saying they are Christian, but also talking about, playing around with, and even giving ascent to other spiritualties, even while claiming the name of Christ. If we were surveyed about our spirituality, we would certainly check, "Christian;" but our actions show another reality.

The difficulty with approaching this topic is that to do so easily comes across as hyper-spiritual, goodie two shoes, and condescending. And yet it's a truth that must be taught. From what I read in the Scriptures, we are called to walk a straight, narrow pathway that doesn't include testing the waters in the kingdom of darkness. We cannot include anything that sounds spiritual, looks spiritual, feels spiritual, talks spiritual, professes great spirituality, but is not from God. In fact, these practices distract us from God because true, eternal spirituality can only be found in Christ.

God's Word is our ultimate authority and in the Scriptures we are taught to seek the Lord and no other. We are to seek His Kingdom above all else; yet we search for anything that gives us some guidance for today and tomorrow. God's Word gives us clear guidance from what the people were doing in Isaiah's day: "And when they say to you, 'Inquire of the mediums and the necromancers who chirp and mutter,' should not a people inquire of their God? Should they inquire of the dead on behalf of the living?" (Isaiah 8:19).

What is today's equivalent to what they were doing in 760 BC? Palm readers, tarot cards, astrology charts, birth signs, games from the dark side and the list goes on and on. There is no lack of distraction to draw us away from true spirituality from above.

The bottom line is that we must inquire of the Lord and no other. It is best to avoid walking on the edge of the kingdom of darkness — we are called to walk in the light. It is for our own good that we walk as far away from the precipice as possible and find safety in the cleft of the Rock.

God's Word speaks to this issue with great clarity:

> *"When you come into the land that the Lord your God is giving you, you shall not learn to follow the abominable practices of those nations. There shall not be found among you anyone*

who burns his son or his daughter as an offering, anyone who practices divination or tells fortunes or interprets omens, or a sorcerer or a charmer or a medium or a necromancer or one who inquires of the dead, for whoever does these things is an abomination to the Lord. And because of these abominations the Lord your God is driving them out before you. You shall be blameless before the Lord your God, for these nations, which you are about to dispossess, listen to fortune tellers and to diviners. But as for you, the Lord your God has not allowed you to do this." (Deuteronomy 18:9-13)

The word, "necromancer," is interesting. The definition is "prediction calling on the spirits of dead people," and "witchcraft." What I see in this word is "one who uses counterfeit spiritualties to romance us away from the true Spirit of Jesus."

"And Samuel said to all the house of Israel, 'If you are returning to the Lord with all your heart, then put away the foreign gods and the Ashtaroth from among you and direct your heart to the Lord and serve him only, and he will deliver you out of the hand of the Philistines.'" (1 Samuel 8:3)

"And all Judah rejoiced over the oath, for they had sworn with all their heart and had sought him with their whole desire, and he was found by them, and the Lord gave them rest all around." (2 Chronicles 15:15)

"Then Jesus said to him, 'Be gone, Satan! For it is written, 'You shall worship the Lord your God.'" (Matthew 4:10)

"No servant can serve two masters, for either he will hate the one and love the other, or he will be devoted to the one and despise the other. You cannot serve God and money." (Luke 16:13)

What do we gain by dabbling in other spiritualties? Are they nothing more than games we play to entertain ourselves? In reality, they are empty promises. What they offer is like getting a lottery ticket from your boss for a Christmas bonus — but it's not the winning number. Even though there's something in us that yearns to know what tomorrow holds, it's a pointless pursuit. "When times are good, be happy; but when times are bad, consider this: God has made the one as well as the other. Therefore, no one can discover anything about their future" (Ecclesiastes 7:14 NIV). Did you get the last sentence of that verse? "No one can discover anything about their future." So why waste your time? The stars and planets don't know your future. Tealeaves haven't a clue about what tomorrow holds for you or for anybody else. So give it up.

Only God knows about tomorrow and He holds your tomorrows in His loving, caring hands. Does a baby need to know about tomorrow? No. His parents will care for him. Does a seven-year-old need to be concerned about tomorrow? Certainly not, if she has loving, caring parents to watch over her. Be encouraged to have the faith of a child and trust in Him. Rest in Him. Have faith in Him alone for He cares for you and holds you close to His heart.

There is no need to look to the stars. We must look to the Light of Life alone for our eyes to see the true Light.

Q & A Chapter 28: God Watches Over You

1. Describe God's watchfulness over His people.

2. What are the dangers of dabbling in a variety of spiritualties?

3. How do you feel about not knowing what the future holds for you?

Your Mission Journal Notes:

29

Knowing Who We Are in Christ

Middle child. That's who I am in the Larson family. There are blessings that come with being the middle child, like having my older siblings "test the waters" to know what I could get away with. But essentially a middle child is the invisible child, the peacemaker, and negotiator. In my family invisibility was a good thing and being inconspicuous became my strong suit. How was it possible to be unnoticed in a tiny house with a family of seven? It wasn't easy, but I became quite skilled at flying under the radar.

Now I've discovered some good news. In the family of God, I'm no longer an invisible middle child. God constantly watches over me with loving kindness and, as needed, He holds me extra close to His heart.

Who are you and what do you become when you obey Christ's call to "believe and be baptized?" Do you have a change of identity? What's all this about a new name? What happens to you within your heart of hearts? Are you a part of the family of God, and what is your place among God's children? Let's search the Scriptures to see the effect of Christ's resurrection power at work in you by means of the hearing of His Word and the waters of baptism. Our Lord Jesus begins this good work to mold you and shape you into a useful servant in the Kingdom of Heaven and to pour out eternal blessings on you.

First of all, why do we say you are, "in Christ"? When you are in Christ, you become a lot more than just another person who shows up at church. Being in Christ is not limited to being a part of a Christian community. As the redeemed of Christ, all you become is because of Christ. All of what you have become is because you are received into

Christ and His body, the church. The seed of faith was planted in your heart as you heard God's Word. And then, through the miraculous waters of baptism you became a part of the church and adopted into the body of Christ. As you obeyed Christ's command to be baptized in the Name of the Father, and the Son, and the Holy Spirit, you became one with Him.

We may well spend an eternity discovering the depths of who we are in the family of God, yet here on terra firma, we find a sampling of our identity to whet our appetite for more kinship.

We are one with Christ in His death, burial, and resurrection.

> *"For in him the whole fullness of deity dwells bodily, and you have come to fullness in him, who is the head of every ruler and authority. In him also you were circumcised with a spiritual circumcision, by putting off the body of the flesh in the circumcision of Christ; when you were buried with him in baptism, you were also raised with him through faith in the power of God, who raised him from the dead."* (Colossians 2:12)

How can we illustrate this beautiful oneness in Christ? In reality, there are no human words to picture how you become one with Christ in his death, burial and resurrection. Like coffee and cream. Once you put them together, they are one — in one cup and one beverage. Like blending varieties of wine: the resulting wine is unlike the old. These are incomplete pictures of this truth, but they are a good beginning. Being one with Christ is foundational and central to our identity as Christians.

How is it possible to become one with Christ in His death, burial, and resurrection when you're in an air conditioned church and the pastor or priest pours water over your head while proclaiming the words, "In the name of the Father, and of the Son and of the Holy Spirit"? Or maybe you're in a nice, white baptismal robe in preparation for being submersed in the preheated baptismal tank in front of the whole church? You give your testimony of faith, hold your nose and down you go. You could be standing beside your

husband in the icy waters of a mountain stream, or in the salty
waters of the ocean, ready for your baptism. What's the connection?
How does this miracle of becoming one in Christ's death, burial and
resurrection happen when baptism is done in so many ways and in
various places?

> *"For if we have been united with him in a death like his, we
> will certainly be united with him in a resurrection like his.
> We know that our old self was crucified with him so that the
> body of sin might be destroyed, and we might no longer be
> enslaved to sin. For whoever has died is freed from sin. But
> if we have died with Christ, we believe that we will also live
> with him. We know that Christ, being raised from the dead,
> will never die again; death no longer has dominion over him.
> The death he died, he died to sin, once for all; but the life he
> lives, he lives to God. So you also must consider yourselves
> dead to sin and alive to God in Christ Jesus." (Romans 6:5-11)*

Does this mean that your new identity is found in death? Beyond
a doubt! When you die in Christ you become a new person, alive like
never before. The Scriptures illustrate this truth, showing us that the
body that was in bondage to sin is now dead, just as Christ died. This
dead, enslaved flesh is buried with Christ, just as our Lord Jesus' body
was buried in a tomb. Now a whole new creation is raised up, just as
Jesus was resurrected from the dead. The apostle Paul illustrates this,
showing us how it is like planting a seed in the garden. The seed must
die before it sprouts and becomes a whole new plant to flourish, grow,
and bear fruit. Jesus taught this truth. "Very truly, I tell you, unless
a grain of wheat falls into the earth and dies, it remains just a single
grain; but if it dies, it bears much fruit" (John 12:24). The Apostle Paul
asserts the same truth. "What is sown is perishable, what is raised is
imperishable. It is sown in dishonor, it is raised in glory. It is sown in
weakness, it is raised in power. It is sown a physical body, it is raised a
spiritual body. If there is a physical body, there is also a spiritual body"
(1 Corinthians 15:42-43).

Who we become in Christ begins with believing, and then continues with the water of baptism.[108] "The one who believes and is baptized will be saved" (Mark 16:16). Why water? "... [B]y the word of God heavens existed long ago and an earth was formed out of water and by means of water" (2 Peter 3:5). Here we see that God creates something brand new out of water by His Word. "This means that anyone who belongs to Christ has become a new person. The old life is gone; a new life has begun!" (2 Corinthians 5:17 NLT).[109]

You have been made a brand new creation. As a new creation, you are a witness of the greatest miracle. God brings together the water and His Word, just as He did at the creation of the world, and makes you brand new in Christ by the power of the cross. You are a miracle brought about by our Creator God, just as the tribes of Israel became a new nation unto God through "baptism" in the Red Sea.[110]

The Gospels teach us that "it was not Jesus himself but his disciples who baptized" (John 4:2). Even today, Jesus appoints His "disciples" to baptize in water.[111] "They serve in a system of worship that is only a copy, a shadow of the real one in heaven" (Hebrews 8:5, NLT).[112] What is baptism? Christian baptism is so much more than showing or illustrating a spiritual reality that already happened when you

---

[108] We must be clear; there is no such thing as a baptism ordained by a parish, local church organization, denomination or synod. There is no Baptist baptism, no Anglican baptism, no Lutheran baptism and no other true baptism that baptizes you into anything other than Christ. There is one baptism and it is into Christ. If anyone claims any other baptism than in the name of the Father, Son and Holy Spirit, their baptism is only by the hands of man and is only a baptism of the flesh.

[109] It is helpful to study with more than one translation, enlightening us with a more complete picture and meaning of the text.) "Therefore, if anyone is in Christ, he is a new creation. The old has passed away; behold, the new has come" (2 Corinthians 2:15 ESV).

[110] In Christ we are not an earthly nation, but one church, one body in Christ, the body of Christ.

[111] Keep in mind that the Kingdom of Heaven is not limited by space and time. Therefore, in our baptism we are taken into Jesus death, burial and resurrection and we become one with Christ in his death, burial and resurrection. It is logical, it is miraculous, and it is entirely possible.

[112] This scripture specifically refers to the rituals prescribed by the law and performed by priests who served under the Mosaic system. Yet, the Old Testament system of worship foreshadowed what was to come, a better covenant ministered by Jesus Christ our High Priest who is serving in the true tabernacle in heaven.

come to faith in Christ Jesus. Baptism through water and the Word is the physical, visible evidence of a spiritual reality. In baptismal waters brought together with God's Word, whether you are baptized in your church, in a river, in a bathtub or in the ocean, you see with your eyes the reality of what is happening to you from above. The baptism you see is a reflection of what is happening in the spiritual realm, an imperfect reflection as if mirrored in rippling waters. An incredible miracle takes place as you become one with Christ in His death, burial, and resurrection and by means of baptism you become a whole new creation.

How should I describe this new creation? We are sons and daughters of God Almighty. We are new creations, invited to partake of the new wine in the new covenant, in communion with the saints. We are welcomed at the Lord's Table to break bread. "This is my body that is for you. Do this in remembrance of me." In the same way he took the cup also, after supper, saying, 'This cup is the new covenant in my blood. Do this, as often as you drink it, in remembrance of me.' For as often as you eat this bread and drink the cup, you proclaim the Lord's death until he comes" (1 Corinthians 11:25-26). There are wonderful blessings as an adopted son or daughter of the Most High God. As you abide in Christ these blessings literally overtake you and overwhelm you like a tsunami wave.

Being a son or daughter of the Most High God is better than anything you have ever imagined, because now you are in Christ who is seated at the right hand of the Father. But Jesus did not leave you on our own because Jesus lifts you up. He holds you in loving His arms, "...and raised us up with him and seated us with him in the heavenly places in Christ Jesus."[113]

> "And when he had said these things, as they were looking on, he was lifted up, and a cloud took him out of their sight. And while they were gazing into heaven as he went, behold, two men stood by them in white robes, and said, 'Men of Galilee, why do you stand looking into heaven? This Jesus, who was

---

[113] Ephesians 2: 6

taken up from you into heaven, will come in the same way as you saw him go into heaven."[114]

"Being therefore exalted at the right hand of God, and having received from the Father the promise of the Holy Spirit, he has poured out this that you yourselves are seeing and hearing."[115]

"And he said, "Behold, I see the heavens opened, and the Son of Man standing at the right hand of God."[116]

"As he was saying these things, a cloud came and overshadowed them, and they were afraid as they entered the cloud. And a voice came out of the cloud, saying, 'This is my Son, my Chosen One; listen to him.'"[117]

"The Lord says to my Lord: 'Sit at my right hand, until I make your enemies your footstool.'"[118]

These Scriptures erase all doubt that you are now in Christ who is seated at the right hand of the Father. This is who you are. "In Christ" is your new identity.

What an incredible and wonderful miracle our Lord has done in us. The slave to sin is dead, and now we become alive in Christ, a new creation in Christ, and we are joined with Christ at the right hand of God the Father Almighty. A holy fear of God comes over me as I think of this, because in reality — in this very moment, I'm standing in Christ in the heavenly sanctuary. I'm so close to God that His presence, His light, His glory, His majesty and His beauty overwhelms me and would consume me if not for being in Christ, if not for the Holy Spirit sealing me from the righteous and just wrath of God. Yet, my knees buckle

---

[114] Acts 1:9—11
[115] Acts 2:33
[116] Acts 7:56
[117] Luke 9:34—35
[118] Ps 110:1

and I'm overcome with trembling and awe. I fall to my knees, my face to the ground to worship a Holy God.

To stand in God's council and enter His Holy presence is only possible when we are in Christ. The reason we can do this is simple: we are now the righteousness of God in Christ. Think of it. Jesus beckons us to His side. He pulls us close and wraps us in His robe of righteousness. Then He brings us forward before our Heavenly Father and says, "This is your daughter. This is now your son," and we stand before God in confidence, secure in Christ. We may now dwell in His presence in peace and in rest as if resting in lush, green pastures — right now.

Consider these beautiful and powerful descriptions of who we are in Christ. You'll be blessed beyond all you can imagine:

1. We are ambassadors (2 Corinthians 5:20).
2. We are disciples in the faith of discipleship (1 Peter 3:5).
3. We are disciple makers (Matthew 28:19).
4. We are a kingdom of priests, a chosen generation, a royal priesthood (1 Peter 2:9, Revelation 5:10, Revelation 1:6, Exodus 19:6).
5. In Christ, we are armored up and battle ready, raising the banner called "love" as a battle flag (Romans 8:37, Ephesians 6:11-17, 2 Timothy 3:7, 1 Peter 1:13-16).
6. We are a holy people, set apart for Christ (1 Peter 1:13-16, 1 Thessalonians. 5:22, Romans 7:1, Deuteronomy 7:6).
7. We are all ministers of the gospel of Jesus Christ (Romans 15:16, 2 Corinthians 5: 18, Acts 17:11, 2 Timothy 2:8, Hebrews 4:2).
8. We are citizens of an eternal kingdom, whose Builder and Maker is God (Hebrews 11:10).
9. We are the redeemed; justified, sanctified, and glorified (Romans 8:29-30, Philemon 3:9-11).
10. We are Christ's hand extended into a lost and dying world (1 Corinthians 12:7).
11. We are sons of the Most High God (Luke 1:32, Psalms 82:6, Galatians 3:26-29).
12. We are joint heirs with Christ (1 Peter 3:7, Romans 8:17, Ephesians 1:11, NLT).

13. We have the mind of Christ (Philippians 2:5-8, 1 Corinthians 2:16).

Sons and daughters of the Most High God are beautiful in His sight. All of what God has given to you is to adorn you as His bride. You are being prepared for His coming just as this Scripture declares: "And I saw the holy city, the new Jerusalem, coming down out of heaven from God, prepared as a bride adorned for her husband" (Revelation 21:2). Disciple, ambassador, priest is your new identity. Redeemed, soldier, citizen of heaven – this is who you are in Christ. Heir, servant, minister – this is you, a new creation in Christ. A new creation by the power of God's holy Word.

Q & A Chapter 29: Knowing Who We are in Christ

1. What does the Bible mean when it says you are "in Christ?"

2. How is it possible to be one with Christ in His death, burial, and resurrection?

3. Describe how your life has changed now that you are "in Christ."

Your Mission Journal Notes:

30

Contrite of Heart

Singing in the shower is one of my favorite things to do. My voice reverberates on the tile walls and the words of songs and Psalms wash through my soul as water and soap wash the outside. The song I sing most often stirs my heart: "Create in me a clean heart, O God, and renew a right spirit in me. Take me not away from thy presence, O God. Take not your Holy Spirit from me. Restore unto me the joy of thy salvation and renew a right spirit in me."[119]

These inspired words from Scripture show us a picture of a contrite heart before God. David called on the Holy Spirit as the source of a right heart. He expressed his fear of the consequences of not having a right heart. David's song teaches us that we need someone to represent us before God. We learn from David that having a contrite heart is an integral part of pursuing a right relationship and drawing closer to God.

Our teacher, David, was described as a man after God's own heart, yet he failed in many ways. The contrite heart of a man or a woman who walks in David's sandals causes them to press forward and move purposefully to grow closer to the heart of God. Yet, in moving closer and closer to God, our sin becomes more evident. The apostle Paul tells of this dichotomy: "I do not understand my own actions. For I do not do what I want, but I do the very thing I hate" (Romans 7:15). A kingdom heart grieves over sin, repents of wrongdoing, seeks forgiveness and cleansing of sin, and then once again goes forward,

---

[119] This chorus is a paraphrase of Psalms 51:10-12. Author unknown. © 1988 MARANATHA! MUSIC.

walking closer to a Holy God. Christians who have the heart of God abide with their Heavenly Father and quickly sense even the slightest bit of distance, the smallest barrier to fellowship with God that is caused by their sin.

"It's frustrating," a friend told me. "I thought that the longer I followed Jesus, the more I would become like Him." All Christians can identify with that feeling of frustration. My friend went on to say: "Instead I find much the opposite – my sinfulness becomes more and more obvious and grievous." My friend is right. As we grow and mature in Christ we do become more like Him, but we also see more and more of our sinfulness and the ways in which we are yet to be like Him. It's like each time we take a step we see two more we need to take. What produces that feeling of frustration is a contrite heart before God.

Without the desire to seek God and become more like Christ, we become like the tribes of Israel who begged that God not speak directly to them. "Now when all the people saw the thunder and the flashes of lightning and the sound of the trumpet and the mountain smoking, the people were afraid and trembled, and they stood far off and said to Moses, 'You speak to us, and we will listen; but do not let God speak to us, lest we die'" (Exodus 20:18-19). The people didn't want to get too close to God because in God's presence they immediately saw their sin and depraved condition. They needed an advocate before God, to stand between them and God or they would be consumed by God's just wrath.

We, like them, need an advocate before God. The first book of the Bible to be written was the book of Job. He too expressed his need of an advocate before God. "Even now my witness is in heaven; my advocate is on high. My intercessor is my friend as my eyes pour out tears to God; on behalf of a man he pleads with God as a man pleads for his friend" (Job 16:20-12 NIV).

Men and women who are in pursuit of God's own heart are quick to recognize and confess sin and then call on God, as did the Psalmist: "Wash me thoroughly from my iniquity, and cleanse me from my sin" (Psalms 51:2). A contrite heart is sensitive to the ministries of the

Holy Spirit who convicts of sin.[120] We submit ourselves to the Holy Spirit who disciplines us, chastens us and corrects us. We receive the comfort of the Holy Spirit who brings to our mind, even as we are convicted, that we have an Advocate, our Lord Jesus who brings us before a Holy God and pleads our case, saying, "I paid the price, I took the penalty for his sin."

"Create in me a clean heart, oh God." This attitude of heart is tender toward God. When our hearts are clean, our ears are willing to listen to the Spirit of God who lovingly confronts our sin. With pure hearts we press on with great confidence, knowing that when we trip and fall down, the Spirit of Jesus advocates on our behalf before the Father. We can go forward in this earthly pilgrimage knowing that our hearts are being made right before God Almighty so that we may draw closer and closer to the heart of God each day of our lives.

Q & A Chapter 30: Contrite of Heart

1. What does it mean to have a contrite heart toward God?

2. As you get closer to God, why do you see your sin more clearly?

3. What is the value of the Holy Spirit's discipline in your life?

Your Mission Journal Notes:

---

[120] Read John 14:16, 26; John 15:26 and John 16:7. In 14:16 the Holy Spirit is referred to as the Spirit of truth. It is truth that convicts of sin, while a lie condones our sin.

31

The Nature of Forgiveness

No Future without Forgiveness is Desmond Tutu's book about the transition South Africa made from despotism to democracy. He spoke words of forgiveness, healing and restoration that laid a solid foundation for a bright national future. His restorative words are rooted in the truths of Scripture.

In stark contrast we look at other places like the tribal regions of Pakistan where people have a culture of vengeance and reciprocity. This kind of social structure is continuously being undermined and destroyed by currents of vengeful anger aimed at another family or tribe that committed an offense against your family, even generations ago. The wound festers until there is vengeful, hate-filled injustice. In any culture where forgiveness cannot take root, the seeds of destruction flourish and bear the fruit of malice.

Forgiveness is so much more than just absolving someone of the wrong done to you. Restorative forgiveness includes discipline in the process. Restorative forgiveness includes loving correction, healed wounds, and rebuilt relationships.

As we search for pearls of wisdom regarding forgiveness, we find there is more to it than letting go of an offense. Giving up our need for getting even is just a good beginning. Restorative forgiveness goes beyond mercy. Absolving someone of his or her wrong, even though it is "mission impossible" from a natural point of view, is just the beginning of forgiveness. For those who wish to search out the heart of God, we find great truth in Jesus' choice of words: "Then Peter came to Jesus and asked, 'Lord, how many times shall I forgive my brother or sister who sins against me? Up to seven times?' Jesus answered, 'I tell you, not seven times, but seventy- seven times'" (Matthew 18:21-22 NIV). His word choice leads us to this Scripture in the Old Testament:

> *"For thus says the Lord: Only when Babylon's seventy years are completed will I visit you, and I will fulfill to you my promise and bring you back to this place. For surely I know the plans I have for you, says the Lord, plans for your welfare and not for harm, to give you a future with hope. Then when you call upon me and come and pray to me, I will hear you. When you search for me, you will find me; if you seek me with all your heart, I will let you find me, says the Lord, and I will restore your fortunes and gather you from all the nations and all the places where I have driven you, says the Lord, and I will bring you back to the place from which I sent you into exile." (Jeremiah 29:10-14).*

In this Scripture we see the work of forgiveness and the heart of forgiveness.

Jeremiah's prophecies were fulfilled: ""Seventy weeks are decreed for your people and your holy city: to finish the transgression, to put an end to sin, and to atone for iniquity, to bring in everlasting righteousness, to seal both vision and prophet, and to anoint a most holy place" (Daniel 9:24). Look at all God accomplished in His people during the seventy years they were in exile. God changed their hearts so they would seek Him. The Lord God restored their fortunes and prepared them for gathering to their homeland. Restoring His people was included in God's work of forgiveness. The forgiveness math Jesus used, seventy-seven times, now adds up.

Forgiveness is certainly about showing mercy, letting go of the offense, giving up your right to revenge, and washing away the stain of the offense. But it is even more than that for those who have kingdom hearts. There is more to forgiveness and this is for our good, a blessing in which we delight. This miracle called forgiveness is a part of a saving sanctification in which God works together with us as He imparts His blessings to the saints.

In forgiveness, we are called to restore the offender. The purpose is to bring him/her back into fellowship with our Heavenly Father, with fellow believers and to the offended. This is a part of restoring the soul. This is the healing oil poured out to cure the sickness of sin. The prophet Hosea spoke of this process. "After two days he will revive us; on the third day he will raise us up, that we may live before him."[121] God is eager to forgive us and yet restoration takes time. Jesus did the math and He did "time" for us as His body lay in a garden tomb at Jerusalem.

Be quick to forgive and then be patient. Take the "time" to restore.

The beginning of forgiveness is to simply and prayerfully intend to have an attitude of forgiveness, a mind set on humbling yourself to forgive; and you will find God's miraculous power at work in you as you do so. You don't have to wait for someone to beg forgiveness, repent of their offense against you before stepping onto the pathway. It is an attitude of heart. This is a great miracle by the work of the Holy Spirit in us that is only possible in Christ.

Once your heart is in the right place, look for an opportunity to express what is in your heart, to forgive, to absolve the person who committed the offense. Please allow me to share some of my own experience.[122] In my family where I grew up, we were taught to forgive — immediately — you must, you shall, you will. It was considered a great sin not to forgive and forget as if it was an automatic reflex action. It was like a two-step formula: offense — forgiveness, offense — forgiveness. And don't you dare mention the offense ever again.

What I've learned about myself is that this is not real forgiveness from the heart, but rather forgiveness by the law. This legalistic kind of forgiveness left the hurt to churn inside me like a bad heartburn. The offense and hurt were repressed in my heart as if I had just put a cork in a bottle. The pressure would build and eventually the cork

---

[121] Hosea's words ring true as the "sign of Jonah" Jesus spoke about in Matthew 12:39. Jesus was placed in a tomb on Thursday before the sun set. He lay in the grave on Friday and Saturday, and after the sun rose on Sunday morning the stone was rolled away to reveal that He had risen so "that we may live before him."

[122] We must keep in mind that experience is not the arbiter of truth. God's Word is the plumb line of truth.

would pop. When the cork popped an ugly mess would pour out, doing harm to those around me, and then I needed mercy and forgiveness more than the original offender. Because of this, I've learned not to forgive by formula or in a legalistic manner. Certainly, there is a time to "get over it," but just as important, there is a time to grieve and there is a time to restore.

Now when I forgive someone it comes from my heart. First I must acknowledge that an offense has occurred, and then I must admit the hurt it has caused me. To deny the offense and to repress the feelings of hurt only serve to keep the offense festering. I needed to learn to be honest with myself first, and then tell God the whole truth about what I was feeling. God always hears our heartfelt cries.

Once I acknowledge the feelings of hurt I have, I can face my offender and show the heart and mind of Christ in my willingness to forgive and restore. I discovered that it was good for my healing process to articulate forgiveness and mercy toward the offender, waiting for an appropriate time. I found that it was better to answer the offender in a manner that restored them to my circle of fellowship, taking time for the process to do its good work. It was good to absolve them of guilt to remove barriers the offense built up between us. For me it is no longer a you-must-do-it-immediately-without-a-thought kind of process, but a course of action that brings offender and offended back into fellowship in Christ.

God's command for us to forgive is not a call to mindless stupidity. When it comes to more extreme forms of offense and abuse, godly wisdom is called for. We are instructed in Matthew 18 to go talk to the offender, one on one, but a few words of godly wisdom regarding forgiveness are in order. A one-on-one talk is the ideal way to resolve an offense, but it is not to be done with reckless abandon. You must not put yourself in danger.

After you have admitted the harm and acknowledged the hurt of what was done to you, take time to grieve. If the offender has not turned from their violent or spiteful ways that caused you harm, it may **not** be wise or safe to confront them on your own or to verbalize forgiveness in private. Again, you must not place yourself in harm's way. Every circumstance is unique, and in some cases it may not even be safe to write a letter or e-mail expressing your heart of forgiveness if that communication would be taken as open an invitation for the one who violated you to come back into your life and harm you again. This is especially true if they have not repented and proven to others they have had a change of heart.

Many abusers claim over and over again that they have changed and it will never happen again. Their promise may hold for a while, maybe a week, a day, or an hour, until the next time they get drunk, stoned, overwhelmed, or stressed. Most often, you will not be the best judge of the offender's change of heart. The bottom line is to be prayerful, be wise, be safe, and get good support and counsel as you undertake the process of forgiveness. Take time before restoring.

This brings us to an important point that I've referred to as restorative forgiveness. The most difficult aspect of forgiveness and restoration is that of discipline. We see this in the way God brought the children of Israel to repentance, through the discipline of exile, so that they might ultimately be restored after seventy years. The Apostle Paul wrote to the church in Corinth instructing them to discipline a person in their church because of his grievous sin. "Drive out the wicked person from among you" (1 Corinthians 5:12). The unrepentant offender was exiled for a time. But it was a time of preparation to be restored.

This is an important principle. We begin to learn as a child that when we do something bad, mom gives us a time out. King David experienced this truth. After his sin with Bathsheba he was expelled from his throne in Jerusalem for a time. Jonah spent three days and nights in the belly of a whale after running from God. The tribes of Israel, because of their sin, spent seventy years in exile as God prepared them and disciplined them so they could be restored.

First and foremost, in the exercise of church discipline, we must always remember mercy, because in mercy there is forgiveness and in forgiveness there is restoration. There are times when the course of wisdom is to discipline using a time out. That may include a time away from fellowship, ministry, and service. Paul's purpose for driving out the wicked person was not to get rid of the bum for good — out of sight, out of mind. It was a part of a discipline plan aimed at bringing the person to repentance, so they could be forgiven and restored to fellowship. In other words, show them the door and then be prepared, by the leading of the Holy Spirit, to bring them back and restore them to the community of believers — for that is the whole purpose of discipline as a part of forgiveness. Paul was clear on this: "When you are assembled, and my spirit is present with the power of our Lord Jesus, you are to hand this man over to Satan for the destruction of the flesh, so that his spirit may be saved in the day of the Lord" (1Corinthians 5:5). The man's temporal flesh had a stranglehold on him and it had to be broken. When the stranglehold of sin was broken, he could be forgiven and restored.

How does this apply in practice for Christians today? Some examples may be: a man who cheats on his wife must be disciplined, learning to be accountable to his wife and his Christian brothers. He may, for a long time, be accountable to his wife for where he is and what he's doing, encouraging her to check his phone log, until the day when his heart is proven to be changed. When he humbles himself and proves himself, he can be restored with trust after a time. An elder, pastor, priest, or church leader who betrays the church and brings shame upon the Holy name of Christ will need to step down from ministry and service for a time, learning to be accountable to his fellow ministers, elders, and deacons until he humbles himself, proves himself, and comes to repentance so that he may be restored. A person caught up in addictive behaviors will need loving, caring discipline, being accountable as necessary to help them come clean, to repent, be forgiven, and ultimately be brought back into complete fellowship. A time of godly discipline serves the purpose of restorative forgiveness.

A Christian leader, the priest of his household, and every member of a congregation, ought to submit to discipline ministered in Christ's love to bring them to repentance so they may be forgiven and brought back into fellowship and into communion with our Lord Jesus Christ. There are no exceptions. No leader or member ought to shun accountability and discipline. No one is above being disciplined. We must all submit ourselves in the same way, in the home and in the church, to God's Word and to Christ who is the head of the church.

Is it your desire to be shown mercy, be forgiven, and brought back into the sweet fellowship of believers in Christ? Then be encouraged to show mercy, forgive, and, in wisdom's time, restore the offender to the blessings of Christian fellowship.

Only in Christ are forgiveness and restoration possible. We begin forgiveness prayerfully, intending to let go of the offense and to restore our relationship with the offender. When necessary, a time of loving discipline is applied for the good of the offender. We humble ourselves, acknowledge our hurt, ask for wisdom, and apply loving correction as we forgive those who cause us harm. In restorative forgiveness you will find God's miraculous power at work in you and in your relationships, because there is no future without forgiveness.

Q & A Chapter 31: The Nature of Forgiveness

1. What are the consequences when forgiveness is withheld?

2. What part does restoration play in an act of forgiveness?

3. How is it possible to forgive from the heart?

Your Mission Journal Notes:

32

Gathering in Community as One

Arizona, especially the Verde Valley in the high desert of northern Arizona, is becoming well known for producing exceptional wine grapes. There are many varieties of wine made from Arizona grapes with unique and distinct appearance, scents, flavors and finish. Today sixty-three bonded wineries produce unique varieties of Arizona grapes. Imagine what would happen if sixty-three vintner's got together to blend their finest red wines. With the blending complete, when they poured a glass of wine for you to sample, would you have sixty-three wines in your glass? No! You would have *one* very special glass of wine — a brand new wine. This kind of "blending" happens when God brings His church together in a gathering. All of us are blended together as one with each other and with the Father, Son, and Holy Spirit.[123]

Our worshipful gatherings were foreshadowed in Old Testament forms of worship. God's command to gather together is important now and forever. The nature of God is revealed in His desire to bring His people together to strengthen us in the bonds of fellowship, to manifest Himself so that we may worship, honor, and serve God, and to prepare us for what is to come.

God gave us a picture of this gathering when He instructed the people of the nation of Israel to come to Jerusalem to gather and celebrate a festival of weeks, called the festival of Shavu'ot.[124] This is the second of the three major annual Jewish festivals. During this

---

[123] The miracle of this blending is that we do not lose our God-given individuality. We are still unique and special.
[124] Leviticus 21:15-16, 21

time, the people commemorated the first fruits of the harvest and brought them to the temple. They gathered the best of their harvest and then came together for a feast at the Lord's temple in Jerusalem. What this festival illustrated for us began in earnest with Peter's sermon on the day of Pentecost. Peter quoted the Old Testament prophet Joel, who many years before had foretold what would happen when Jesus established His church: "Then afterward I will pour out my spirit on all flesh; your sons and your daughters shall prophesy, your old men shall dream dreams, and your young men shall see visions" (Joel 2:28).

Think about what happens when you enter the candy store at the mall. As soon as you walk through the door they give you a free sample of their butternut candy, fudge, or some other delicious confection. Why? Because they know you'll like it and want to buy some. The feast gatherings of the nation of Israel were like samples of good things to come. A festive table is also set before the church to strengthen our faith and to bond us together as a cohesive community. This satisfying communion feast prepares us for the great and final gathering of God's people who will dwell with Him forever. But the great gathering won't be just a lot more of what we have now. What we have now is like tiny droplets of moisture; then it will be like oceans of water.

As we gather together to worship, God continues to work in our lives to bind us together. The bonds become stronger with each gathering, making us one with the Father, the Son, the Holy Spirit, and the whole community of faith. Our assemblies prepare us to be brought together in the great feast, just as God planned from the beginning. You are called to be a part of this ingathering, and you can have a festive taste of this as you gather with the congregation today.

There are very few "do not" statements in the New Testament, so when we read one, we know it's of great importance. "And let us consider how to provoke one another to love and good deeds, not neglecting to meet together, as is the habit of some, but encouraging one another, and all the more as you see the Day approaching" (Hebrews 10:24-25). Let's be clear in our understanding of this Scripture. Do not neglect gathering together. Gathering is for our good because of its great benefits. First and foremost, in our gatherings we come to delight in God: "Happy are those who live in your house, ever singing your praise. Selah" (Psalms 84:4). What God has for us, as a congregation, is a blessing beyond compare. It is glory upon glory.

In the house of the Lord we are blessed as we sing His praise. We come to the blessings of forgiveness, mercy, strengthening, encouragement, accountability, caring support, restoration, and renewal of relationships. What we give is an even greater blessing than what we receive. We give glory and honor to God, we lift up our voices in praise, we minister to our brothers and sisters in Christ by the power of the Spirit, and we receive the blessings of fellowship with our fellow believers and our Holy God. In these times of worship, God manifests His living, active presence, causing others to exclaim, "God is truly among you."[125]

I'm always in awe of how creative our God is. After all, He is Creator of all heaven and earth, but He still amazes me. He does things in different ways at different times. In one gathering there may be shouts of praise, initiated and inspired in the Holy Spirit. In another assembly a holy hush may come over the church. Each and every gathering may be somewhat different, and God manifests himself in various ways. He keeps us on our toes because we tend to get in a rut and say to ourselves, "if we do this and that like we always do, then we know God is here." This principle may be likened to looking at a beautiful, perfect diamond with many facets, one diamond refracting the light in many different ways. In the countless manifestations of His creative presence in our worshipful gatherings, we are strengthened in His bond of fellowship.

We ought not discount any means that God will use to manifest his presence to each person in a gathering. He may make Himself known to a seven-year-old girl looking through a stained glass window during the sermon, her eyes opened to the reality of the living Christ for the first time. God may manifest his presence to a boy who takes in his hands the bread and the cup of communion for the very first time. He may well manifest His living, active, ministering presence

---

[125] 1 Corinthians 14:25.

in miraculous ways — an elderly gentleman struggling to the front to receive communion, gripping tight to his cane and then walking away without need of it. The Lord Almighty may manifest himself through the prayers and laying on of hands to gift and empower a young mom with a spiritual gift for ministry. Manifestations of His presence may come through the ministries of the spiritual gift of prophecy, words of wisdom, knowledge, or words of encouragement. We serve an awesome God and we must not attempt to limit what He will do. God's living, active presence will, at times, make us uncomfortable, and we must not limit God for the sake of comfort. We must not attempt to restrain a boundless God who desires to minister to His people and join us together as a family.

God brings us together as one, as a congregation, and as the church universal. As we gather to worship and minister before God, we are strengthened in our faith today and prepared for that one final gathering when "the Spirit and the bride say, 'Come.' And let everyone who hears say, 'Come.' And let everyone who is thirsty come. Let anyone who wishes take the water of life as a gift" (Revelation 22:17).

> "But you have come to Mount Zion and to the city of the living God, the heavenly Jerusalem, and to innumerable angels in festal gathering, and to the assembly of the firstborn who are enrolled in heaven, and to God the judge of all, and to the spirits of the righteous made perfect, and to Jesus, the mediator of a new covenant, and to the sprinkled blood that speaks a better word than the blood of Abel." (Hebrews 12:22)

Join together with me and let's enjoy the new wine of the new covenant as we prepare for that great Day of the Lord. [126]

---

[126] Luke 5:37-39.

Q & A Chapter 32: Gathering in Community as One

1. What is God's good purpose in commanding Christians to gather together?

2. What are the benefits of gathering together in Christ?

3. How does Jesus reveal His living, active presence in a gathering of believers?

Your Mission Journal Notes:

33

Faith Proven in Action

Grab your Bible, a highlighter, notepaper, and pen and let's jump into learning about the righteousness that is in Christ and about good things we do as a result of His righteousness at work in us. We'll learn about the dangers of being complacent in our own self-righteousness. Finally, we will see the powerful effects of Jesus' righteousness and its eternal value.

Within the American church as a whole, we find ourselves conflicted regarding what we do versus what we believe. Our understanding of the righteousness of Christ and our own righteousness is confused. Too often we think, "My doctrine is correct, my world view is Biblical, I partake in the sacraments of the church, I confess my sins, and I'm not a bad person, so what else is there to do?" Beyond the shadow of a doubt, righteousness that is true and eternal can only be present when we are in Christ Jesus our Lord and Savior. In Him we come into righteousness that is truly attributed to us and not of our own doing. In His righteousness, we stand before a Holy God and are not consumed in the fire of His presence. By contrast, our own righteousness is no better than a filthy rag that is to be burned.

Take a look at this Scripture: "Though I say to the righteous that they shall surely live, yet if they trust in their righteousness and commit iniquity, none of their righteous deeds shall be remembered" (Ezekiel 33:13).

Your true heart is revealed in the way you perceive the meaning of this spiritual truth. There are some who would say, "I'm not under the law; I fully trust in the righteousness of Jesus Christ and my own deeds are of little or no consequence."

It took me some time to grasp this chapter's concept and my hope is to communicate this in a clear and simple way. We must trust in the righteousness of Christ because when we trust in our own righteousness we are deceived — self-deceived. In our own righteousness we chart our own course, we see ourselves as right, we esteem ourselves as a cut above the rest, we give advice but can't accept it, and we see ourselves as innocent.[127]

Read your Bible from Genesis to Revelation and you will see that deeds are of great consequence, and yet, there is no righteousness of eternal value apart from Christ. So you must trust in the righteousness of Christ. His righteousness in you is *not* a matter of Christ having done all these righteous deeds and now He gives you credit for what He has done. Here is the reality of it. Jesus wraps His robe of righteousness around you and now your Heavenly Father looks upon you as righteous.[128] Because you are wrapped in Jesus' righteousness, you will naturally do what He is doing, say what He is saying, and go where He is going. "...[W]hoever says, 'I abide in him,' ought to walk just as he walked" (1 John 2:6). Therefore your righteousness and righteous deeds are in Him, because of Him, by the power of His Spirit and they are not your own.

Yet you must be aware that your deeds create an immediate effect, whether good or bad. Elihu spoke of this. "Look up at the heavens and see; gaze at the clouds so high above you. If you sin, how does that affect him? If your sins are many, what does that do to him? If you are righteous, what do you give to him or what does he receive from your hand? Your wickedness affects others like you, and your righteousness, other human beings" (Job 35:5-8 NIV). Elihu was not completely right in what he spoke, as we see in this Scripture: "So the Lord was sorry he had ever made them and put them on the earth. It broke his heart" (Genesis 6:6 NLT). Our sin does not change who God is, but sin does grieve the Holy Spirit. Our good deeds do not

---

[127] Proverbs 12:15, 20:6, 30:12, Jeremiah 2:35, 2 Corinthians 10:12
[128] "I will greatly rejoice in the Lord, my whole being shall exult in my God; for he has clothed me with the garments of salvation, he has covered me with the robe of righteousness, as a bridegroom decks himself with a garland, and as a bride adorns herself with her jewels" (Isaiah 61:10).

change God, but there is great joy in the kingdom of heaven when God's people manifest His righteousness in the earth. We must be aware that wickedness harms those around us but godly deeds serve to strengthen them. The righteousness of Christ, manifested in us, will have a miraculous effect on all the people we rub elbows with every day.

It's worth repeating. Your sin or righteousness does not change who God is in the least, and yet unrighteousness has immediate consequences. Your sin stains all those you interact with every day. Your sin will blemish a whole church. Your sin brings shame upon the very name of Christ. Now consider that the righteousness of Christ at work through you is like a light to those around you. It is warmth that draws them to Christ. It is a flame that burns brightly as a witness of His righteousness manifested in you.

"We have all become like one who is unclean, and all our righteous deeds are like a filthy cloth" (Isaiah 64:6). Here is an important question: If I am the righteousness of God in Jesus Christ, and my own righteousness is likened to a filthy cloth, why should I be concerned for my righteousness which is likened to trash? The answer is simple. If you are truly "in Christ," His righteousness becomes a part of who you are. It's a matter of the love of your heart, and of what you treasure in your heart. If your heart and soul are bound up in the righteousness of Christ, the desire of your heart will be to live, act, work, and serve in the likeness of Christ. You will do what Jesus would do if He were wearing your flip-flops. His righteousness at work in you is of utmost importance because you are "in Christ" and seek to live *in* and not apart from the righteousness of Christ.

Remember that God made us in His image – body, soul, and spirit. For those who are called by His name, He has restored our soul and lit the fire, bringing our spirit to life. Now our body must be brought continually into subjection to the Word of God. We *are* the righteousness of God in Jesus Christ, and still we struggle against the flesh that must constantly be brought into subjection to Christ. To say, "my deeds as are of no consequence" is to compartmentalize, living a part of your life outside of His robe of righteousness. And that's a formula for disaster.

I'm compelled to press you with this question because it's a matter of the love of your heart. It's the same question Jesus asked of Peter in John 21:15: "Simon son of John, do you love me more than these?" We too must answer this question. Do we love the pleasures and so-called fun things of this world more than we love our Lord Jesus?[129]

Stop to think about it. Pause for a moment to examine yourself and take account of your heart's attitude. Jesus was asking Peter, in essence, "Are you going fishing, doing the work you love, or will you feed my sheep because you love me even more?" Jesus pressed Peter three times with penetrating, heart wrenching questions, "Are you going to do what you've always loved doing, or will you nurture my little lambs because of your love for me?" Jesus questioned Peter regarding the love of his heart. Now it's your turn to face your Lord Jesus to answer. What pathway will you choose? What acts of love will you pursue?

It's too easy to say or think that we depend totally on the righteousness of Jesus Christ, and this is certainly good. "For our sake he made him to be sin who knew no sin, so that in him we might become the righteousness of God" (2 Corinthians 5:21). Because of this great truth, from the depths of our heart of hearts will flow righteous deeds in the likeness of Christ.

Now that we've given up on the idea that our own goodness can save us, we can no longer be self-satisfied and secure because of all the good stuff we do on our own. We can delight in the security of being wrapped in Jesus' robe of righteousness and do what His righteousness empowers us to do. Now we have a great sense of purpose, knowing that what we do in Christ has an eternal effect on all those whose lives we touch.

In the epistle of James this truth is made clear: "You see that faith was active along with his works, and faith was brought to completion by the works" (James 2:22). The NIV expresses it slightly differently: "You see that his faith and his actions were working together, and his faith was made complete by what he did."

---

[129] So many of the things we thought were so much fun in our B.C. days (before Christ) in reality were not all that much fun compared to the fun, fellowship and laughter we share with our brothers and sisters in Christ. This is where the fun begins.

Q & A Chapter 33: Faith Proven in Action

1. How are we given righteous standing before a Holy God?

2. What is the effect of our righteous deeds upon those around us every day?

3. Describe your first love, the love of your heart.

Your Mission Journal Notes:

34

The Power of Self-discipline

How many times did mom have to tell you "Don't be scratching at that"? But refusing to scratch an itch requires self-discipline when mom isn't watching. And, of course, doing the stretch exercises the doctor told you to do every day requires self-discipline. You need self-discipline to put a clip on the potato chip bag instead of eating all of them. Self-discipline is saying "no" to yourself to attain a greater good. Disciplining yourself means doing what you don't want to do in order to have what is of greater value.

In the realm of the kingdom of heaven, self-discipline is most important. "For the Spirit God gave us does not make us timid, but gives us power, love and self-discipline" (2 Timothy 1:7). For all those who minister in a spiritual gift, whether it be a gift of helps that enables you to set up tables and chairs for a pot luck, ministering in the gift of prophecy in a gathering of believers, or preparing to teach a Bible study lesson, you cannot constantly pour yourself out without something being poured back in. I'm not talking about a vacation or sabbatical time to rest your body and refresh your mind, even though that is valuable. Like our body, the soul and spirit also need to be recharged. One of God's gifts for strengthening soul and spirit is spiritual disciplines. What I'm speaking of is beyond your ability, and once again, it is mission impossible.

We have a great need for self-discipline simply because of how we are made. Let's look at why that is, how to be self-disciplined, and what spiritual disciplines are.

A person is a three part being because God has made us in His image.[130] We are body, soul and spirit. We all understand what the body is because we have to feed it, exercise it, use it to do our work, and keep it clean and healthy. It's the part of us that gravity effects, keeping our feet planted on the ground. This body is together with soul and spirit, one part of the three-part vessel I'm referring to in this chapter. Spirit, soul and body all require strengthening and refreshing in Christ.

When we minister in our spiritual gifts, we serve in the power of the Spirit of Jesus. Together with the Spirit, we become God's instruments in the kingdom of heaven. But accomplishing this mission requires all of who we are – not just this body, but soul and spirit as well. This Scripture confirms we are a three-part creation. "May the God of peace himself sanctify you entirely; and may your **spirit and soul and body** be kept sound and blameless at the coming of our Lord Jesus Christ" (1Thessalonians 5:23, *emphasis added*).

Soul: "Bless the Lord, O my soul, and all that is within me, bless his holy name" (Psalms 103:1). The soul is not visible to the human eye, but it is evident to human perception. What people can see of your soul are the feelings you have and express, the kind of heart you have toward others, your unique way of thinking, the choices you make that impact those around you, your passions, and your motivations.[131] The soul includes all that affects your social relationships, your interactions with the world, and also how you relate to your Creator. Of course, other people can't read your thoughts or know your inner feelings, but beyond a doubt, what you think and feel in your heart is eventually expressed in some manner or another, and becomes known to others. "The good person out of the good treasure of his heart produces good, and the evil person out of his evil treasure produces evil, for out of the abundance of the heart his mouth speaks" (Luke 5:45). The soul brings body and spirit together and completes the formation of the individual. "Love the Lord your God with all your heart and with all

---

[130] Genesis 1:27

[131] Your heart, mind, will, emotions, personality, expressions of love, sense of humor and even that twinkle in your eye: these are all parts of the soul.

your soul and with all your strength and with all your mind" (Luke 10:27).[132] Loving the Lord is from the soul and each of us has one.

Spirit: Soul and spirit are unique and separate. "Indeed, the word of God is living and active, sharper than any two- edged sword, piercing until it divides soul from spirit" (Hebrews 4:12). Consider the spirit of men and women, the part of you that is brought to life in Christ and made to be a new creation by the power of the cross.[133] The spirit is likened to a seed that is planted in the ground to die, awaiting the light of spring to awaken it.[134] The spirit is like a candle whose light cannot shine, but now by the miracle of the cross of Jesus Christ, the fire is lit and the light shines out.

Your spirit connects with God, worships God, exalts God, serves God, and ministers in God's presence. "God is spirit, and those who worship him must worship in spirit and truth" (John 4:24). Our confusion of soul and spirit comes from the need of our soul and spirit to work together in agreement as we serve in the Kingdom of Heaven and worship a Holy God. If we served in spirit alone, apart from our personalities, varying emotions, ministering without benefit our personal uniqueness, our service would be manifested in cookie cutter style — and that's not God's style. "I praise you, for I am fearfully and wonderfully made. Wonderful are your works; that I know very well" (Psalms 139:14).

This is the spirit of a man or woman and the part of us that connects with the Spirit of God. Our spirit must be strengthened to overcome the weaknesses of the body.

Body: It's doubtful you need to be reminded that without a body, no ministry here on earth is possible.[135] Our spirit and soul are joined together and need this earth suit as the vehicle to minister here on terra firma. Yet we need to keep in mind that we get ourselves into trouble when our flesh (our sinful nature) is strengthened, rather

---

[132] This Scripture depicts heart and soul as one together with our strength and our mind. A look at the Greek meaning of the words helps to see how all of these work together as part of the soul. Heart - καρδία (kardia); soul - ψυχή (psyche); strength - ἰσχύς (ischys); mind - διάνοια (dianoia).

[133] 2 Corinthians 5:17

[134] John 12:24, 1 Corinthians 15:36

[135] Psalms 6:5

than our spirit. When this happens the soul will join together with the flesh, and it's downhill from there, until the Lord intervenes to turn us around. "Live by the Spirit, I say, and do not gratify the desires of the flesh. For what the flesh desires is opposed to the Spirit, and what the Spirit desires is opposed to the flesh; for these are opposed to each other, to prevent you from doing what you want" (Galatians 5:16-17).

The Scriptures emphasize the necessity of strengthening our spirits.[136] The strength we receive from above is a great need among Christians, today more than ever.[137] First, it is necessary that our spirits be strong in Christ to overcome temptations that would bring us to ruin, given half a chance.[138] And certainly, after we pour ourselves out in the ministries of spiritual gifts in service to God's people, we will need to have the Holy Spirit refresh us and strengthen us again and again. We need to keep on being filled with the Spirit of Jesus (see Ephesians 5:18).

God has given us many ways to strengthen our spirits, all of them are important and require us to do our part. First of all, our spirits are fortified in fellowship with other Christians.[139] Partaking of the body and blood of our Lord and Savior Jesus Christ as we share communion in a gathering of the saints unites and strengthens us.[140] Hearing God's Word strengthens our spirits.[141] In exalting, praising, offering thanksgiving in holy worship, prayer and intercession, our spirits are strengthened for victory.[142] As Christians "break bread," having lunch together, the strength of our Lord Jesus is poured out.[143] These are all gifts God has given to build us up. Incredibly, God has given to us even more in the form of spiritual disciplines to strengthen the saints.

Christian disciplines are the "work out your salvation" part: "... work out your own salvation with fear and trembling; for it is God who is at work in you, enabling you both to will and to work for his good

---

[136] "Finally, be strong in the Lord and in the strength of his power" (Ephesians 6:10).
[137] 1 Peter 4:11
[138] 1 Corinthians 10:13
[139] Ecclesiastes 4:12, John 1:7
[140] 1 Corinthians 10:17
[141] Romans 10:17
[142] 2 Chronicles 20:21
[143] Acts 2:42-46

pleasure" (Philippians 2:12). This requires effort on our part. In this effort we work together with the Holy Spirit to transform ourselves, to bring our minds in conformity to Christ, and to restore us to the fullness of life in Christ. This is not effort that earns your salvation, but it is a necessary part of saving sanctification. All Christian disciplines are within our power and bring us to the point of being able to do what we cannot do by our own effort. In spiritual disciplines, we are brought into agreement with God's order of things to further strengthen us.

With this understanding of the created human being, you can now see the importance of spiritual disciplines to the Christian believer, because in them, we are strengthened in spirit, our soul rises up to bless the Lord and our bodies become useful instruments in the kingdom of heaven.

Here are some useful spiritual disciplines that help to strengthen us, refresh us, and restore us in ministries of spiritual gifts:

Solitude and silence are incredibly important and too often neglected. In solitude and silence we find a powerful means of God's grace. In these quiet times we put aside our priorities, burn the to-do list, reschedule the "honey-do" list, hide the cell phone, turn off the T.V., leave behind all the expectations (both our own and others) and allow our exhausted, work-worn bodies some peace and quiet. Take your unmarked Bible on your lap and begin to listen to the Spirit of Jesus minister to you as He speaks words of life into your heart of hearts.

Christian meditation has very little in common with Eastern meditation techniques and transcendental meditation. Christian meditation does not involve techniques to clear the mind in order to achieve a spiritual state of being. We do not employ repetitive mantras. We do not use ritual objects accompanied by rhythmic chants. There is no need to sit in a Lotus position or any other special position. You don't need to burn incense to help you meditate. Breathing in special ways is of no use to a meditating Christian.

For Christians, meditation simply means to focus our attention on God's Word, possibly one verse, thinking it through and listening to the Holy Spirit minister God's truth. It is a kind of thinking that brings us to the very depth of what we are meditating on. It's a kind of thinking that may be likened to creating a mental schematic of a particular Scripture, a godly principle or truth. Praying the Scriptures is one excellent means for Christian meditation.

For your times of meditation, find a quiet place and try to minimize interruptions. Find a relaxing spot to help you enter into the blessings of this discipline. Setting aside a specific amount of time is good, but this is not something you can do with manmade techniques — it is by the Spirit of the Lord alone in agreement with your spirit that makes this possible.

Bible study helps you dig into the depths of God's Word. A new course of personal study will often be inspired in a time of meditation. As a part of your study, the Holy Spirit will lead you to delve into comparative Scriptures to prove or to challenge your meditative thoughts. A useful form of study may be to choose a topic like "the names of God," and search through what all of Scripture says about this.[144] There are many different methods of Bible study, and some are useful. Be encouraged to do what works for you and not get into you-have-to-do-it-this-way style of study.

It is always such a blessing to me when I'm preparing to teach a Bible class, study group or a message, because God pours into me so much more than I can possibly speak of as His words overflow from me. Serving in this way is a beautiful expression of God's nature. My mouth speaks words that are uniquely expressed because God has made my soul to be one of a kind. My ministries are powerful as I serve by means of the Holy Spirit's gifting and empowering work in my spirit. You will also find this to be true. Your ministries will also be powerful and effective beyond what you could have imagined.

Other spiritual disciplines are covered in other chapters. The list in this chapter is not intended as a complete list because there are many powerful, beneficial spiritual disciplines given to us for our good. You will find these topics covered in the chapters as listed.

---

[144] Topical studies are excellent until you become so focused on one topic at the expense of other Scriptural truths that bring balance to the topic you're studying. A word study is excellent until you begin to focus completely on specific words and ignore the whole of Scripture that interpret the word you are examining.

Prayer, Intercessions: See chapter 15.

Fasting: See chapter 17.

Are you feeling empty? Do you have that "burned out" feeling? You're exhausted and your feet feel like you're wearing lead shoes. You just can't resist scratching that itch. Close your eyes and look up, for your Redeemer is right there with you. Jesus strengthens you in spirit and because of this, your soul is made strong. He strengthens your body to reach out your hands in ministry as the hands of Christ Jesus, reaching out to those our Lord Jesus wants to touch. God provides all you need for strengthening you in body, soul and spirit. Be encouraged to make spiritual disciplines a part of your walk with the Lord and you will become stronger in the power of His might to do the work of the kingdom of heaven.

Q & A Chapter 34: The Power of Self-discipline

1. Define Christian disciplines.

2. Why is it so important to strengthen our spirit?

3. What disciplines of the faith will you begin to practice? Why?

Your Mission Journal Notes:

35

Overcomers

"We shall overcome, we shall overcome,
We shall overcome someday;
Oh, deep in my heart, I do believe,
We shall overcome someday."[145]

For the voting rights protesters and segregation demonstrators in the 1960's and 70's, this was a familiar and powerful song that brought their voices together in common cause, a just cause. This song was the cry of their hearts, yearning to be free from the tyranny of repressive discrimination. Their cause was right. Their purpose was to overcome the injustice against those repressed by their fellow man. The lyrics of the song spoke of their yearning to overcome someday, and yet as they stood up for what was right and just, they were already overcomers.

Emphasis is often achieved by repetition. The word "overcome" appears often in this book and is the focus of this chapter. In the book of Revelation there is a phrase repeated seven times in the letters to the churches. We do well to take note of this emphasis. The apostle John was instructed to write a letter to each of the seven churches. He was to write the very words of Jesus as they were given to him. In each of the seven letters one phrase is repeated: "To him who overcomes" (Revelation 2: 7, 11, 17, 26; 3:5, 12, & 21 NIV 1983).

Take up your shield, put on your helmet, grab your sword and strap on your armor. We're going into battle. We, like Noah, are called to overcome in Christ in this present life. "I have said these things

---

[145] Unofficial anthem of American civil rights movement; author unknown.

to you, that in me you may have peace. In the world you will have tribulation. But take heart; I have overcome the world" (John 16:33 ESV). Let's charge forward and we will see what it means to be an overcomer. We will learn the source of our strength. Together, we will identify what we must overcome. It's a battle, but we are not alone in this battle because we stand side by side with our Lord Jesus.

The meaning of the Greek word "overcome" used in the Revelation verses, "νικάω," tells us that God's people are called to be victorious over all temptations and trials that come against the church. The saints are given authority to conquer, overcoming spiritual darkness in the world.[146] The sheep of His pasture are given power to do battle as soldiers of the cross.[147] Christians are given strength to persevere, and we must armor up against the schemes of the devil.[148]

We are all called to overcome, but what is it that we must overcome? Each and every Christian has this battle to fight. We have personal weaknesses and a sin nature to conquer. Every family has challenges to face, to overcome, and turn around for good. The forces of darkness confront every church, and they must be defeated. Nations, states, cities and communities are constantly assailed with ungodly ambitions of those who oppose Christ, and they must be resisted with all the strength and power of the kingdom of heaven. We must overcome the darkness with light. "The light shines in the darkness, and the darkness did not overcome it" (John 1:5).

The best way to illustrate this principle is to relate to the heroes of the faith who overcame. These champions of the faith surround us like a grand stand full of witnesses who cheer us on in this day and age.[149] All of these heroes were people who had great hope, looking forward to what they could not see.[150] They were champions of faith, certain of something they could not touch. In fact, their faith was more than just trusting in something they couldn't feel or see. They lived by faith in spite of crushing, overwhelming circumstances. They

---

[146] Luke 9:1-2
[147] Ephesians 6:10-11
[148] Ephesians 6:11
[149] Hebrews 12:1
[150] Hebrews 11:1

were "up to their necks in alligators," and yet they could see beyond the jaws of death that encompassed them. Let's focus on one Bible hero, Noah.

Noah lived in a time of great violence and evil upon the earth.[151] He was surrounded by a culture of wickedness and corruption. People of his time were self-serving and narcissistic at their best. Whatever they desired, they pursued and took for themselves. But Noah held strong to his faith in a God his eyes could not see.[152] Noah overcame the desires of vain pursuits and self-satisfaction to love and serve the Creator of all heaven and earth. He stood alone in a depraved society. He stood in a pinpoint of light while everyone around him stumbled around in a dark cloud.

Not only did he stand apart, but God also commanded him to do something that just didn't make sense. Why would anyone build a sea-worthy ship 450 feet long, 75 feet wide, and 45 feet high with no ocean in sight? Why would he build a boat made to survive a flood when there had never been such a flood in all of time? Was the word "flood" even in their vocabulary? Yet "Noah did everything just as God commanded him" (Genesis 6:22).

It's difficult for us to grasp Noah's dilemma. He was literally surrounded by the filth of a depraved and evil people. Violence knocked at his door. Corruption badgered him at every step along the way. Wickedness laid a trap in his pathway. Bullying tyrants surely opposed this righteous man at every turn and were elevated to hero status by the people.[153] Uprightness was constantly belittled and Noah was their only target. I can only imagine the crowds chanting as they sneered at Noah's shipbuilding, "The boat won't float, the boat won't float."

Even though inundated by evil on every side, "Noah did everything just as God commanded him." In obedience, Noah conquered, overcame evil, and won a glorious victory. We too are called to be conquerors. "...[I]n all these things we are more than conquerors through him who loved us" (Romans 8:37). God's first command and covenant to

---

[151] Genesis 6:13
[152] Genesis 6:9
[153] Genesis 6:4

His created people was to overcome: "...fill the earth and subdue it" (Genesis 1:28). The Hebrew word for subdue is כָּבַשׁ *kabash* and means to conquer, to overcome, to bring into subjection. This command and covenant stand to this day for all who are called by His name.

To overcome in this world is impossible; but it's totally possible by faith in Jesus Christ, and by the power of the blood of the Lamb. We must not yield to the pressures of the world around us. We must press on to victory, triumphing over the enemies of Cross. We must stand firm, persevering for the faith. As we fight this battle we find that, in reality, Christ has overcome on our behalf. He has already declared victory in the war, but there are still battles he has called us to fight. Armor up!

Have you ever known someone who comes through the door and the whole room brightens? You're sitting in the shadows, fighting back tears and your heart is breaking with grief. Someone enters the room and suddenly it's filled with sunshine. Before long you're wiping away the tears and you can't help but smile and even laugh. This is the hand of God manifested in His people. The Psalmist sings of this truth: "Happy are those whose strength is in you, in whose heart are the highways to Zion. As they go through the valley of Baca they make it a place of springs; the early rain also covers it with pools. They go from strength to strength; the God of gods will be seen in Zion" (Psalms 84:5-7).

What an incredible truth. Our pilgrimage to the mountain of God leads us on a path through the valley of weeping (Baca). Yet, even while drowning in a valley of tears we are called to overcome. Our journey to the courts of the Almighty takes us through the garbage pit (Baca). But while our feet are mucking through the garbage we are empowered to conquer. In place of weeping, we leave behind springs of cool, clear water. Instead of a garbage pit, the trash is replaced with refreshing pools. By the power of God's Word, we build seaworthy ships even when there is nothing but a dried up creek bed in sight.

It just keeps getting better. As overcomers, we are given a great and precious promise. "To the one who is victorious, I will give some of the hidden manna. I will also give that person a white stone with a new name written on it, known only to the one who receives it" (Revelation 2:17).

Grasp hold of this promise in your hand as if you would this white stone. Treasure your new name. Hold fast and be fully satisfied, partaking of His hidden manna. You need God's assurance as you seek to ascend to the courts of God Almighty, because you will be blocked, tripped, scorned, humiliated, gossiped about, abused, accused, misused, lied about, verbally assaulted, threatened, deceived and mistreated; but take joy — take great joy in knowing you can overcome all these obstacles in Christ.

You can taste the sweetness of victory. You are an overcomer in Christ, overcoming as you pass through life on this pilgrimage, turning valleys of weeping into refreshing pools. You stand strong to oppose those who come against soldiers of the kingdom of heaven and strike down fiery darts and words thrown at you — hard as rocks. Lift up your sword and shield. Shout in victorious praise because now you are an overcomer in Christ Jesus.

We must all be prepared because there is coming a time right here in the good old U.S.A. when our lives will be threatened, we will be accused, convicted and imprisoned. No constitution can protect us when evil men prevail. No law or legal system will shield us when good is called evil and evil is called good (Isaiah 5:20). Christian persecution is commonplace all around the world right now and is rapidly accelerating. And yet, even if we are left to shiver on a cold concrete floor behind iron bars, we can be overcomers, victorious in Christ. Those who oppose Christ can snuff the life out of this physical body, but they cannot take away the life we have in Jesus Christ, because we live for eternity and we are overcomers in Christ.

Q & A Chapter 35: Overcomers

1. What are we called to overcome?

2. How do we become overcomers?

3. What promises are given to those who overcome?

Your Mission Journal Notes:

36

Reading the Signs

Blaring T.V. commercials proclaim the healing virtues of a revolutionary new pharmaceutical called "Avotarg." The advertisement shows people dancing that could never dance before. Couples run barefoot on the beach, hand in hand, who had previously lost the ability to run — but "Avotarg" changed their lives. And then, with the two beautiful people still running on the beach, wind in their hair, waves washing gently across their toes, the deep voice an announcer spoils the fun, giving a list of side-effects: loss of appetite, ulcers, and the list goes on and on. It's as if the side effects are sure signs that you're taking this medication.

Did you know that following the Scriptures has side effects? Beyond a doubt there are many good things that result from doing what the Scriptures admonish us to do. Did you catch that? These are good side effects, incredible blessings that come with taking that Scripture prescription. Get your stethoscope and let's check for signs of life in our patient. We'll see that the wonderful medicine labeled "true and real worship" offers incredible side effects as written on the label.

Here is an example of this principle from my personal life. Because I knew how desperately I needed godly wisdom in my daily life, I began each day with reading a chapter from Proverbs — chapters one through thirty-one, corresponding with the day of the month. The side effect was that godly wisdom increasingly showed up in my work and family life. Here's a great example from Scripture. "The fear of the Lord is the beginning of wisdom; all those who practice it have a good understanding. His praise endures forever" (Psalms 111:10). Did you catch the side effect of the fear of the Lord? Wisdom and good understanding. What I love about the healing medicine our Lord gives us is that no disclaimers are required. The side effects are wonderful. Father God forgives our sins, cures our sin disease, and leaves us with fantastic benefits that overflow from our hearts in joy and laughter.

Now let's look at how this truth effects our Christian gatherings. When we come together to hear preaching of the Word, to sing God's praise, and to minister in the gifts of the Spirit, there are wonderful side effects. The Bible calls these "signs."

When the *whole* truth of Scripture is taught in the church, withholding nothing, ignoring not a word, adding nothing to it, and then this whole truth of the Word is received, believed, lived and confessed, signs and wonders will confirm that the true Gospel has been rightly taught and received. "And they devoted themselves to the apostles' teaching and the fellowship, to the breaking of bread and the prayers. And awe came upon every soul, and many wonders and signs were being done through the apostles" (Acts 2:42-43 ESV). See also Mark 6:17.

Do you see it? When we come together to worship in spirit and in truth, when our worship is spiritual and real, when we proclaim the whole truth of Scripture and live the Scripture, signs and wonders are the side effect. This is not a cause and effect kind of thing. It's God's mighty hand at work among His people as a sure sign that we have completely stepped under the "umbrella" of His Word, where His showers of blessing fall upon us. One great side effect, or a sign of true worship in a gathering of Christians, is the ministry of spiritual gifts. People of the congregation using the spiritual gifts of prophecy, words of wisdom, words of knowledge, singing in the spirit, and so many more beautiful expressions of ministry: these ministries will take place as a sign of true worship.

But a note of caution is in order. When the "side effects" are not manifested in a church, too often we are tempted to manufacture them to reassure ourselves of God's presence. Over and over I've witnessed people fake it after being prayed for to receive God's provision or His healing touch. It's as if they feel a need to immediately proclaim an answer to prayer for the benefit of those who prayed. It's like they are on the "Jesus is Real" reality show and they're on camera. They try so hard to walk without a limp. They work at letting go of their walker. It's a natural, emotional response, as if they need to tell those who prayed, "You're prayers are so powerful." The truth is, prayers are powerful and they are heard by an Almighty, powerful God. There is no need to attempt to manufacture something. Simply rest in it and wait upon God's "Yes."

There is no need to proclaim what is not yet true unless, of course, it begins to be true in the present moment. Be encouraged to thankfully look to a loving God and our Good Shepherd to receive his blessed touch. There is no need to hype the moment or fake the good side effects. Just believe, receive, and revel in it. You will see the manifestation of God's touch in His best time.

When you see God's signs and wonders at work in His church and when you see ministries of spiritual gifts in the church, you may be assured that the whole of Scripture has been taught, believed, and received by those who God has called to gather with you in your assembly of believers.[154] There is no need for manufactured, captivating, trumped proclamations of what has not happened. Our Lord, God and Savior longs to show His living, active presence among His people as a sign that His resurrection power is at work, even today.

"And these signs will accompany those who believe" (Mark 16:17).

Q & A Chapter 36: Reading the Signs

1. What signs indicate that the whole truth of Scripture is being taught, received, lived, and confessed?

2. What is the "side effect" of the fear of the Lord?

---

[154] I'm not saying that if you don't see something spectacular happen in church every Sunday, your worship isn't spiritual and real. Unrealistic expectations of the extraordinary quickly become self-defeating and often self-serving.

3. When the ministries and service of spiritual gifts are evident in a gathering of believers, what can you know to be true about the people who are gathered?

Your Mission Journal Notes:

37

Tested and Tried

Daddy held Jimmy under his tiny arms, helping him to steady his feet so he could step out on his own — to take his first steps. His fuzzy jammies wiggled and jostled with excitement and his stocking feet were dancing. Mommy held her breath and with hands to her face, she cried out, "Don't let him fall." Jimmy had been trying to walk for several days now, letting go of the coffee table while trying to get his feet to step out. Now Daddy let go, but held his hands close. At first Jimmy just stood there and wobbled a bit. And then Mom squealed and laughed while taking video with her cell phone. She captured Jimmy taking his first steps. Two and a half faltering steps on his own before Dad, who was always right behind him, caught him in a fall.

Are you feeling abandoned? Feeling alone, with no one to hear you crying out? Is there anyone to catch you in a fall? You're not alone. How many times, I can't count, I've felt the hand of God withdrawn from me for a time. My first inclination was to think, "What is my sin?" I found my reassurance in God's Word: "Consider it pure joy, my brothers and sisters, whenever you face trials of many kinds, because you know that the testing of your faith produces perseverance" (James 1:2-3). Indeed, little Jimmy would not have walked if Daddy hadn't taken his hands away for a moment.

This "tested and tried" road might feel bumpy, but God accomplishes the good work of sanctification in us as He tests us. His purpose is good, refining us like precious metal, making us ready, as a bride prepared for her bridegroom. Heroes of the faith were tested and tried. When we fall down — God's mercy and forgiveness are revealed. Our faith is strengthened knowing that God works in this way, withdrawing His hand only for a moment.

Our impurities come to the surface when we are tested. When God tests us, what is hidden is revealed. In the times when God lets go and steps back, our repressed desires boil up to prove what is in our hearts. "Search me, God, and know my heart; test me and know my anxious thoughts. See if there is any offensive way in me, and lead me in the way everlasting" (Psalms 139:23).

When Daddy let go of little Jimmy it became perfectly evident that what was in Jimmy's heart was to walk on his own. Mommy and Daddy had been encouraging him, "Come to daddy! Come to mommy," holding out their hands. When dad let go, Jimmy did what was in his heart to do. And it was good.

We see an example of a sin revealing test played out in Scripture: "But when envoys were sent by the rulers of Babylon to ask [King Hezekiah] about the miraculous sign that had occurred in the land, God left him to test him and to know everything that was in his heart" (2 Chronicles 32:31). Do you see what happened? In an opportune moment, God withdrew his hand from King Hezekiah to reveal what was in his heart. God already knew what was in the king's heart, but now God brought it to the surface to be revealed so his sin could be confessed and forgiven.

We are tested in many ways. Fear comes over us, testing our faith, just as Peter was tested at Jesus' trial before the crucifixion.[155] Joseph was tested, being sold into slavery and then thrown into prison.[156] The pain of physical disorders can test us. Potentially wrongful relationships may test us. The desire for power and control can make its demands upon us. Loss of those who are precious to us leaves a huge void that tests us to the core. I've grieved and prayed with dear friends who were tested with fears of rejection. And the greatest of

---

[155] Matthew 26:69-75
[156] Genesis 39:20

all tests comes when Christians are persecuted for their faith in Jesus Christ.[157]

Many times I've been tempted to be prideful. I've thought, "Wow, I'm doing great." I begin to think about the bad things I haven't been doing that I used to do. I throw my shoulder out of joint patting myself on the back for all the wonderful things *I'm* doing. *I* teach Sunday school, *I* lead a Bible study group, *I* go to the prayer time before Sunday morning services, and *I* am just doing so many grand things. This may be true, but the deep, hidden things in my heart must be exposed to the light. What is it that lurks in the dark corners of my being like a cockroach that hides, waiting for the lights to go out?

My flesh waits for an opportunity to live in the limelight. My natural man is filled with ungodly desires, waiting for a chance to dash about when the lights are turned off. These are the things that God reveals when he draws back his protective hand. In these moments the Holy Spirit withdraws His restraining influence and our hidden weaknesses are revealed.

God's purpose in pulling back is to open my eyes to see what is lurking in the dark corners of my heart. Beyond the shadow of doubt, I know that there are many things God has not yet dealt with in my life. God, in His mercy, does not require that we conquer these things in one day, or even in a year. If we had all of our waywardness revealed to us at once, we would feel totally overwhelmed, discouraged and want to give up. God in His mercy works with us, one issue at a time. He is merciful and gracious and His loving kindness is abundant.

God did not require the tribes of Israel to conquer the land of Canaan all at once. "But I will not drive them out in a single year, because the land would become desolate and the wild animals too numerous for you. Little by little I will drive them out before you, until

---

[157] We must be clear. God does not make someone ill. God does not inflict us with pain. God will not put us too close to an irresistible relationship. God will not put servile fear in our hearts. "When tempted, no one should say, 'God is tempting me.' For God cannot be tempted by evil, nor does he tempt anyone; but each person is tempted when they are dragged away by their own evil desire and enticed. Then, after desire has conceived, it gives birth to sin; and sin, when it is full- grown, gives birth to death" (James 1:13-15). Always remember and take comfort that when these grievous things happen to us, God uses them for good (Genesis 50:20).

you have increased enough to take possession of the land" (Exodus 23:29). What a gracious and merciful God we serve. He is patient, compassionate, and longsuffering as He waits while we grow in the faith.

Even the thought of God pulling back the Presence of His Holy Spirit from me is a frightening prospect. I have nightmarish memories of the many times temptation raised its ugly head and tripped me up. I must remind myself that temptation was always resistible when I was at my strongest. The temptations that tripped me up were not in my area of strength but in my weakness; the things I kept secret, things I denied until what was in my heart boiled to the surface. I'm well acquainted with many of my frailties. The temptations that come my way are all too familiar to me. Just the thought of God pulling back his protective covering that keeps me from succumbing to these sins is too much for me to think about because I know that I'm fallible. I have no strength of my own. Lord, have mercy.

But there is great hope that I can grab onto like a lifeline. I cling to God's sure promise; "I will never leave you nor forsake you."[158] This promise assures me He is always close by, ready to catch me when I fall. I know the Rock on which my feet are planted. "No temptation has overtaken you except what is common to mankind. And God is faithful; he will not let you be tempted beyond what you can bear. But when you are tempted, he will also provide a way out so that you can endure it" (1 Corinthians 10:13).

It strengthens me to personalize this truth to remind myself of this great promise: "God will not let Cho be tempted beyond what Cho can bear." Why then did I fall into sin? It was because of my own evil desire that I refused to confess, keeping it secreted away in some dark corner in my heart. It was because, upon becoming aware of my sin, I did the Adam thing and attempted to cover it up with a fig leaf. And fig leaf moments always lead to my undoing.

I'm sighing with relief as I write this. My God is awesome. Never will I be tempted beyond what I can, in Christ, resist. Never! He is my strength to resist. He reveals the secrets of my heart for my own good

---

[158] Deuteronomy 31:6, Hebrews 13:5

by drawing back His hand for a time. He is the hope of my salvation. God lovingly reveals my sin to me in times of testing. The Spirit of God gives me a contrite heart, leading me to repent and confess my sin. God forgives me of my sin, showing me abundant mercy. By the blood of my Lord Jesus I'm washed clean of the stain of my sin. He restores my soul, He heals my sin sickness, He gets rid of the fig leaves[159] I've used to cover up my sins and He wraps me in His robe of righteousness, presenting me to the Father completely forgiven and restored. In all this there is overwhelming joy. "Consider it pure joy, my brothers and sisters, whenever you face trials of many kinds, because you know that the testing of your faith produces perseverance. Let perseverance finish its work so that you may be mature and complete, not lacking anything" (James 1:2-4).

Blessed be the Name of the Lord, for He is mighty in battle. "Indeed, we live as human beings, but we do not wage war according to human standards; for the weapons of our warfare are not merely human, but they have divine power to destroy strongholds" (2 Corinthians 10:3).

The great cover-up is over. No more fig leaf moments. When God withdraws His hand from you, for just a moment, what is in your heart to do will be revealed — to your great benefit. With your sin revealed, you can confess it and receive God's forgiveness, mercy and cleansing. The Lord's testing will happen again and again as you walk with the Lord because He does not require you to conquer all your sin in one day. When the test comes your way, you will feel as if you are being tested by fire — but it is a refining fire that reveals pure gold. God is your strength in these times, and He is always close by. Rest assured, He will hold His hands close to you as you take your steps of faith.[160]

---

[159] Genesis 3:7

[160] Additional guiding scriptures: 2 Chronicles 32:31, Psalms 7:9, Psalms 11:5.

Q & A Chapter 37: Tested and Tried

1. What is God's purpose in testing us?

2. What good things does God accomplish in us as He pulls back his hand for a moment?

3. In whom do you find strength in times of testing?

Your Mission Journal Notes:

38

Through Water and Fire

From beginning to end, from Genesis to Revelation, we witness water and fire in the hand of God, the Creator of all heaven and earth. God used water to form the earth: "...an earth was formed out of water and by means of water" (2 Peter 3:5). In Genesis chapter seven, God cleaned up a violent, corrupt world in a great flood that encompassed the whole earth. Modern science has discovered that our bodies consist of about nine-tenths water, while newborn babies are born with an even higher percentage of water. Jesus used dust and spittle (water from His mouth) to heal a man born blind,[161] creating whole new eyes for him. This is the power of an Almighty Creator God using the element of water, which He created and then used to create the heavens and the earth.

So, put on your fireproof armor, grab your life jacket, and let's jump into the fire and water of God's Word. Our goal is to see what God has provided as the means for us to come to Him, made pure and whole, and empowered to do the work of the kingdom of heaven. Through water we are cleansed, and through fire we are refined and empowered. God has planned to bring us into His presence "...to comfort all who mourn, and provide for those who grieve in Zion — to bestow on them a crown of beauty instead of ashes, the oil of joy instead of mourning, and a garment of praise instead of a spirit of despair" (Isaiah 61:2-3 NIV).

In the age of the church, by means of water and the Word, God makes us whole new creations in Christ. "He saved us, not because

---

[161] John 9:1-12

227

of any works of righteousness that we had done, but according to his mercy, through the water of rebirth and renewal by the Holy Spirit" (Titus 3:5). By means of baptism in water we become new born babies in the realm of the Spirit. And by words God has spoken through the apostles and prophets, as recorded in Scripture, we are baptized into fellowship with Christ and His church — the body of Christ. "You have been born anew, not of perishable but of imperishable seed, through the living and enduring word of God" (1 Peter 1:23). In the waters of baptism and the words Christ Jesus proclaimed, we are made one with the Father, Son and Holy Spirit, in whose name we are baptized.

By means of the most basic element of creation, water, and by means of His spoken Word, an incredible miracle is accomplished in everyone who answers God's call. The heavens and earth came into being by His Word and this same miraculous Word restores us to right standing and fellowship with our Creator God. Consider the power of His Word as He spoke to bring all His creation into existence. The Word is no less mighty, no less present, no less active among God's people today. As time passes, the Light of creation has not dimmed. "In the beginning was the Word, and the Word was with God, and the Word was God. He was with God in the beginning. Through him all things were made; without him nothing was made that has been made. In him was life, and that life was the light of all mankind" (John 1:1-4).

All who are called out of the world's darkness into God's glorious light are led by the Spirit to be baptized by means of water and the Word. In baptism, we are made a new creation in Christ. In holy baptism, we are adopted into the family of God and given a new name.

God also works through fire. Indeed, He is God who speaks out of fire.[162] The first mention of fire is found the first book in the Bible. Adam's sin separated him from the fellowship he had known, walking together in the cool of the day in sweet communion with his Heavenly Father. The destructiveness and divisive power of sin drove Adam and Eve from this perfect paradise, never to see it again in their lifetimes on earth. "He drove out the man; and at the east of the garden of Eden he placed the cherubim, and a sword flaming and turning to guard the

---

[162] Deuteronomy 4:33

228

way to the tree of life" (Genesis 3:24). God set a guard over the garden with a blazing sword brandished at the entrance, so they might not enter and eat of the tree of life.[163]

In Daniel's prophetic writings, he tells of a "river of fire" flowing from God's presence.[164] In Revelation we look on as the Apostle John hears a voice behind him:

> *"Then I turned to see whose voice it was that spoke to me, and on turning I saw seven golden lampstands, and in the midst of the lampstands I saw one like the Son of Man, clothed with a long robe and with a golden sash across his chest. His head and his hair were white as white wool, white as snow; his eyes were like a flame of fire, his feet were like burnished bronze, refined as in a furnace, and his voice was like the sound of many waters. In his right hand he held seven stars, and from his mouth came a sharp, two- edged sword, and his face was like the sun shining with full force." (Revelation 1:12-16)*

What the Apostle John witnessed is clearly a revelation of Jesus Christ, His nature, and His blazing presence. He didn't see a figurative representation or a 3-D projection of Jesus the Christ. John's eyes were opened to what was present and real in the spiritual realm. We can be sure that John wrote down exactly, precisely what he saw, because he was instructed, "Write in a book what you see and send it to the seven churches" (Revelation 1:11). He didn't write an allegory of what he saw. He didn't record impressions of what he observed. John wrote to describe exactly what he saw, just as he was instructed.

Walk with me through this Scripture in Revelation. Let us rightly divide[165] the Scriptures to know the truth, so that we too

---

[163] The tree of life is not inaccessible. Jesus is the way to the Tree of Life, for indeed He is the Tree of Life. He is the Way and the Truth and the Life.

[164] Daniel 7:10

[165] The KJV uses the words, "rightly dividing" while the NSRV translates this "rightly explaining" and the NIV uses "Correctly handling." I believe "Rightly dividing" is inspired in that as we give out, pass on and proclaim God's Word (like the five loaves and two fish Jesus used to feed the five thousand,) the Word is divided and multiplied to supply all those in need. And yet, it is never depleted or diminished.

may see the revelation of Jesus Christ by means of the writings of the Apostle John. [Notes added in italics.] "Then I turned to see whose voice it was that spoke to me, and on turning I saw seven golden lampstands, *[Seven lampstands, with seven flames of fire[166]]*, and in the midst of the lampstands I saw one like the Son of Man, clothed with a long robe and with a golden sash across his chest. His head and his hair were white as white wool, white as snow; his eyes were like a flame of fire *[His eyes blazed with flames of fire – John saw fire in His eyes]*, his feet were like bronze, refined as in a furnace *[Refined in a furnace of fire, hot as a refining fire, and shimmering with the light of refining fire]*, and his voice was like the sound of many waters. In his right hand he held seven stars *[blazing, burning, flaming stars of light]*, and from his mouth came a sharp, two-edged sword, and his face was like the sun shining with full force *[The earth's sun flames so brightly that we cannot look straight into it. The light of His face blazed like the sun. The light of his face was not a reflection of light like the moon, but like the suns glowing light]*."

There was a hint of this blazing fire in the face of Moses: "When Aaron and all the Israelites saw Moses, the skin of his face was shining, and they were afraid to come near him" (Exodus 34:30). The effect of this shining fire in the face of Jesus had a similar effect upon John as he turned to see who was speaking to him: "When I saw him, I fell at his feet as though dead" (Revelation 1:17).

This mystery of God is worth the effort necessary to understand it. We must dig into the Scriptures to know the truth of the nature of God whom we serve. The earth was formed by water and the earth will be cleansed by fire, burning up the very elements of the earth. "But the day of the Lord will come like a thief, and then the heavens will pass away with a loud noise, and the elements will be dissolved with fire, and the earth and everything that is done on it will be disclosed" (2 Peter 3:10). Disclosed? Everything done on the earth, revealed? How can this be? All that has been done on the earth by men and women of every century will be revealed by fire. It will be tested by fire. For those whose work is nothing but wood, hay, and stubble, they would

---

[166] Zechariah 4:2.

do well if left with a few ashes to hold in their hands. For those who make straw in this life, it will turn to nothing but smoking embers.

But take heart, for we have the greatest of hope. As we reach out with empty hands, God is a God of grace and mercy. "Is not this man a burning stick snatched from the fire?" (Zechariah 3:2 NIV). Take comfort, for those with ashes in their hands may be like that smoldering stick snatched from the fire. Paul confirms the words of Zechariah. "If it is burned up, the builder will suffer loss but yet will be saved — even though only as one escaping through the flames"[167] (1 Corinthians 3:15).

God's plan is to take these weak, fallen human creations of His and prepare them to withstand the testing of fire and enter through the Gate and to partake of the Tree of Life. The prophets proclaimed this great day. "When you walk through the fire, you will not be burned, the flames will not set you ablaze" (Isaiah 43:3). A beautiful example of this is found in chapter three of the book of Daniel. Because three Jewish administrators refused to bow down to worship the king's golden statue, the monarch went into a rage and commanded that they be thrown into a furnace stoked seven times hotter just for them. In this Biblical account we're given a picture of coming through the fire just as Isaiah proclaimed. The end of their story is a great testimony of God's power and might to save.

> *"So Shadrach, Meshach, and Abednego came out from the fire. And the satraps, the prefects, the governors, and the king's counselors gathered together and saw that the fire had not had any power over the bodies of those men; the hair of their heads was not singed, their tunics were not harmed, and not even the smell of fire came from them." (Daniel 3:26-27)*[168]

The Lord set His guardian cherub at the entrance to the Tree of Life, with a flaming sword in hand to guard the way. But now we have

---

[167] Read 1 Corinthians 3:10-15.

[168] I heard of a young mom whose children loved this story as their favorite for bedtime. But she renamed it as the story of Shadrach, Meshach and To-bed-we-go.

a way that is made possible by our Lord and Savior Jesus Christ. He prepares us to pass through the fire, to test our metal, so to speak.

> "Now if anyone builds on the foundation with gold, silver, precious stones, wood, hay, straw — the work of each builder will become visible, for the Day will disclose it, because it will be revealed with fire, and the fire will test what sort of work each has done. If what has been built on the foundation survives, the builder will receive a reward. If the work is burned up, the builder will suffer loss; the builder will be saved, but only as through fire." (1 Corinthians 3:12-15)

The truth of this is confirmed again.

> "The sinners in Zion are terrified; trembling grips the godless: 'Who of us can dwell with the consuming fire? Who of us can dwell with everlasting burning?' Those who walk righteously and speak what is right, who reject gain from extortion and keep their hands from accepting bribes, who stop their ears against plots of murder and shut their eyes against contemplating evil — they are the ones who will dwell on the heights, whose refuge will be the mountain fortress. Their bread will be supplied, and water will not fail them. Your eyes will see the king in his beauty and view a land that stretches afar." (Isaiah 33:14-17)

Once again, God reveals His very nature to us and we see that He is a consuming fire. Who of us can approach God, who is a refining inferno? Isaiah tells us that it is he who walks righteously and speaks what is right will dwell on the heights, that is, in Mount Zion the mountain of God.

I'll speak for myself. I'm certainly not a man who always walks righteously and always speaks rightly. And yet, I have an eternal hope in Jesus Christ, because He is my righteousness and in Him I walk righteously and speak what is right. "God made him who had no sin to be sin for us, so that in him we might become the righteousness of God" (2 Corinthians 5:21). And in Christ I will see the King in His beauty and view a land that stretches afar, for I pass through the fire, that flaming sword brandished at the entrance of the Tree of Life to partake of Christ in His fullness. The wood, the chaff, and the straw have been burned to ashes and what remains is precious metal and precious stones that may come into the presence of our God who is a consuming fire. Now we may bring what is acceptable to be cast before Him as our offering of love and devotion.

It's important to see this truth. A brandished, flaming sword protects the way to the Tree of Life, but Jesus made a way for us to enter and partake of this life-giving tree. We must pass through the fire to test the work of our hands. Fire tests what we have done to reveal what is like precious metal. Is our service the work of the Spirit, accomplished by the power of the Spirit and by the anointing of the Spirit? Or is it a good work done by our own strength, by our own initiative, by our own means? All the things we do will be tested and proved as we pass through the fire. Elijah saw this protective blaze first hand as chariots of fire were all around him, to protect him from his enemies.[169]

This is our great hope. By water and through fire we are prepared to come into God's holy presence and to our eternal promised land where neither tear nor sorrow will weigh upon us. Think about it. Did Jesus baptize anyone with water? There is certainly no record of it. But John the Baptist proclaimed, "I baptize you with water for repentance, but one who is more powerful than I is coming after me; I am not worthy to carry his sandals. He will baptize you with the Holy Spirit and fire" (Luke 3:16).

By means of the waters of baptism we become a new creation in Christ. Through the testing, purifying fire of the Holy Spirit, we may enter His blessed presence. And now our Lord Jesus Christ baptizes us with the Holy Spirit and with fire. This Holy Spirit fire is a baptism that lights a flame in you to gift and empower you for works of service for the good of His church. God's fire burning in you gives you the power necessary to minister in the sanctuary before a Holy God — that is, to do the work of the church as an anointed, worshipful ministry before the Lord God Almighty.

---

[169] 2 Kings 6: 17

This baptism with fire is a baptism of love. "Place me like a seal over your heart, like a seal on your arm; for love is as strong as death, its jealousy unyielding as the grave. It burns like blazing fire, like a mighty flame. Many waters cannot quench love; rivers cannot sweep it away" (Song of Songs 8:6-7 NIV).

Come be baptized in the fire of His overwhelming love. The fire of His love protects you from the burning of His just and rightful wrath. This love will guard you like a shield that is formed with the elements of His tender, protective jealousy.[170] His fire will flare up in your heart of hearts cleansing you of the wood, hay, and stubble.

Elijah, God's prophet in Israel, gave a beautiful demonstration of water and fire brought together to fulfill God's purpose. As the people gathered on Mount Carmel, he told them:

> "'Fill four large jars with water and pour it on the offering and on the wood.' 'Do it again,' he said, and they did it again. 'Do it a third time,' he ordered, and they did it the third time. The water ran down around the altar and even filled the trench. At the time of sacrifice, the prophet Elijah stepped forward and prayed: 'Lord, the God of Abraham, Isaac and Israel, let it be known today that you are God in Israel and that I am your servant and have done all these things at your command. Answer me, Lord, answer me, so these people will know that you, Lord, are God, and that you are turning their hearts back again.' Then the fire of the Lord fell and burned up the sacrifice, the wood, the stones and the soil, and also licked up the water in the trench. When all the people saw this, they fell prostrate and cried, 'The Lord — he is God! The Lord — he is God!'" (I Kings 18:33-39)

Water and Fire in the hands of God performs a great, life-changing miracle in all who believe in the Lord, Jesus Christ. In the waters of baptism He washes us to make us pure and whole, washing away the

---

[170] We must understand that God's tender jealousy is not a humanlike destructive jealousy, but a jealousy that is altruistic, gentle and protective.

ashes and giving beauty in its place. Baptismal water cleanses us, preparing us to be baptized in His holy fire — prepared for works of service and ministry within the body of Christ, the church, so that what we do in Christ is of eternal effect and everlasting value.

On Elijah's altar, the water prepared the altar for God's consuming fire. We too are prepared as a living sacrifice,[171] i.e. made one with Christ, in the waters of baptism. Drenched in water three times; in the name of the Father, Son and Holy Spirit; now prepared for being baptized by our Lord Jesus, baptized by fire. "...[W]e went through fire and through water; yet you have brought us out to a place of abundance" (Psalms 66:12).

Q & A Chapter 38: Through Water and Fire

1. Describe the power of the water and God's Word brought together in baptism.

2. How will fire disclose or reveal what you have done in your life?

3. What materials will you use to build with so they can pass the test of fire?

Your Mission Journal Notes:

---

[171] Romans 12:1

39

Depending upon Christ Alone

Robins feed worms and bugs to their hatchlings until they grow strong enough to fly away on their own. The mountain lion teaches her cubs to fend for themselves before they go off to carve out their own territory. The young eagle is pushed from the nest at the top of the cliff and must fly to survive on its own. In this temporal world, a child grows up to become independent of his or her parents. So then, wouldn't it be natural for us to become more independent as we mature in the Lord?

The above examples give us a small picture of nature's way of forcing the young ones to venture out on their own, but this is not a perfect picture of the Spirit of the Father with His children. He commands us to grow up, to be mature, and to totally depend upon Him rather than being independent or self-dependent. In fact, as we mature, we see clearly our weaknesses and learn that everything we are called to do depends upon Christ alone. This is foundational for Christian maturity. Depending upon Christ alone is essential to prepare us for the work, service, and ministries God has prepared in advance for us to do.[172] Mature dependence is what we will explore in this chapter.

In this I find a great dichotomy. The question occurs to me. Are we more independent or dependent as we grow up in Christ? We learn that our dependence upon Christ is not an infantile kind of dependence. It's not like a baby's dependence, crying out because they're hungry

---

[172] Ephesians 2:10

and need milk. In fact, leaning on Christ is not a sign of weakness, but a sign of strength. So what is it? How should we describe it?

Depending on Christ is walking in the Spirit.[173] It is trust in a living Redeemer. It is God confidence. It is hope that is eternal. It is saving faith in a risen Savior. But where is the line to be drawn between newborn dependence and mature dependence?

Scriptures instruct us to have a child-like faith,[174] and yet we are also taught to be mature, to get beyond the milk of the Word and start chewing on some solid food. Is there a conflict that we must have child-like faith and yet stop being childish and eat real meat? "When I was a child, I spoke like a child, I thought like a child, I reasoned like a child; when I became an adult, I put an end to childish ways" (1 Corinthians 13:11). The apostle Peter instructs us to grow up "in the grace and knowledge of our Lord and Savior Jesus Christ" (2 Peter 3:18).

Have you ever known someone who was mature and yet remained vulnerable, with a child-like innocence about her? It's a rare combination that comes from a lot of Holy Spirit refining to remove the rough edges.

We are like wild olive branches, grafted into the true Olive Tree, who is Jesus Christ.[175] We are like shriveled twigs, brought to life as we are joined to the True Vine and given sustenance to bear good fruit. We are like the seed planted in fallow ground, and provided with water, sun, and nourishment to grow and bear, some thirty, some sixty and some a hundred times what was sown in the ground.[176] And yet we are not automatons, robots, or puppets with strings attached to our limbs to control our every movement. We are not like ventriloquist dummies that have no voices of their own. This is the dichotomy of Christian freedom and dependence upon Christ.

To accomplish God's eternal purpose for us, we need to be grafted into (baptized into) the eternal, Almighty God. God has no desire to pull our strings or make us move around, run and jump with a joystick from heaven. Instead, he uses unique and flawed people; people who

---

[173] Galatians 5:16
[174] Matthew 18:3
[175] Romans 11:24
[176] Matthew 13:8

freely choose right and wrong, and choose to abide in Him, to walk in the Spirit, and to press forward in Christ, by faith.

Impossible? Totally possible in Christ! When I'm exhausted, Christ is strength in me.[177] When I'm overwhelmed, Christ Jesus lifts the burden from me.[178] When I'm fearful, Christ's love drives out the fear.[179] When I'm sick, in Christ I find healing power.[180] When I'm discouraged, I have courage in Christ.[181] When I'm attacked and insulted, my Lord Jesus is my shield and defender.[182] I'm wringing my hands in an anxious sweat, His hand touches me to comfort.[183] In my weakness, Christ's power is made known.[184] Impossible odds overwhelm me, but it becomes possible to overcome in Christ.[185] God calls me to do what I cannot otherwise do, and Christ Jesus sends His Holy Spirit to gift and empower me for the work of His kingdom.

In every circumstance, in any impossible difficulty you face, Christ is beside you, indwelling you, enveloping you, and surrounding you.[186] All who are in Christ are called to come before a Holy God with childlike trust, holding nothing back.[187] We are instructed to be teachable[188] and walk humbly with our God.[189] Allow the Holy Spirit to instruct your heart even in the night[190] and awaken your ears to be instructed in the morning.[191] Chew on the meat of the Word and begin to mature in Christ.[192] Ask for what you need! The Good Shepherd will give you His armor, His shield, and His sword to do battle against the forces of

---

[177] Psalms 46:1
[178] 1 Peter 5:7
[179] 1 John 4:18
[180] Jeremiah 17:14, Psalms 30:2
[181] Psalms 31:24, Deuteronomy 31:6
[182] Psalms 28:7
[183] Philippians 2:1
[184] 2 Corinthians 12:9
[185] Philippians 4:13
[186] 1 Corinthians 12:9, God's name is El-Shaddai, meaning All Sufficient One or Almighty One. Genesis 17:1
[187] Luke 18:17
[188] 2 Timothy 2:15
[189] Micah 6:8
[190] Psalms 16:7
[191] Isaiah 50:4
[192] Hebrews 5:14

darkness that would assault you. "Finally, be strong in the Lord and in the strength of his power" (Ephesians 6:10). He is El-Shaddai, your All Sufficient One. Remain in Him.

This is the work of our Lord and Savior Jesus Christ in you. With a simple, child-like faith you can depend on Him, trusting your Lord Jesus Christ because you are in Him and He is in you. As you stand on the Rock, you will be at rest, at peace, comforted while at the same time strengthened and prepared to be mighty in battle – all because you abide in Christ.

Q & A Chapter 39: Depending on Christ Alone

1. Describe mature dependence.

2. How is it possible to have child-like faith and to be mature as the same time — putting aside childish ways?

3. Describe the power you find as you depend on Christ alone.

Your Mission Journal Notes:

40

Knowing What is of God

The call came from my national sales manager. I could hardly believe what he was offering. It was the perfect stepping-stone to building my career. My employer offered me a position as head of a new company division, adding a new product line for our marketing department. I wasn't excited about moving to Dallas, but there are much worse places to live.

I told my boss, "Give me two days to give you an answer." I prayed, asking to know the heart of God in the matter. Beyond a doubt, my answer would determine my future with the company, because turning down a major promotion in our corporate culture meant they would offer no further opportunities — it was a deal breaker.

The answer I got from the Lord was "No." I was not to accept the offer. It bothered me, because I didn't know why, but I made the phone call and let them know I wouldn't be moving to corporate headquarters. For six months I puzzled about why, because it seemed like such a good move for me. Then I got the news of a corporate take over. A larger conglomerate was buying us out and planned to sell our division to another company. Not only would I have been out of a job, but I would also have been stuck in Dallas during an oil slump. It would have been bad in every way and the good Lord rescued me from disaster.

So often, Christians struggle to know what God desires of them. We struggle to know the will of God in personal circumstances. We struggle with questions like, "Do we accept the job offer that would require uprooting the family? Do we risk our retirement savings to invest in church bonds? Should we step up and take on the responsibility of teaching the fourth grade Sunday school class? Is it good to serve as head usher and have to be at church every Sunday, giving up family weekend outings?" How can we know what is good and right in every circumstance? Let's examine the Scripture to see what God has for us, to guide us, and to give us wisdom so we can charge into battle with great confidence.

In the book of James we find our first clue to the answer. "If you lack wisdom..... ASK!" Ask for wisdom. The wisdom we seek is simply to know or discern what is right and what is wrong. Wisdom is the means for getting on the right track in every day decisions and especially life changing decisions. Wisdom is light for your pathway.

There are times in each of our lives when things happen around us that stir up turmoil in our spirits. At these times we turn to the Giver of Wisdom to seek the mind of Christ in the matter. We search the Scriptures for insights, for direction, for enlightenment. And our search is sure to provide us with the wisdom we need so we can know the direction we ought to go.

My church once called a new pastor who came with a new message to the church. He explained the Scriptures in a way that seemed to enlighten us to "truths" that we had never heard before. He connected Scriptures that we never connected before. He created a new excitement by digging into the Scriptures and discovering things we might have missed. But something kept nagging at my spirit. Something was grating in my soul. A part of me liked what I heard. This was exciting stuff that I never knew was possible. It was like an unexpected gift.

But was it of God? Was the message truly consistent with God's Word and could it stand the test of Scripture? Could it pass the test of truth when evaluated like when the prophet Amos tested God's people with God's plumb line?[193]

The first line of defense in a local body of Christian believers is God's Word, the Holy Scriptures. God also gives us other lines of defense, like the spiritual gift of discernment. God, in His wisdom and goodness, has ordained this precious gift to be active and working

---

[193] Amos 7:7—9

in every local body of believers. It is not a gift without purpose, for God knows our needs even before we know and he has prepared this good gift for each and every local church, and for the wellbeing of the church. This gift is one line of defense to protect us from those who would deceive and lead us astray.

The next line of defense is common discernment. This is discernment that is based upon knowledge that is washed in prayer and strengthened by the power of God's living Word. There are clues that we can use to discern what is right and what is wrong. Test these by the truth of Scripture to see how they may apply to your need for wisdom and discernment in your local body of believers.

What are you concerned about in your home church? You can know by the testing of Scripture whether it is right and good. Scripture is the plumb line for us to know if a church is walking in the truth or beginning to stray. There are often warning signs to alert us. When we see the warning signs, we do well to dig into the Word and get on our knees to prayerfully seek the Spirit for guidance. Some of the warning signs are listed here.

a. Is your church dependent upon one particular charismatic leader?[194] Would your church fall apart without the overwhelming strength and energies of one person?[195]
b. Has one person pushed himself to the forefront by his or her own doing?[196]
c. Has one person gathered around herself a group of loyal, dedicated followers who would likely support her no matter what?[197]
d. Is one person claiming to have all the answers? He acts as if no one else has insights and understanding of God's Word like he does?[198]

---

[194] In Titus 1:5 and Acts 20:17 we see that the church was led by a plurality of elders and not by one person.
[195] Ephesians 4:12 teaches us that a leader's work is to prepare all believers to serve and minister in the church.
[196] 3 John 1:9-10
[197] 1 Corinthians 1:10-17
[198] Philippians 2:3-5, 2 Corinthians 4:5, Mark 10:43-45

e. Is what he teaches consistent with the historic orthodox Christian doctrines of the church? Can his teachings stand the test of time?[199]

f. Does the teaching stand the test of the whole of Scripture or is she dependent upon just one or a few Scriptures?[200]

g. Are the teachings consistent with forgiveness, grace and mercy, or are they dogmatic "do's and don'ts" to govern our lives?[201]

h. Is the teaching consistent with the nature of God as revealed to us throughout the whole of Scripture?[202]

i. Is the message in harmony with God's order of things as revealed in all of His creation?[203]

j. Is the teaching consistent with the fruit of the Spirit? Does it line up beside the fruit that comes with being grafted into the True Vine?[204]

k. Are the claims offered in the teaching simply counterintuitive? They just don't make sense?[205]

l. Are there two or three witnesses to confirm the truth being taught?[206] Here are some proven and trustworthy witnesses you can trust: Witness # 1) Confirmed in the Scriptures. Witness # 2) Confirmed in wise and godly counsel. Witness # 3) Confirmed in a peace that passes all understanding, which washes away the doubt in your mind.

God is faithful, even when we are not. When a church or its members get off track, God provides many ways to bring us back to the pathway of wisdom and the fear of the Lord. He does this by

---

[199] 1 Thessalonians 5:19-21

[200] 2 Peter 1:20

[201] Hebrews 4:16

[202] 1 John 4:8

[203] 1 Corinthians 14:33, Genesis 1:1-3.

[204] Matthew 7:16

[205] Nehemiah 4:9, This is one of the most common sense prayers and actions I've found in the Bible.

[206] 2 Corinthians 13:1, This Scripture is based on the Biblical principle of all things being established by two or three witnesses.

the faithful preaching and teaching of His Word. In addition, God will gift and empower people in a local church with the spiritual gifts of prophecy, the gifts of words of wisdom, words of knowledge and discerning of spirits. Our loving Heavenly Father will manifest His living, active presence in a gathering of believers through the ministries of spiritual gifts to speak His Word and bring us back into right standing with Him.

When we despise the gifts God has given to bring a church back on track and when we follow the path of least resistance, not applying godly wisdom and using God's plumb line, we are in great danger.

I'm a witness of these dangers. The end result of our new pastor with his new message was disaster and chaos. The church split, more than once. Many of my dear friends left church for good, never returning to any church. But we could have avoided all the painful consequences if we had first examined his message using a Scriptural plumb line.

Come before your loving Heavenly Father with the simple faith of a child. Be disciplined to grow in the grace and knowledge of our Lord and Savior. Be a good Berean[207] and prove what you are being taught. Prayerfully confirm the direction you would go, asking for godly wisdom to light your pathway. Test the pathway you are led to choose by two or three trustworthy witnesses. Check out what you desire with a Scriptural plumb line. Seek wise and godly council. Let God's peace give you rest and quiet in your soul, and then step out with boldness and great confidence in Christ Jesus our Lord. Be mature in the great hope we are promised. "...[A]nd let endurance have its full effect, so that you may be mature and complete, lacking in nothing" (James 1:4).

---

[207] "These Jews *(Bereans)* were more receptive than those in Thessalonica, for they welcomed the message very eagerly and examined the scriptures every day to see whether these things were so" (Acts 17:11 italics added).

Q & A Chapter 40: Knowing What is of God

1. What is wisdom? Why do we need it? How do we get it?

2. What spiritual gifts has the Spirit given to the church to protect us from evil?

3. Describe the "plumb line" test and its purpose. What is a Christian's plumbline?

Your Mission Journal Notes:

41

Accomplish What God Has Ordained

Albert William Estavon leaned against his cane and eased himself onto the lush, green grass of the hillside punctuated with marble tombstones. The stone to his right was engraved "William Walker Estavon, 1812 - 1865." He sighed as he got settled. He pulled great grandfather's journal out of his vest pocket. Several brittle papers fell into his lap as he started to open it. The papers, stained and stiff with age, crinkled as he opened them up.

He looked over the valley, painted with the light of dusk fading from the cedar shake rooftops, all lined up in neat rows with straight, wide streets. Albert laughed to himself, for indeed, the fruit of all great-grandfathers' planning was evident in the thriving town of Estaville that had grown up by the river. He shook his head with amazement as he looked from the paper to the town. The plan was perfect and the town was wonderful. Out of the corner of his eye Albert spotted a doe with her speckled fawn grazing nearby. Squirrels busily raced up and down the oak tree.

Albert shaded his eyes from the setting sun, getting a sense of comfort as he looked at the towering white steeple crested with a cross that graced the center of town. The church was surrounded with stores, shops, civic buildings, a livery stable, a school, a bank, a boarding house, large and small homes, a train station and all the other necessary components of a fully functioning community. Trees of every variety graced the landscape. Orchards and vineyards looked like colorful postage stamps across the terrain. What Albert saw before his eyes was a real and living manifestation of what his great grandfather William had put on paper so many years before.

Albert thumbed through great-grandfathers' journal. The first date was "January 1, 1841." As he continued scanning through the pages he noted that William had started the careful, meticulous planning for this town even before leaving Ohio. As he turned a page he found a list of what William thought was necessary for a thriving community. Farmers, ranchers, blacksmiths, lawmen, civic leaders, teachers, judges, merchants, doctors – each profession was listed with the names of William's descendants beside each.

His name, "Albert," was written beside "banker." He shook his head, puzzled. How did William know? His brothers, aunts, uncles and cousins, like him, filled the needs of a thriving community. He laughed as he carefully folded the papers along the creases long embedded in the paper and put them back in the age-stained journal for safe keeping. He'd heard the story many times of Grandfather taking newborn Albert on his lap, looking into his brown eyes, examining his tiny hands and then declaring, "His name is Albert and he's going to be a banker."

Have you ever wondered how it happens that a community, a county, or state function so efficiently (or inefficiently at times)? What if we were all lawyers? What if we were all shopkeepers? What if we all wanted to be mayor? The wheel, so to speak, would be heavy on one side and wouldn't turn. Instead, we find ourselves in fully functioning communities with a vast array of talents. In the same way, God provides the gifts, abilities, skills and the strength required for the orderly functioning of a church.

Are you aware that there are many spiritual gifts necessary for the functioning of the body in your local church? I'm not speaking of an organizational diagram that lists jobs and names: "4th grade girls: Sandra Timson" — but a God-ordained order of things that He predestined.

Knowing just a little of the nature of God as He has revealed Himself in His Word, there is no doubt that God, before He began to create the heavens and the earth, created a plan for all the ages, beginning to end. God planned for civic communities, for nations, for tribes, for religious communities, for churches, for families, for the orderly functioning of everything. What God created was formulated for the good of all, for all time. Before the first words of creation were spoken He knew your name, He knew the time of your birth and the day of your death. God knew each and every component necessary for the people of the earth to function and flourish within His established order. He ordained natural gifts for people to perform the work necessary for the wheels of communities, states and nations to function.

In the same way, before time began, God ordained spiritual gifts for His people for the orderly functioning of His kingdom and His church. Too often, we mess up what God has planned for us, but by His forgiveness, grace, and mercy, He restores and sets us on the right path. Now, on the right pathway, the Spirit of Jesus gifts and empowers us to do what God has ordained.

God knew you by name before you were born into this world. He knew the date of your adoption as His son or daughter and He ordained a work for you to accomplish. As He knit you together in your mother's womb, God began to remake you so that you could accomplish all that He has called you to do. By the work of His Holy Spirit, He gives you custom made spiritual gifts to enable you to be a fully functioning part of His kingdom and His church. His Holy Spirit empowers you in those gifts to produce in you the strength to do all you are called to do.

Walk according to what God has called you to do in His kingdom and His church. He will join together with you and work side by side with you in all He has called you to do. If you refuse, is God able to accomplish what He has ordained for you to do? Undoubtedly. But in His great love He has brought you into a bond of fellowship and given you the responsibility to accomplish a good and eternally valuable work. His burden is light. He will make a way for you.

Your work was planned for you from the beginning of time. From the moment you were conceived, and from the moment you were born, God has molded you to accomplish all that He planned for you. Put your hand to the work especially planned for you to accomplish.

Your heart may feel heavy because you have gone your own way for most of your life and are just now beginning to see the Light. Time has slipped away and you're feeling a sense of loss. Now you've had a change of heart and your desire is to do all that God has prepared for you, for once in your life. Take heart because God is God who restores. "I will restore to you the years that the swarming locust has eaten, the hopper, the destroyer, and the cutter, my great army, which I sent among you" (Joel 2:25 ESV). This Scripture is, in essence, saying that God will restore to you the years that your sin has devoured. All those fruitless, destructive years will be forgiven and forgotten and the work ordained for you in His kingdom and His church will be done in the time remaining.

God is to be praised and exalted. God is worthy of your reverence, awe and delighted obedience. Now — repent, turn from your sin and be restored to this special and unique work God has called you to do, a work He has determined that only you can do. Roll up your sleeves, put on your spiritual work gloves and get ready to serve.

Kingdom hearts carry out all that God desires of them. The apostle Paul proclaimed this again regarding King David: "I have found David, son of Jesse, to be a man after my heart, who will carry out all my wishes" (Acts 13:22). God has ordained a work for each of us to accomplish. He ordained this work even before you were known to be. He didn't wait to ordain this work until He found out what kind of person you would turn out to be, because He already knew.

For the purpose of accomplishing this work, God doesn't send us out as free agents to figure it out and tough it out on our own.[208] The desire of God's heart is for us to be under His authority, to be people with a heart like His, and to fully dwell in His counsel so we may accomplish all that He has called us to do in His strength.

The Lord Almighty doesn't leave us to guess what He has called us to do. God will not leave you to flounder about, trying to find your gift. Trying to discover your spiritual gift by taking a test is futile.[209] A weekend seminar on spiritual gifts isn't the key. Instead, the Holy Spirit is Giver of all good gifts to be used in the church. He will prepare

---

[208] An example of this principle is found in Matthew 25:14, the parable of the talents. We would be in great error if we interpreted this parable with a deistic bent. Those to whom the talents were given remained his servants and the property continued to belong to the landowner. They were not given five, two and one talents and sent out as free agents to carve out a niche for themselves.
[209] A written test will reveal your God given natural gifts, but is not useful for spiritual gifts.

you, gift you, and empower you in the gifts needed for you to serve His people.[210]

Aim to become a man or woman after God's own heart and carry out God's purpose and plan for you. Ask for and receive His Spirit's gifts because He has a job for you to fill in His eternal purpose and plan. Jesus is knocking on your door. Be encouraged, today, to open the door and step onto His pathway to fulfill all He desires for your life. Right now is a good time to begin.

Q & A Chapter 41: Accomplish what God has Ordained

1. What is necessary for a church to function as God has planned?

2. We are God's handiwork (Ephesians 2:10). What is our purpose in Christ?

3. If you have missed your purpose so far, what hope do you have?

Your Mission Journal Notes:

---

[210] Book Number two in the Kingdom series, *Kingdom Treasures*, goes into depth on how to receive spiritual gifts, the purpose of spiritual gifts in the church, and the blessings of the Lord working through us by means of spiritual gifts.

42

Don't Burn Out

When Sally and Todd moved to Wachetta Falls, they set out to find a church that was more than just a busy place with a lot of programs. On their third Sunday, they found a church in the center of town that appeared to meet their goals. The people were a good mix of working class, professionals, young and old. Some dressed casually, a few looked like they just wandered in off the street, and some of the older folks wore jackets and ties. And a lively bunch of kids were running around the church.

The following week, one of the church elders visited them at home to welcome them and tell them more about the congregation. Todd and Sally talked about their careers and Sally shared that she was looking for a job teaching public grade school.

"A teacher?" the elder's eyes brightened. Before Sally knew what happened, she was teaching the fourth grade girls Sunday school class. She was given a teacher's book, some scissors, glue sticks, and craft supplies, and sent into a tiny room in the church basement with twelve active girls who had eaten too much sugar for breakfast.

It wasn't long before she began to dread Sunday mornings. She woke up exhausted. Nightmares of classroom walls closing in on her disturbed her sleep. Even before the weekend started she was looking for a good reason to call the church to say, "I can't make it on Sunday. Will you find a substitute for me?" Because of her personal tenacity she lasted a year, but couldn't make herself do it any longer and she resigned.

Tragic stories of fallen, broken, worn out people have been related to me over the years. Accounts of dedicated, faithful servants who served in the church year upon year, event after event, and Sunday after Sunday until that fatal day when they could not go on. They were busy with Sunday School, Vacation Bible School, leading women's ministries, church family camp outs, Christmas parties for the kids, mid-week kid's clubs, Bible studies, setting up communion, weekly care and prayer groups, the church prayer chain and then, besides all that, they took a turn cleaning the church. Just thinking about all the activities should make you tired.

Managing all the demands of church isn't just a matter of learning to say "no" when you're asked to do more than is good for you. Burning out both physically and emotionally comes from trying to do too much, for too long in our own strength. The consequence of this is physical and emotional exhaustion, feeling cynical and detached, and feeling like a failure. Symptoms of chronic fatigue overcome you. You wake up at two a.m. with your mind racing. You have trouble concentrating during meetings. You may feel anxious, depressed, and angry; you snap at your kids knowing it wasn't their fault.

There is a better way. If you don't want to do a slow burn out in service to the church, commit your body, soul, and spirit to be under the anointing and empowering work of the Holy Spirit, joined together in Christ and under the authority of Christ to accomplish what God has called and prepared you to do. God has provided a way for you to receive His power for ministry.

Serving in the church is a great honor and privilege and certainly it is excellent to serve as a part of your Christian life. Yet when we serve only by means of our own strength in our human strength, we set ourselves up to crash. We cannot do the work of the kingdom of heaven with tools made for common tasks.

This Scriptures give us great insight: "So we do not lose heart. Even though our outer nature is wasting away, our inner nature is being renewed day by day. For this slight momentary affliction is preparing us for an eternal weight of glory beyond all measure, because we look not at what can be seen but at what cannot be seen; for what can be seen is temporary, but what cannot be seen is eternal" (1 Corinthians 4:16-18). The apostle Paul makes this point clear: "...but be filled with the Spirit" (Ephesians 5:18). An image of the cause of burn out is becoming clear as we read these Scriptures. Our bodies wear out, and yet our spirit can be continually renewed and strengthened in the Holy Spirit. The weakness of this temporary earth suit, what can be seen, suffers in weakness; but this weakness makes room for God's power to be manifested in us — and in His strength there is no burn out.

Zechariah, the prophet, offers further evidence of the causes of burn out: "Not by might, nor by power, but by my spirit, says the Lord of hosts" (Zechariah 4:6). Examining the original Hebrew of this text offers a good understanding of it. "Might" comes from לֹּ֫חַ chayil (the strength of armies, wealth, and human methods). "Power" comes from כֹּחַ koach (human power, might, force, ability). It is not by human might, not by the power of mortal man, but by the power and anointing of the Holy Spirit that God's work is to be accomplished.

There is a better plan, but it's a difficult plan to choose because we must humble ourselves. With regard to our natural leadership skills, organizational abilities, hard earned education, impeccable résumé, and family and personal connections, we are called to consider them all rubbish. I'm not saying to toss them out, but give them only their appropriate value. Certainly they are good in their place, but for the purposes of the Kingdom economy, consider them rubbish. "For his sake I have suffered the loss of all things, and I regard them as rubbish, in order that I may gain Christ" (Philippians 3:8).

We are getting to the core of a foundational principle in the Kingdom of Heaven. When you attempt to do Kingdom work by means of earth bound talents and abilities, serving in the church using your human energies and temporal strengths, you are setting yourself up for a fall. Instead, begin your work by means of the gifting and empowering work of the Holy Spirit and then continue being filled, refilled, and refreshed in the Spirit of Jesus. In this you will find a continuous flow of strength and power to accomplish the kingdom work ordained for you.

Be encouraged to worship God in spirit and truth, and serve the Kingdom of Heaven in the power of the Spirit. Keep your heart, soul, and spirit wholly and completely dedicated to Christ and His church. Offer up your body as a living sacrifice unto God to serve under the authority of our Lord Jesus.

Mission impossible? Certainly.

Be willing to count your personal assets as "rubbish." Be willing to humble yourself, and admit that your temporal abilities have limited value in the kingdom of heaven. Submit to the Spirit of God and He will accomplish a good work in you. Continually be refreshed in the Spirit and the Word. In this you will find new strength and renewed power to serve and minister in the church, and in the Kingdom of Heaven.

Have you been working, serving and ministering in the strength of your earth suit? Instead, apply your effort in a more fruitful way. Cry out to a Holy God to "Create in me a clean heart, O God, and put a new and right spirit within me. Do not cast me away from your presence, and do not take your Holy Spirit from me. Restore to me the joy of your salvation, and sustain in me a willing spirit" (Psalms 51:10). God is faithful. He forgives, cleanses, and restores our soul. Sally's church leaders could have made all the difference in her service to the church by imparting the Spirit's empowering work and gifting for ministry by praying for her and laying hands upon her as the Lord has called them to do. Timothy was anointed in this way, and later the apostle Paul wrote to him. "Do not neglect the gift that is in you, which was given to you through prophecy with the laying on of hands by the council of elders" (1 Timothy 4:14).[211]

When we do things in this way, that exhausted, angry, and helpless feeling will be washed away because you have come to see that the work of the kingdom of heaven is no longer a burden you must bear on your shoulders, for His burden is light.[212] "Finally, be strong in the Lord and in the strength of his power" (Ephesians 6:10).

God is our strength in all He calls us to do.

---

[211] The elders' laying hands on a person who is called to ministry is not only for pastors, elders, deacons, bishops and other leaders. All of us need God's power at work through us to minister God's Word, and to live God's Word, touching all those who live and work with us every day.

[212] Matthew 11:30

Q & A Chapter 42: Don't Burn Out

1. What causes some Christians to burn out?

2. What does it mean to "serve in your own strength?"

3. Where does your real strength and power come from for Christian ministry and service?

Your Mission Journal Notes:

43

Empowering Moments

The rafters shook with sounds like the blast of a powerful wind. Tongues like fire appeared and rested on all of them and they spoke in other languages as the Spirit gave them ability. As Jesus was preparing to ascend to the Father, He made a promise to the disciples: "'This,' he said, 'is what you have heard from me; for John baptized with water, but you will be baptized with the Holy Spirit not many days from now'" (Acts 1:4-5).

Empowering moments may also be referred to as Pentecost moments. This is the promised work of the Holy Spirit and we do well to learn of our need for this work of the Spirit and its effect upon us in the work of the church. When reading the first chapter of Acts, it's easy to come to the conclusion that this was their Pentecost moment, but it was the first of many outpourings of the Holy Spirit upon Jesus' followers. Reading on though the book of Acts we see that there were other times when the Holy Spirit came upon believers in a similar manner. This empowering work of the Spirit was necessary to establish a foundation for the church in that day and it is equally important throughout all of the church age.

Throughout the history of the orthodox Christian church, we find records of the work of the Holy Spirit in ways similar to what is recorded in Acts. Later manifestations of the Holy Spirit have often been less dramatic, but no less powerful. The apostle Paul had his personal encounter with the Holy Spirit as he was prepared for ministry to the Gentiles. Is there any doubt that the Holy Spirit empowered Martin Luther to do the work of a reformer in a corrupted church? Would anyone dare to claim that Dietrich Bonheoffer did not serve by means of the power of the Holy Spirit? Could you possibly claim that Mother Teresa served as a light in the darkness of Calcutta, India apart from a mighty work of the Holy Spirit in her? Another giant of the faith, D. L. Moody, had his Pentecost moment, after which he preached the same sermons, but with powerful effect upon the hearts of the people, convicting them of sin and bringing them to saving grace.

Baptism in the Holy Spirit is not necessarily an ecstatic experience, and yet you cannot have this empowering work without knowing it has happening to you. The proof is not in the experience but in the manifestation of the Spirit in the ministries the Spirit accomplishes through you. The ongoing manifestation of the Spirit in you is for the glory of God, extoling our Lord Jesus as He is shown to be real, true, and actively present in you (the church) as the Spirit works and ministers through you. To be clear, the Holy Spirit pours out His living, working presence into you and in doing so, gifts you and empowers you for service and ministries of the church that God has foreordained for you to accomplish. As an example, you may be gifted with a spiritual gift of helps and become the designated kitchen manager. In this work, you may well accomplish (in the Spirit) a powerful, bonding effect upon all those who receive the blessings of the food they share together that you have prepared.

You may be thinking, but that's not very glamorous — kitchen manager? Do I really need the gifting and empowering baptism of the Holy Spirit to wash the dishes and mop the floors? Beyond a doubt, yes, you do. The difference you will see between mopping the floors in the strength of the flesh and the power of the Holy Spirit is the difference between darkness and light. It is for you to choose. Will your service in the church be a work of beauty, or will it be ashes?[213] Will it be a matter of get-it-done so you can go home or will it be a blessing of life changing, eternal value to those you serve?

And yet it is important to understand that the gifting and empowering work of the Holy Spirit is never a one time, you-got-it-for-all-time experience. The baptism of the Spirit of Jesus, no matter how it begins in you, is a continual, continuous, pouring out and refreshing

---

[213] Isaiah 61:3

work of the Spirit to perpetually refill you for works of ministry. As you pour yourself out in ministry, the Spirit pours Himself into you to refill you again and again.

When the Holy Spirit's fire has poured into you, giving you power for service, go and serve in the strength of the Holy Spirit, bringing glory and honor to the holy name of our Lord and God, our Almighty Abba Father. Through you, God will extend His hand to all those in need around you. As you pour yourself out in the ministries of the Spirit, you will become strengthened for even greater service in the kingdom.

Q & A Chapter 43: Empowering Moments

1. What is God's purpose in gifting and empowering His people?

2. What is the difference the between mopping floors in your own strength and the strength of the Spirit?

3. Why is it so important to keep on being refilled and re-powered in the Spirit?

Your Mission Journal Notes:

44

Treasure God's Word

King Archemius in the great kingdom of Archemia, on the day of celebration for his thirty-third birthday, put on His royal robes, took his golden scepter in hand and appeared before the people. He commanded his representatives to distribute to each of his subjects paper notes marked with his seal. He called the notes "Archbacks." Each paper note certified that on the day of his natural death they could come to his treasury and claim a one ounce gold coin. But even though he was still quite young, the people began to use the certificates as if they had current value, offering and accepting them in trade. Before long, it was impossible to do business in the kingdom without using the king's Archbacks.

The kingdom grew and prospered in his lifetime, and after many years the king died at the fine old age of ninety-eight. His casket was carried throughout the kingdom on a golden carriage pulled by eight dappled Clydesdale horses with golden bells on their leather harnesses. The people mourned for their king, assembling in a great ceremony to pay their respects, and they continued to mourn for thirty days.

With the king dead and buried and the thirty days of mourning behind them, the people completely forgot the promise printed on the Archback certificates and continued to use the paper for trade, never claiming their promised gold from the king's treasury.

It was much the same in Jesus' day. Leaders of the people refused to accept what was promised them. Jesus confronted this hypocrisy of the Pharisees saying, "You search the Scriptures because you think that in them you have eternal life; and it is they that testify on my behalf. Yet you refuse to come to me to have life" (John 5:39-40). The teachers of the Law were diligent students, memorizing, analyzing, and discussing at great length the words written on the scrolls of the prophets. They could quote Scripture, chapter after chapter. They studied the subtle connotations of the written words. They were men of intellect with a detailed understanding of the Scriptures.

In reality, the teachers of the Law had in their hands scrolls made of papyrus with ink markings, but no more than that. The words of the prophets were embedded into their brains, but not their hearts. They were proud to quote verse after verse to display their Scriptural acumen and personal self-discipline, but God's Word was not embedded into their hearts and they refused to live the words of Scripture in their daily lives. In Jesus' own words, "If you know these things, you are blessed if you do them" (John 13:17). Knowledge alone isn't enough to truly motivate you. A change of heart is necessary, and that is impossible by our own doing.

The teachers of the Law said long, beautiful, even poetic prayers in public. They wore the tefillin[214] on their hands and forehead. They wore robes and tallit prayer shawls with special Tzitzit or fringes on each corner of the shawl. They had Scriptures on their doorposts, and in essence they were surrounded by Holy words. The teachers of the law may have been somewhat like a man today who dresses in a sharp Brook's Brothers business suit, a silk tie with a perfect knot, a matching kerchief in his pocket, and embossed business cards in his wallet, but he has no job and no car to get there if he had one. But no! The religious leaders were much worse than a man with a business suit and no business. It was all too common for them to evict widows and orphans from their homes. I can only imagine how it was done. "Oh, your husband just died and you can't pay the rent?" His face would harden with his dark eyes glaring at her. "Well, go find someone else's shoulder to cry on. I've got a business to

---

[214] Tefillin are black boxes worn by men; one is worn upon the left arm so that it may rest against the heart, with a leather strap that is wound around the left hand, and around the middle finger. The other box is worn upon the head, above the forehead, resting upon the cerebrum. This is in fulfillment of the Torah commandment in the Sh'ma.

run and bills to pay. Get out before dark and take all those children with you."

The ultimate evidence of their great hypocrisy is their rejection of Jesus. They despised Emmanuel, God with us. They attempted to trap him with His own words and plotted His downfall – His death.

We must take warning from their example. Our treasure isn't found in the paper, ink and leather binding of the book with the gold foil lettering that says, "Holy Bible." What we ought to value instead is the Word illuminated for us by the Spirit of God — the power of the living Scriptures. God has gifted us with the invention of paper, ink, and binding as a means to keep this all together in a useful book, and it truly is a useful vessel for revealing the real thing — the Living Word, the Spring of Living Water. A Thompson Chain Reference NIV on your library shelf means nothing. An unopened Gideon Bible in your hotel room can't help you. Carrying the Good Book to church under your arm is meaningless if it's only for show. Even memorizing Scriptures does you no good if you don't take it into your heart and allow the power of God's Word to change your heart.

We must pray for, seek, and depend upon the Holy Spirit of Jesus to do a mighty and powerful work in our hearts, changing our minds, renewing us, and refreshing us by means of His Holy Scriptures. May I encourage you to be washed in the Word, be immersed in the Word, to be saturated in the Scriptures and allow God's Word to do a spring-cleaning kind of scrubbing in your life, every day of your life.

The Holy Spirit inspired the writers of the Holy Scriptures, giving them the words to write. To receive the full benefit, depth, meaning and power of those words, the Holy Spirit must minister those words to you. The Spirit of Jesus must open your understanding and your heart to reveal the Resurrected Christ to you as you prayerfully study, meditate on, and read your Bible. A study of the Scriptures must not be limited to an intellectual pursuit, because your knowledge of the Bible will only bring you to be proud of yourself for what you have accomplished.

The Pharisees thought that by the Scriptures they had life. But listen to what the apostle Paul had to say in a letter to Timothy: "All scripture is inspired by God and is useful for teaching, for reproof, for correction, and for training in righteousness, so that everyone who belongs to God may be proficient, equipped for every good work" (2 Timothy 3:16-17).

Paul is not referring to a finger wagging, tongue lashing, Bible thumping lecture to put you in your place. What he is saying is that by the teaching of God's Word, when the Holy Spirit is at work in your heart and mind, He will bring about correction, admonishing you and giving you the means to live a righteous and godly life. This is the work of the Spirit of Jesus whom Jesus sent to us as promised, and it is a work of the Spirit's tender love.

Now you can take your "Archback certificate" to the treasury in the kingdom of heaven and cash it in for the real thing. You no longer have nothing but paper and ink; you have real gold, a true treasure found only in God's Word. Allow God's Word to be your lamppost to light your pathway — yes, to change the direction of your life and to lead you in paths of righteousness.

In reality, every day of your life Jesus is walking along in front of you. His sandals are leaving footprints on the pathway as He goes ahead of you. All you need to do is walk in His footsteps. The power of the Word and the work of the Holy Spirit through the Word are light to your eyes so you may see where Jesus has walked.

God's Word is a great treasure. Open your hands and receive the riches of the kingdom of heaven.

Q & A Chapter 44: Treasure God's Word

1. How does God's Word get from the page into your heart?

2. What is the effect of the Holy Spirit ministering and interpreting God's Word to you?

3. What does it mean, to "have God's Word in your heart?"

Your Mission Journal Notes:

45

Overflowing with Thanksgiving

The kids were wide eyed with anticipation as they wiggled in their chairs and highchairs. Four-year-old Jimmy Junior was proud that he was big enough to sit in his own seat with the help of a Webster dictionary. The family celebration began amid the noise. The children and parents reached out, joining hands around the table to pray. With a well-browned turkey steaming on a platter in the center of the table, accompanied with stuffing, cranberry sauce and all the trimmings and, of course, pumpkin pies cooling on the kitchen counter, the celebration began. It was as if they all inhaled the beautiful aromas of seasonings and sweet spices in unison as the prayers of thanksgiving began.

Jimmy Junior opened his eyes a peep to look around to see all their heads bowed, except for baby Teanna Mae who was waving her spoon and chattering along as if saying baby prayers. Jimmy watched as she pinched Cheerios between her tiny fingers and bit into them with her new baby teeth. He wanted to eat too, and his empty stomach gurgled while dad prayed lots of "Thank You" prayers.

"Enter his gates with thanksgiving, and his courts with praise. Give thanks to him, bless his name" (Psalms 100:4). Indeed, the expression of our thanksgiving is very telling. My own saying goes, "the rendition of your thanksgiving reveals the condition of your heart."

We've all known a teenager who, despite being provided with every possible earthly comfort, complains and wants more. This human weakness is as old as time. We see examples of this principle in Old Testament accounts of the tribes of Israel. These stories are written for us to see the error of their ways so we can avoid the same dumb mistakes. Speaking through His prophet Moses, God warned the people against complacency and discontent.

> "Has any people ever heard the voice of a god speaking out of a fire, as you have heard, and lived? Or has any god ever attempted to go and take a nation for himself from the midst of another nation, by trials, by signs and wonders, by war, by a mighty hand and an outstretched arm, and by terrifying displays of power, as the Lord your God did for you in Egypt before your very eyes?" (Deuteronomy 4:33-34)

We are warned about complacency that leads to ungratefulness. When we refuse to acknowledge the blessings given to us, too often our next step is to start looking around for something better. You know, those proverbial greener pastures off in the distance. We become prodigals, we look for something that will satisfy our feelings of being deprived and we become resentful if we don't get it. Some have walked away from the good blessings given to them, despising the precious gifts they have, to seek something better. When they can't find it, they become bitter.

But God in His abundant mercy has made a way for us. He is faithful even when we are not. He is quick to forgive a repentant heart. He hears our prayers and the cries of our heart. King David cried out to the Lord when his sin was revealed to him and his heart was torn with grief because of his sin against a holy God. "Create in me a clean heart, O God, and put a new and right spirit within me. Do not cast me away from your presence, and do not take your holy spirit from me. Restore to me the joy of your salvation, and sustain in me a willing spirit" (Psalms 51:10-12). David knew the joy of being forgiven, restored, and comforted as we see in the Psalm he wrote. "The Lord is my shepherd, I shall not want. He makes me lie down in green pastures; he leads me beside still waters; he restores my soul. He leads me in right paths for his name's sake" (Psalms 23:1-3).

Thanksgiving is restorative, healing, life changing, and an excellent attitude fixer. Thanksgiving changes our self focus to a God focus. Thanksgiving lifts a burden off our shoulders and prepares us to give up our whiny, cranky attitudes, casting burdens upon the Lord. Seriously, that's what he wants us to do. "Cast your cares on the Lord and he will sustain you; he will never let the righteous be shaken (Psalms 55:22 NIV).

In the Old Testament system of worship, specific gifts were to be presented as thanksgiving offerings in response to the bounty God had provided them. David sang songs of thanksgiving, and choirs were appointed to sing words of thanksgiving to the Lord. Thanksgiving opens the gates of heaven, giving us entry into the courts of our Lord. Our thanksgiving honors our God. Thanksgiving opens our eyes to His gates of deliverance.

Listen to what God says of those who offer their thanksgiving: "Those who bring thanksgiving as their sacrifice honor me; to those who go the right way I will show the salvation of God" (Psalms 50:23).

There is an old cliché, "Do a check-up from the neck up." It is good for us to take account of what comes out of our mouths. Is it cursing? Check your heart and you'll know why. Are they abusive or manipulative words? Your heart needs a check up. Do you spill venomous accusations out of your mouth in those high-pressure moments? You may need a heart monitor.

Jesus made this principle clear. "For out of the abundance of the heart the mouth speaks" (Matthew 12:34). Do words of thanksgiving overflow from your mouth as naturally someone saying, "I love you" to his fiancé? When this is what comes out of your mouth, you know your heart is right toward the Lord. Does your heart overflow with songs filled with grateful expressions? Your heart is blessed indeed. Are your prayers bursting with thankful utterances? You've been given a heart filled with an abundance of joy.

You'll be blessed when you read through all the Scriptures about thanksgiving and thankfulness.[215] You'll quickly see some beautiful aspects of giving thanks before a Holy God. There is an altar of thanksgiving, specific places set aside for offering prayers from a

---

[215] A topical Bible is highly recommended for this purpose. NIV Nave's Topical Bible by Zondervan is excellent. Good online resources: blueletterbible.org, biblehub.org and biblegateway.org are all excellent resources.

grateful heart, both in a gathering of believers and in the privacy of your home. Offering thanks is to be a joyful, festive occasion. Prayers, songs, and psalms of thanksgiving are to be continuous, commemorating God's goodness. Thankfulness is expressed in spiritual songs and thankful expressions go together with our prayers, like an orchestra and its music. We do well to give thanks together with an offering, making our thankful expressions more than words. Thanksgiving is to be a part of every gathering for the church and in all private times of prayer.

Fill your heart with an attitude of gratitude because it is healing, restoring, and refreshing. Gratefulness is the gateway that brings us before the Lord — to His saving graces, to His mercies, to His abundant blessings. Thanksgiving is the way into true praise and worship. Expressions of thanks are like stepping-stones in kingdom of heaven. "As you therefore have received Christ Jesus the Lord, continue to live your lives in him, rooted and built up in him and established in the faith, just as you were taught, abounding in thanksgiving" (Colossians 2:6-7).

Mighty is the name of the Lord for You, Lord, are gracious and merciful to Your servants. Your favor overwhelms us like a flood and Your goodness reaches from the depths to the heights. Your faithfulness extends like outstretched arms from east to west. Thank you, Lord God Almighty, for this season of your blessings. Your faithfulness is greater than we could have asked or imagined. Blessed be the name of the Lord.

Q & A Chapter 45: Overflowing with Thanksgiving

1. How does a grateful heart change your life?

2. Can you know a person's true heart by the words that come out of his mouth?

3. What are you thankful for?

Your Mission Journal Notes:

46

Let us Break Bread Together

Happy kid noises, family chatter, and youthful laughter from all around the table filled the room with a symphony of pleasing sounds. All the conversations came together like an improvised song with grandpa's deep baritone voice, grandma's alto tones, mom and dad's soprano and bass voices, the little girl's mezzo soprano, a hungry baby's staccato whimpering and a cranky toddler's whine in high C — a family song shared around the dinner table.

A family dinner, a gathering around the table, entertaining guests over a shared meal, inviting a friend to join you for lunch – all of these bring us together in a great purpose and this is given to us as a special gift.

I'm continually amazed. The more that is revealed to me of God's nature, the more I'm overwhelmed with His majesty. In fact, the word "amazing" seems so inadequate. God has given His created beings so many good gifts that it's hard to comprehend the full scope and to take them in. The precious gift I'm thinking of is the gift of gathering around the table to break bread together, i.e. to share a meal. This is an incredible blessing with great power in it.

In our daily rush, in the clamor of our daily lives, as we struggle to survive the jungle that entangles us in this American culture, we sacrifice some of God's precious gifts on the altar of convenience. God has purposely designed us to need a break during the day to nourish our bodies, and fuel this working machine of bones, muscle, and skin that God gave us. But our Creator gave us something better than just grabbing greasy chicken nuggets in a bag at the drive through window so we can keep running the rat race. He gave us the gift of gathering together to "break bread" and share a meal.

We have been designed to come together and form a special bond when we share food at a common table. There's great power in this, and it is a healing, strengthening power for our benefit. This principle is true for all people God has created, of every language, nation, and tribe. There are few cultures without traditions that bring people together with a shared meal. This is the way God made us and it's a part of our DNA to need the fellowship of a gathering.

Why are so many business deals made over lunch or dinner? Do you suppose that negotiations are finalized with a shared toast for good reason? What is a birthday party without cake, candles, and friends? Wedding celebrations often include a common meal, or at least a shared cake that brings the celebrants into a bond with the bride and groom — for better or for worse. Sampling your friend Betty's chicken casserole with all your other Christian friends at a church potluck binds you together in a way that is unique and special. A prayer breakfast is a powerful means of coming together in agreement. But why is it so powerful and effective? How does this happen?

The Scriptures gives us a sense of the depth and meaning of dining together. A shared meal is one of the greatest and most powerful God-given blessings. These are gatherings with a purpose — to create a common bond. On top of all that, laughter is often a part of this time-honored custom.

Take a moment to remember the meals you have shared with family and special guests in your home. Can you recount the blessings and the memories of stories told while breaking bread together? One of my most memorable meals happened at our little house on Cleveland Street in Spokane. A missionary from India visited and prepared one of his favorite rice curry dishes. He reduced the spices to about a quarter of what he normally used, and still it was so hot that we drank a lot of water trying to cool our burning mouths. But I remember hearing stories of life in India that broadened my perspective of the world around me. That time of fellowship strengthened my family and the family we call "church."

Throughout the Scriptures we find many references to the tables people gathered around. And especially, what a great honor it was to receive an invitation to dine at the king's table. It was a great privilege implying the king's favor.

First King David's invitation to dine was a show of gratitude to his faithful subjects. "Deal loyally, however, with the sons of Barzillai the Gileadite, and let them be among those who eat at your table; for with such loyalty they met me when I fled from your brother Absalom" (1 Kings 2:7). In this next Scripture we see it as a show of forgiveness and mercy: "So Jehoiachin put aside his prison clothes. Every day of his life he dined regularly in the king's presence. For his allowance, a regular allowance was given him by the king, a portion every day, as long as he lived" (2 Kings 25:29). Even as a captive in a foreign land, food from the king's table meant that Daniel was being brought into the king's good graces: "The king assigned them a daily portion of the royal rations of food and wine (Daniel 1:5). Another of King David's invitations to dine with him was fulfillment of a promise: "[B]ut your master's grandson Mephibosheth shall always eat at my table" (2 Samuel 9:10).

The tribes of Israel were blessed with manna so they could dine at the Father's table as they wandered in the desert for forty years. Jesus multiplied the bread and the fish to feed four thousand men and their families and then again over five thousand men and their families dined together at a picnic on the grassy hills above the shores of the Sea of Galilee. For three years while the disciples attended "Jesus University" they broke bread over breakfast, lunch, and dinner. They talked, they learned, their bodies were nourished and their spirits grew strong as they shared meals together. After Zacchaeus had his life-changing encounter with Jesus, he invited Him and his disciples to his house to stay and share a meal.

Jesus led his disciples into the significance of the greatest and most powerful God given blessing: a shared meal around a holy table. The Last Supper changed everything. It was a shared meal that changed the world forever. With the breaking of bread and sharing of a cup, nothing would ever be the same again, for indeed, our Lord and Savior Jesus Christ bound together His disciples in a way that established a firm foundation for His church. The disciples broke bread with their

King. They received the Lord's favor. They were bound together with Him as never before.

To this day, Christian churches around the world celebrate this moment, remembering the saving work of Christ to redeem sinners from a lost and dying world. In each of these remembrances, during every church communion celebration, we too are brought together in a bond of fellowship. Indeed, we break bread in the company of our Lord Jesus for He is ever present in the bread and the wine. We receive the Lord's favor for forgiveness of sins. We were bound together with Him in His church with a renewed and strengthened fellowship.

> "While they were eating, Jesus took a loaf of bread, and after blessing it he broke it, gave it to the disciples, and said, 'Take, eat; this is my body.' Then he took a cup, and after giving thanks he gave it to them, saying, 'Drink from it, all of you; for this is my blood of the covenant, which is poured out for many for the forgiveness of sins. I tell you, I will never again drink of this fruit of the vine until that day when I drink it new with you in my Father's kingdom.'" (Matthew 26:26-29) [216]

We are so blessed to have regular celebrations remembering Jesus' saving work accomplished on our behalf, giving His body to be broken so that we might be redeemed, to make us whole in body, soul, and spirit. We are blessed to partake of the cup, remembering that His blood was shed for the remission of our sin, so that we might be washed clean — cleaner and whiter then fresh fallen snow.

A greater blessing awaits us. A grand celebration is being prepared for us. It is the wedding supper of the Lamb. "And the angel said to me, 'Write this: Blessed are those who are invited to the marriage supper of the Lamb.' And he said to me, 'These are true words of God'" (Revelation 19:9).

Reading, studying, and meditating on this next Scripture will cause your heart to well up with great joy.

---

[216] Also found in Mark 14:17-25; Luke 22:7-22; and John 13:21-30.

"Then I heard what seemed to be the voice of a great multitude, like the sound of many waters and like the sound of mighty thunder peals, crying out, 'Hallelujah! For the Lord our God the Almighty reigns. Let us rejoice and exult and give him the glory, for the marriage of the Lamb has come, and his bride has made herself ready; to her it has been granted to be clothed with fine linen, bright and pure'—for the fine linen is the righteous deeds of the saints." (Revelation 19:6-8)

Now that I think about it, there could be nothing grander than to have all of my readers come to my house, gather around my table in Jesus' name to share and celebrate over a bountiful meal. Oh, what a festive occasion it would be because our Lord Jesus would be feasting with us.

"Finally, be strong in the Lord and in the strength of his power" (Ephesians 6:10). God has given us many wonderful blessings to strengthen us and to bind us together as one in Christ. And together, we are stronger. Gathering around a shared meal is a practice that is powerful in its effect upon us. It's an added bonus that a get together is a lot of fun. Consider yourself invited to come celebrate as we prepare for the greatest of all wedding celebrations. "Blessed are those who are invited to the marriage supper of the Lamb" (Revelation 19:9).

Q & A Chapter 46: Let us Break Bread Together

1. Describe the gift of gathering around a table to "break bread" together. What is its value to God's people?

2. Write about the most memorable shared meal you have experienced.

3. What means has God given to the church to bring us together in the unity of faith?

Your Mission Journal Notes:

47

Keys of the Kingdom of Heaven

The unclad doors of the temple swung in the wind, the wood rotted and splintered. It was serving no purpose. A tarnished key lay on the cluttered floor. The door was once ornamented with white, yellow, and amber gold. The metal clad door was patterned with panels, arches, and curves, each with various colors of gold. The key was made of pure gold in elegant trefoil patterns. It was beautiful beyond description. There was never a latch or knob, only a key to open it.

A stormy blast rips the door from its hinges. The exposed wood, tears, cracked and worn away by sun and storm. The carved panels of the door were long since kicked out. It is about to be tossed aside in the rubble. As I observed the ruined door, it occurred to me that if the door were closed, it's as if it was open. If it were opened, it would make no difference. It would blow in the wind — open, closed. Closed, open. It wouldn't matter. The neglected, weather worn, rotting pieces of wood serve no useful purpose. The door I see is useless to either let someone in or to close someone out. I wonder, can it ever be restored?

But I have great hope because I know the One who renews and restores. He forgives and rebuilds. He picks us up and cleans us up and sets us our feet on solid rock to start again. We must not turn away from the One who holds out the keys to the kingdom. Too often we reject what is held out to us.

Jesus said, "I am the door. If anyone enters by me, he will be saved and will go in and out and find pasture. The thief comes only to steal and kill and destroy. I came that they may have life and have it abundantly" (John 10:9-10 ESV). We must not rip away the beauty and majesty of the Door by rejecting the precious treasures He holds out to us in His nail scarred hands. Jesus is not only the Door to great treasure, He is the key. "I will place on his shoulder the key of the house of David; he shall open, and no one shall shut; he shall shut, and no one shall open" (Isaiah 22:22). We must not reject the Key of David, and leave it to thieves.

We must consider the words of the prophet: "Oh, that someone among you would shut the temple doors, so that you would not kindle fire on my altar in vain! I have no pleasure in you, says the Lord of hosts, and I will not accept an offering from your hands" (Malachi 1:10). Why did God speak such devastating words?

Hezekiah is a grievous example for us today, showing us how far down we can go. He was a great reformer in his early days as king. He destroyed the idolatrous altars on the hillsides, mountains, and under the trees where people set up altars to worship false gods. He restored the feasts of Israel and temple worship in Jerusalem. But in the last years of his life his heart changed.

One of the most shameful acts of his reign was to strip the gold from the doors of God's holy temple so he could pay off King Sennacherib to break off his attack on Jerusalem and march his armies back to Assyria. This was not Hezekiah's gold; it belonged to the temple where the people came to worship their Jehovah God, Lord and King. Hezekiah took what was not his and tossed it away. In doing this, he was like Esau who despised his birthright.[217] He despised the precious treasures of the temple of worship. "At that time Hezekiah stripped the gold from the doors of the temple of the Lord, and from the doorposts that King Hezekiah of Judah had overlaid and gave it to the king of Assyria" (2 Kings 18:16).

After Hezekiah stripped the gold from the doors of the temple it was not many years before the Babylonian armies led by King Nebuchadnezzar marched against Jerusalem and conquered the city. The people were exiled and the temple was abandoned.

There is no cause for us to look down on King Hezekiah with righteous indignation. We too, in our day, have despised the treasures of the kingdom of heaven. We are like him in too many ways. We have

---

[217] Genesis 25:34

thrown away the precious ornaments of the church to appease the world that surrounds us — to become more like the world. We have despised the Holy Spirit's gifts, given to adorn His bride and to beautify and strengthen His church. We have failed to distinguish common gifts from holy spiritual gifts and in this also we have rejected what is true and real, what is spirit and truth.

As Jesus prepared to ascend into heaven, He promised to send His Holy Spirit for the good of His church. He didn't send the Holy Spirit to us empty handed, but with a treasure trove of precious gifts to adorn the bride of Christ — the church. The Holy Spirit of Jesus holds out these precious gifts to the church, but we either reject them, redefine them, or pick and choose only the gifts we like. In this, we have given away, despised, and even forbidden the precious treasures of the kingdom of heaven.

If we reject and despise what our Christ Jesus, the Bridegroom offers, it's as if the door swings in the wind. The key gets lost in the dust. Think of the Holy Spirit's grief when we reject the good gifts He holds out to us. In the account of King Hezekiah we find a parallel for Christians in this day to help us learn from our Old Testament brothers. The Scriptures state it clearly. When we reject the Son, our Lord Jesus Christ, we also reject the Father.[218] When we reject the Holy Spirit and His good gifts, it's like standing on ground with a sinkhole developing underneath. You cannot reject one person of the trinity without rejecting the whole. If you reject the gift, you are also rejecting the Giver of the gift.

My prayer is that the Holy Spirit will break your heart with grief over the sin of the church and give you a repentant heart on behalf of the church. This broken repentance is for a good purpose, because upon this foundation of repentance, the Lord God Almighty will renew, restore, rebuild, and revive His church.

Be encouraged. Reach out your hand to receive the treasures of the kingdom of heaven. Say "yes" to the Key to the kingdom of heaven, for our Lord Jesus is the Key. As Jesus promised, He has sent His Holy

---

[218] 1 John 2:23: "No one who denies the Son has the Father; everyone who confesses the Son has the Father also."

Spirit to give us good gifts and to empower us in the use of these gifts to prepare you and to adorn you, His bride, with Kingdom Treasures.[219]

Q & A Chapter 47: Keys of the Kingdom

1. Who is the Key to God's Kingdom?

2. How ought we to distinguish between common and holy? Why is it important?

3. How will you respond when the precious treasures of God's kingdom are held out to you?

Your Mission Journal Notes:

---

[219] To continue to study and to discover your kingdom treasures, the precious gifts of the Spirit, we recommend book number two of this series, *Kingdom Treasures.*

Mission Possible

The grandstands are filled with witnesses[220] shouting and applauding those whose mission is to run the race. With banners held high, each contender presses on. Runners sweating, muscles straining, crossing the marker, on the way to the finish line. As you pressed on in this pursuit, chapter by chapter through *Hearts for the Kingdom*, you have completed the first leg of your preparation for your mission.

This course started with a saving knowledge of Jesus Christ, and by the power of the Word of God, it has revealed to you our Lord and Savior. You have reached your first marker in the race; though impossible, you have accomplished it by faith, being fortified in the strength of God Almighty. You obeyed the Lord's command to believe and be baptized, and in this, you have become a new creation in Christ. You have been adopted into the family of the King of all kings and you have been given his name as your own. You are part of a whole new family, your new name is Christian and your family is called "church."

You have found assurance of your newfound faith being solid in the Rock, Christ Jesus. Your feet are on solid ground and you have confidence that is only possible in Christ. In Christ you have found strength to lift up His banner[221] and run the race. You have been given the gift of faith that gives you confidence to come before a Holy God, to dwell in His counsel, to lay your petitions before Him, to exalt His holy name, and to lift up holy hands in worship and praise before a Holy God.

You are now ready to continue to go forward on your mission and take part in the disciplines of the Christian faith – a pilgrimage, a faith walk, that every Christian is called to. You now have the opportunity to take up the disciplines God's people have practiced from the very beginning of the church so that you too may be strengthened in the faith and stand against the evil one. Like your forerunners in the

---

[220] Hebrews 12:1

[221] "He brought me to the banqueting house, and his banner over me was love" (Song of Songs 2:4 ESV).

faith, you are strengthened in the disciplines of prayer, fasting, and meditating on God's Word, so you too can be an overcomer in the turmoil of these last days.

To run this race with a heart for Christ, a kingdom heart, is to run with His love as your banner. This was once mission impossible, but it is now totally possible in Christ[222] who lifts you up when you falter. Your kingdom heart is the effect of the righteousness of Jesus Christ and its continuing work in you, effecting righteous deeds of eternal value. Your kingdom heart truly reveals Christ to a world in need of His saving grace. Kingdom hearts reveal Christ's living, active presence to a world in need of His touch. And Jesus extends His hand to them through your hand.

Christ Jesus, our Lord, has overcome the world[223] and has made us overcomers and champions in this race. He has gained the victory and has led us in a victorious parade. "But thanks be to God, who in Christ always leads us in triumphal procession, and through us spreads in every place the fragrance that comes from knowing him. For we are the aroma of Christ to God among those who are being saved" (2 Corinthians 2:14).

When you finish the race you will stand shoulder to shoulder with the cloud of witnesses in the grandstands who have already finished their race, and say, "I have fought the good fight, I have finished the race, I have kept the faith" (1 Timothy 4:7).

The first leg of the race is a training course — preparation for what lies ahead. God has given great and precious treasures to His church, to build and strengthen the church, and to prepare His bride for His coming. His bride is to be adorned with precious jewels and beautiful robes.

> "I will greatly rejoice in the Lord, my whole being shall exult in my God; for he has clothed me with the garments of salvation, he has covered me with the robe of righteousness, as a bridegroom decks himself with a garland, and as a bride adorns herself with her jewels." (Isaiah 61:10)

---

[222] Philippians 4:13
[223] John 16:33

Isaiah teaches us three miraculous works God does in the hearts of all who are called by His name. First we are clothed in garments of salvation. Next we are covered with a robe of righteousness and then we are given the beauty of Christ with the jewels of the kingdom. Do you recognize the person I've described? It is you!

I'm inviting you to continue the pilgrimage you have started by reading and studying through *Kingdom Treasures*. This second study book in the Kingdom Series takes the learner through an in-depth study of the treasures of the Kingdom our Bridegroom has given to strengthen us as conquerors for the Kingdom of Heaven, and to give us bridal ornaments, making us ready for His triumphant return. This study book takes us through a thorough study of spiritual gifts. But the approach is not a typical, take a test, discover-your-gift study. Through *Kingdom Treasure,* you learn the purpose, power, and beauty to be exercised in the use of spiritual gifts in the church, and to learn how to receive your ministry/service gift.

Recommended reading and study books

"The Divine Conspiracy" by Dallas Willard
"The Great Omission" by Dallas Willard
"Systematic Theology" by Wayne Grudem
"The Spiritual Man" by Watchman Nee
"Mystery of the Holy Spirit" by A. W. Tozer
"The Pursuit of God" by A. W. Tozer

Online Study Tools

blueletterbible.org
biblehub.com

This study book was prepared by Cho Larson for the purpose of revealing Christ to those who are called to saving faith; for those who desire assurance of their faith and all who long to grow in grace and knowledge, i.e. to be strengthened and mature in their Christian faith. My prayer is that the truth of God's Word will be manifested in the hearts of all those who will receive this message.

Many of the thoughts and themes included here have long incubated in my heart during years of study, teaching and writing. After completing the study book, Kingdom Treasures it came to me that the best stewards of the precious treasures of the kingdom are Christians who are maturing in their walk of faith. God is always faithful to help in what He calls us to do. The Holy Spirit instructed my heart even in the night and then awakened my ears to hear what He would teach me as He stirred me from sleep every morning. As I prayed through and dug through the Scriptures; God's Word became increasingly alive to me. In researching each topic, the Holy Spirit guided me, taught me and helped me find the words to write.

My understanding of the need for practicing Christian disciplines and for spiritual gifts at work in the church was shaped by about six years serving as Christian Education Director at a church that grew from 450 to over 900 members. It was my job to recruit, train and then help teachers to teach and prepare learners, bringing them to our Lord and Savior to receive of His saving grace.

Serving in various positions of Christian leadership has opened my eyes to the struggles each of us face when we attempt to serve by the strength and power of the natural man. I've been a first hand witness of churches being weakened rather than being ministering to in love with a servant's heart and by the power of the Spirit.

There is a better way and it is the way of the cross. I pray that the Holy Spirit has revealed this pathway as you searched numerous Scripture references with me. In testing what is taught, my hope is that you found this study to be clearly and solidly grounded in God's

Word. May the Word be opened to all who will ask and receive. God is always faithful to teach me the truth of His Word and redirect me when I'm on a wrong path. I'm not unique in this and He will certainly be faithful to teach all who have ears to hear.

Many Blessings in Christ.

Cho Larson.